TWO WHO WERE THERE

Margaret and Stanley Nowak. Drawing by John Gelsavage.

TWO WHO WERE THERE
A Biography of Stanley Nowak

Margaret Collingwood Nowak

Introduction by Thaddeus C. Radzilowski

Wayne State University Press Detroit 1989

93 92 91 90 89 5 4 3 2 1

Library of Congress Cataloging-in-Publication Data

Nowak, Margaret Collingwood, 1908-

Two who were there : a biography of Stanley Nowak / Margaret Collingwood Nowak; with an introduction by Thaddeus C. Radzilowski.

p. cm.

Includes index.

ISBN 0-8143-1883-5 (alk. paper). ISBN 0-8143-1878-9 (pbk.: alk. paper).

1. Nowak, Stanley, 1903- . 2. Nowak, Margaret Collingwood, 1908- . 3. Trade-unions—United States—Biography. 4. Polish Americans—Michigan—Detroit—Political activity. I. Title.

HD6509.N68N68 1989

331.88'092'2—dc19

[B] 88-39057

CIP

The manuscript was edited by Michael K. Lane. The book was designed by Joanne Elkin Kinney. The typeface for the text is Palatino. The display type is Lubalin Graph Medium. The book is printed on 50-lb. white offset text paper and is bound in Holliston Mills' Roxite Linen.

Manufactured in the United States of America.

This book is dedicated to those brave foreign-born U.S. citizens who, like Stanley Nowak, were special targets of McCarthyism and the infamous Walter-McCarran Act. This was indicated by Eisenhower's newly appointed attorney general, Herbert Brownell, in a speech reported in the New York Times *of 18 March 1953, declaring that ten thousand naturalized citizens and twelve thousand aliens were under investigation by the Department of Justice for possible denaturalization and deportation as "subversives."*

We have been a nation of dissenters from our beginning. Yet during the McCarthy period, any dissent from the current definition of patriotism or the exercising of our traditional freedoms of speech and assembly on behalf of unpopular causes might cost one of foreign birth the revocation of citizenship and deportation under the Walter-McCarran Act, which sought to reduce citizenship to little more than a permit that could be revoked at the whim of the government.

It took a very special kind of courage to pursue one's convictions in the face of such a threat; yet thousands of foreign-born men and women stubbornly clung to their belief in our great democratic traditions and never ceased working in the spirit of that faith, cost what it might. They marched in picket lines to support strikes and establish unions, demonstrated for social security, unemployment compensation, civil rights, and worked for the election of people's legislators like Stanley Nowak. They valiantly bore opprobrium, indignities, persecution, imprisonment, revocation of citizenship, and sometimes deportation.

Besides enriching U.S. life with their cultural heritage, they worked in U.S. mines, mills, and factories to make this a great industrial nation; fought in our armed forces; embraced our great historic traditions of freedom and responsibility and worked to keep them alive. We owe them a great deal, and this is my small tribute to their gallant efforts in the face of truly un-American forces that would have destroyed what had made us a great nation.

Contents

Illustrations

Preface

I was impelled to write this book by a number of factors. Very early in our marriage, when Stanley became one of the first five organizers hired by the UAW, I realized the historic nature of his work and that of other activists. In addition to that, Stanley represents a number of historic firsts, one of which is that he became the first labor legislator in Michigan history, representing labor and the common people in the Michigan State Senate against great odds, both personal and political. Another first was the joint campaign with his Senate colleague, Charles C. Diggs, Sr., in 1941, for election to the Detroit common council, bringing together Black and white people at all levels in a common endeavor.

When denaturalization proceedings were initiated against Stanley in 1952, friends urged me to write the book as a weapon in his defense. I undertook the task with some understandable reluctance, for I was up to my ears in the work of Stanley's defense committee, was trying to run an insurance business from our home, care for my mother, who was blind and somewhat incapacitated, look after our teenage daughter, and manage a very busy household that had become the center of our political activities and of the campaign for his defense. By the time the book was finished, the Supreme Court had issued its landmark decision in favor of Stanley in 1958, and the publisher lost interest. So I put away the book.

In the 1960s, college and university students from around the country were reading my manuscript in the Nowak Collection at the Labor Archives of the Walter Reuther Library of Labor and Urban Affairs at Wayne State

University in Detroit and came to interview us for their dissertations on various aspects of labor history. I realized that much of what they asked about was in my manuscript but needed documentation and the establishment of time sequences. I decided to rewrite the book.

By then I was working full-time in Ernest Goodman's law office and had to work on the manuscript in the early morning before leaving for work, doing the research on weekends. Partial retirement in 1975 eased the time situation and enabled me to do more research. In April of 1976 my working years were ended when an automobile accident left me with a broken neck, broken shoulder bone, cracked ribs, and a severe concussion. In the long months of convalescence, with a circle cast held by four screws to my head, and a body cast to my hips, I had ample time to think and read and to begin researching the materials we had at home.

We had in our possession bound volumes of the Polish paper *Glos ludowy* (People's voice) going back to 1932, when I had met Stanley. With some knowledge of the Polish language and some help from Stanley, I was able to translate relevant items. Also, I found in the paper's English pages a wealth of material on the struggles in which Stanley had played a major part. We also had a copy of the official court transcript of the denaturalization hearing of 1954 before Judge Frank Picard. I studied this long and carefully, recalling vividly those painful days. Every quoted word in the chapter on the hearing is taken directly from the court transcript, with silent omissions not affecting the meaning.

When I was finally able to return to normal life, I went to the Detroit Public Library, where I found the following sources:

Microfilms of the Chicago daily papers of 1920 and 1921, borrowed through the Inter-Library File Exchange Service

Microfilms of all Detroit daily papers going back to 1929

The *Michigan Manual* for each of Stanley's Senate terms, 1939 through 1949

The *Senate Journal* (recorded daily proceedings) for each of Stanley's Senate terms

Bound volumes of proceedings of the House Un-American Activities Committee, where Stanley had been interrogated on several occasions

As I finished writing each chapter about a specific strike led by Stanley, we called together people who had participated in the strike, read the chapter to them and obtained verification, corrections, or additional details that both of us had overlooked or forgotten.

Since I had shared much of Stanley's work so intimately, it was inevitable that the book became *our* story. When we appeared in 1978 at one of Warner Pflug's labor history classes at the Walter Reuther Library, he introduced us as "two who were there." This gave me the title for my book.

University students and academics, some from Europe, still come to interview us as veterans of the struggles of the twenties and thirties and as targets of McCarthyism. I hope my book will answer some of the questions repeatedly asked of us. More than that, I hope readers may learn from our story the tremendous role that U.S. Poles and other ethnic groups played in organizing the UAW and in helping to preserve our democratic traditions. Their story has never been fully told, and without their aid in the very early days of the UAW it would have been much more difficult to organize. They provided meeting places when no other halls were to be had; they publicized on their language radio programs, and in their language newspapers the news of organizing drives and affairs; they provided cultural entertainment at UAW gatherings; and most of all, they provided courageous, aggressive people to picket or to hand out literature in the cold and rain, brave the tear gas and the clubs, raise funds, and provide an example to other U.S. workers. These were the people Stanley largely worked with, and their contribution should never be forgotten.

Above all, we hope that our story will demonstrate that the organizing and building of a labor organization is never a one-man show but is made up of the efforts of numberless people. Organizers may offer some leadership and know-how, but the people provide the manpower and womanpower to do the job.

Today's problems are much more complex than ours were when the UAW was coming into being and providing a focal point to put into action the anger and frustration of people long denied their basic needs and rights. But today's generation will find a way, as we did, and may perhaps learn something from our story.

Acknowledgments

My deepest thanks to the following, who have helped at various stages in my writing and my efforts to be published. To the authors of *Working Detroit*, Steve Babson, David Elsila, and Ron Alpern, for their suggestions and encouragement. To Professor Chris Johnson of the History Department of Wayne State University for advice and suggestions in calling my manuscript to the attention of publishers. To Henry Kraus, first editor of the early UAW paper, the *Autoworker*, and to his wife, Dorothy, for prodding me to write this book. To Professor Neil Leighton of the Michigan State University campus in Flint, Michigan for suggestions on chapter arrangement to point up the role of women as labor organizers and activists. To the late Dr. Charles A. Lewis, who for years conducted a writers' workshop on Saturdays at Wayne State University, where I read most of my chapters and received guidance from Dr. Lewis and suggestions from workshop members. To Dr. Philip Mason of the Labor Archives of the Walter Reuther Library of Labor and Urban Affairs for his attempts to get my book published earlier. To Warner Pflug, also of the Labor Archives, who, along with Di Miles, facilitated my research there. To the copy-editor, Michael Lane, who helped me bring order out of confusion. To my editor, Kathryn Peterson Wildfong, whose patience and helpfulness in the final preparation of my manuscript made it a real pleasure to work with her. Last, and perhaps most of all, to Professor Thaddeus Radzilowski, a historian thoroughly familiar with the role of the Poles and other Slav groups in the period about which I write, for reading my book, correcting some errors, and writing the Introduction.

Introduction

by Thaddeus C. Radzilowski

Every historical period—and our own is no exception—constructs a past that it finds useful and comfortable. Some parts of its past are relegated to oblivion, others develop a new and even exaggerated significance. The social and political climate can make even distant eras seem accessible and immediate and doom the most recent past to incomprehensibility. The thirties is one of those periods that have become alien and remote to us. Separated as we are from it by the great chasms of the Second World War, the cold war and the postwar period of prosperity and empire, the thirties with its hunger and social desperation, its class struggles and violence, seems like a period from another place or another century. A Polish immigrant woman who participated in the heroic 1937 sit-down of the cigarworkers in Detroit remembered forty years later that her children and grandchildren greeted her stories with disbelief and suspicions of senility. One grandson told her, "That couldn't have happened in America, grandma. You must be remembering something that happened under the Russians in Poland when you were a little girl."

Margaret Collingwood Nowak's memoir, *Two Who Were There,* helps us to rescue the thirties and especially the workers' struggle of that period from the shadows into which they have slipped. Through the stories of Margaret and Stanley Nowak, we get a fresh perspective on that crucial decade in U.S. history and the echoes of the struggles of that time as they reverberated across postwar history. It is perhaps appropriate that her story opens with an account of the yet little-known 1937 strike by immigrant women in the cigar factories that turned into one of the longest sit-downs in the history of the labor movement. By beginning her narrative with one of the more dramatic events of that turbulent decade in Detroit, she not only establishes the centrality of the thirties to her story but also highlights the key role women and immigrants played in it.

Margaret Nowak's introduction to Polish and other East and South European immigrant communities and to the labor movement came through her husband, Stanley. His life represents an interesting variant of the classic immigrant success story. He came to Chicago's back-of-the-yards neighborhood from Austrian Poland as a boy with his family shortly before the First World War. After a few years of primary education in the parish school, he dropped out to find work. He continued his education by self-study and wide reading guided by the actors of the Polish theaters in his neighborhood and by local socialists. Until after the First World War, the Polish Socialist party (PPS) maintained a strong presence in Polish immigrant neighborhoods. The association of the Polish Socialists with the Central Powers during the war and their struggle under the aegis of Austria-Hungary for a reconstituted Poland combined with the postwar repression in the United States to reduce their strength to only a shadow by the midtwenties. Their influence continued to be felt long afterwards, however, in the activities and ideas of young people like Stanley Nowak who emerged as leaders in the struggle for CIO unions.

The Palmer raids and the postwar strikes in the packing houses that broke the unions gave Stanley Nowak his first opportunities to act as an advocate for the sorely pressed immigrant workers of his neighborhood. That advocacy cost him his first newspaper job and started him on what was to be his life's work.

In the course of his career as organizer and advocate, he was to become as classic an example of an ethnic leader as the churchmen and businessmen with whom he contended for the loyalty of the immigrant workers and their children. He had all of the characteristics ascribed to ethnic leaders: a broader education and more cosmopolitan outlook than his constituents, knowledge of the workings of the institutions of the ethnic community and the wider society, extensive contacts in both worlds and the ability to broker between them. The work of organizers such as Nowak made the new union locals quasi-ethnic institutions during the early period of their existence.

Nothing characterized Stanley Nowak's career as a leader more than his willingness to build coalitions and make alliances across ethnic and political lines in the interest of his working class and immigrant constituency and in the name of the vision of the society in which he had come to believe as a young man. The two indictments he suffered during his career highlighted his close association with Communists both inside and outside the Polish community. He worked closely with the National Lawyers Guild during his legislative career and in the course of his many activities he associated with party members as diverse as William McKie, Johnny Gallo, Tony Marinovich, Boleslaw Gebert, and Oskar Lange. His long association with the newspaper *Glos ludowy* (People's voice) as reporter and editor kept him in close contact with the Communist party and its members. But to concentrate on those ties to the exclusion of others is to miss the reasons for his remarkable success as an organizer and politician.[1]

In the course of his long career as a union organizer, politician, legislator, and relief administrator, Stanley Nowak initiated alliances with a wide variety of socialists and liberals, Democratic and Republican politicians, and conservative churchmen. The goals of building strong unions and winning progressive reforms always superseded, for both Stanley and Margaret, considerations of ideological purity. They welcomed anyone who would work for the causes they deemed important. Margaret Nowak's account of her husband's alliance with Archbishop Woznicki on the issue of post–World War II Polish relief and their agreement not to raise any political considerations that would hamper it is a case in point.

The willingness to raise the creation of broad alliances to the level of strategic principle rather than narrow tactic kept the Nowaks out of most of the ideological and sectarian battles that affected the Left in the thirties. Even more important to that end was the overwhelming and all-consuming nature of the union organizing and the local political work in which they were involved. As Margaret's memoir indicates, there was barely time to eat and sleep during those hectic days in the late thirties and early forties.

Margaret's story of her early life provides another dimension to the history of the U.S. Left in the twentieth century. Of English–Pennsylvania Dutch ancestry and a pietistic, sectarian religious background, she was converted to left-wing views as a young woman by a debate in 1931 between Al Renner of the Proletarian party and William Lovett of the Michigan Association of Manufacturers. That experience crystalized her growing anger at the lot of her family, especially the plight of her father, during the depression and the strong imperative she felt for communal service as a result of her upbringing in the Church of the Brethren into a commitment to work toward a change in the social and economic system. It also led her to the Proletarian party. The two met at a meeting of the Proletarian party at which Stanley Nowak spoke.

The Proletarian party was a peculiar offshoot of the 1919 split that divided the socialist movement and led to the creation of the American Communist party. A group of Michigan leftists unable to make common cause with either the truncated Socialist party or the new Communist party formed a new party. With most of its strength in southern Michigan, the new Proletarian party established its headquarters in Detroit in 1920. It also had centers of support in a few other cities of the Great Lakes region such as Buffalo, New York. The party rejected all compromise with the existing social order and any struggle for immediate demands. It was committed to a notion of a majoritarian revolution achieved by election, in which a conscious and educated proletariat took power fully prepared for the task of managing a humane and progressive industrial society. The party thus eschewed all participation in the electoral process for the immediate future and committed itself to the massive task of the education of the working class through party schools, public lectures, political demonstrations, and publications of all kinds. Membership in the Proletarian party swelled during the depression as disillusioned young people like Margaret Collingwood joined in search of a social vision better than the one that had so apparently failed the United States' people. Its strong emphasis on education made it the ideal entry point to the Left for many who later moved on to other work and new commitments.[2]

The depression also radicalized the immigrant working class of Detroit. Even before the depression of the thirties, they had been a marginal group. When the Great Crash came, they were still recovering from the post–World War I depression. In 1921–22, cases of serious malnutrition and even starvation had been reported among Polish immigrants in the industrial enclave of Hamtramck on the city's east side. By 1922, relief funds in Hamtramck had run out completely leaving thousands destitute.[3] The depression of the thirties hit the weakened immigrant communities even more severely than its predecessor. It threatened—as nothing had before—the homes, churches, and other institutions on which immigrant workers had painstakingly built up their communities.

By 1932 as many as forty-five hundred families a month in the Detroit area were being evicted from their homes. In Hamtramck, candidates for election to the constable's office campaigned for the homeowner's vote with promises to conduct evictions in a dignified and humane manner. Those who lost homes or were evicted from rented quarters often took up residence with neighbors or relatives. Three or even four families living in a single home was not a rare situation in Detroit's working-class neighborhoods.

Unemployment among immigrant workers reached almost 50 percent by 1932. Public assistance in Detroit fell to fifteen cents a day before running out completely. In Hamtramck, where half the population was on relief, families with less than three children were removed from the welfare rolls in order to target scarce resources to the neediest and most vulnerable. Long lines of children queued up daily at parish convents to get a warm breakfast before school.[4] In one Polish Catholic parish, almost 20 percent of the families could afford to contribute less than a dollar for the year 1933. Some gave only a penny or two in order to keep their names on the parish roster.[5]

Those lucky enough to have employment suffered intolerable conditions that continued to deteriorate as the crisis deepened. They faced reductions in their already low wages, irregular work, incessant speedups, and dismissals over the most trivial matters. Women workers were subjected to constant sexual harrassment. Older workers who could not keep up with the ever increasing rate of production were dismissed as a regular practice as corporations took full advantage of the favorable labor market. The Ford Motor Company was one of the worst offenders. A study of the families of laid off Ford workers by the welfare department of the city of Hamtramck showed that in 45 percent of cases the head of the family was between 41 and 50 years of age when permanently laid off by the company. Many had from fifteen to twenty-five years of seniority.[6]

The threatened dissolution of the bases of communities built on homeownership and secure jobs caused a rising wave of militancy among Detroit's immigrant groups. Thousands of East and South European immigrant workers and their families marched in the demonstrations organized by Unemployed Councils. Joe York (Joseph Jurkiewicz), a young Polish-American worker, one of the leaders of a march of unemployed workers to the Ford plant in March 1932 was killed when the Dearborn police department opened fire on the crowd. His funeral and that of the other slain brought out into the streets of Detroit over 100 thousand people, the majority from its immigrant neighborhoods.[7]

Community-based militancy continued to develop even as the economic situation began to improve and employment increased. During the summer of 1935, when the autoworkers union was still in its embryonic stage, demonstrations by women broke out in Polish neighborhoods to protest the high cost of living. Led by the wife of an unemployed autoworker, Mary Zuk, the protests turned into a meat boycott. The boycott soon spread to other immigrant neighborhoods and to adjacent black areas of the city. Within a few weeks, the meat strikes spread to other cities in Michigan and across the Midwest. In the Polish neighborhoods, where the boycott action and picketing were most intense, confrontations between boycott supporters and customers at butcher shops sometimes become violent; and police arrested increasing numbers of demonstrators, most of them housewives.

On 16 August 1935 the boycott committee held a rally at Perrin Park in the heart of Detroit's east-side Polish neighborhood that drew five thousand supporters. The leaders were sent to Washington to testify before a congressional committee whose inquiry into the high cost of food was provoked by the action of the women. The boycott petered out by fall without a marked effect on the prices of food and other necessities; but it did launch the political career of Mary Zuk in Hamtramck, where the boycott action began, and led to the founding of a People's League. She was elected to the city council in 1936 and got increasingly involved in the fledgling labor movement, as Margaret Nowak's memoir points out.

The People's League of Hamtramck, which she helped to organize, was instrumental in mustering community support for CIO organizing drives and sit-downs, especially at Dodge Main Plant. Its program was a mixture of ethnic, community, and union demands including demands for the end of ethnic and racial discrimination; construction of more playgrounds, recreation centers, libraries, public toilets and medical facilities; the end to use of police in labor disputes; and the payment of union scale on public projects.[8]

Thus at the time Stanley and Margaret Nowak became involved in the work of organizing an autoworkers union, a strong streak of militancy was already running through the immigrant neighborhoods; and some segments of it had developed considerable experience with organized protest. In addition, although Detroit had a notorious reputation as an "open-shop" town, there were small groups of workers who had previous union experience and who provided an important shop-floor cadre for the new union. These included workers who had participated in earlier attempts to form an autoworkers union in the twenties; workers who had worked in factories in Europe and who had been members of European Socialist parties; and former members of the mineworkers union who had come to Detroit from Pennsylvania, West Virginia, and southern Ohio seeking work. The last group was the largest and most important, as the migration of both English-speaking and Slavic miners to the auto factories had been particularly heavy during the previous two decades. For many immigrant workers Detroit was a place of second settlement.

Immigrant workers and their children were to be the main focus of the Nowaks' organizing work for the United Auto Workers Union. Everywhere in the Midwest, East and South European workers were the key groups that had to be won over if the CIO was to succeed. East Europeans, with Poles as the predominant group among them, were the largest minority group in the key industries around which the CIO was building: steel, auto, agricultural machinery, coal, and meat packing. If they had not come over, the effort to build industrial unions would have collapsed. But they did come over en masse. One organizer noted that between 500 and 600 thousand Polish Americans came over to CIO unions between 1936 and 1938. Margaret Nowak's memoir illuminates for us a segment of the Detroit part of that little-known story.[9]

In 1930, 25 percent of Detroit's population was foreign-born. The majority of these were East and South Europeans, who together with their children made up more than half of Detroit's working class. Polish Americans composed more than 20 percent of Detroit's population when the Great Depression started. Organizing the foreign-born and their sons and daughters was obviously as crucial to the union's success in Detroit as it was in other cities. But organizing among the ethnic workers meant something more than printing and speaking the union message in their native tongues. It also meant gaining entree to the rich variety of institutions and resources that the immigrant communities had built. This entree provided access to workers who could not be reached in the hectic, repressive, spy-ridden atmosphere of the shop floor; and it legitimized the union message. Just as importantly, it provided the poor, fledgling unions with the media, networks, and meeting halls they lacked. Denied access to most of Detroit's public meeting places and having few of their own, the unions in the early days held their meetings and rallies and conducted a great deal of their business in ethnic halls located in the immigrant neighborhoods that bordered the auto plants.[10] The ethnic groups of Detroit thus provided the unions with a substitute institutional infrastructure during the critical opening phases of the union drive. Margaret Nowak's account of those years gives us some idea of how important that contribution was.

Stanley Nowak and his associates did not of course invent the idea of using ethnic networks and institutions to reach immigrant workers and their U.S.-born children. They refined and perfected a strategy that had been first used in Detroit in the twenties by the Auto Workers Union (AWU). The Communist-dominated AWU led by Phil Raymond tried to get its message to autoworkers through ethnic fraternals and clubs and often used ethnic halls for meetings. Later, during the depression, the same techniques were used with even greater success by the Unemployed Councils. In Hamtramck, for example, the councils worked with several fraternal groups and used their facilities for meetings. Many of the organizers of the Unemployed Councils—like Raymond—had previously been with the AWU.[11] The Action Committee against the High Cost of Living that organized the meat boycott also used ethnic halls, in particular the Dom Polski (Polish Home) for its meetings and rallies.

Nowak and his associates in the UAW not only used the ethnic networks and resources more intensively than did their predecessors but developed a new wrinkle. As a result of his contacts in Polish theater Nowak was able to get on one of the most popular programs on Polish radio to spread the union message. Ethnic radio proved to be one of the most effective organizing tools the UAW developed to rally foreign-born workers to its cause. In cities such as Chicago, in which it proved impossible to get regular access to ethnic radio programs, the task of reaching the workers and keeping them informed was immeasurably more difficult.[12]

The use of Polish radio by Nowak revealed an interesting aspect of the acculturation of East European workers to the U.S. scene. They accommodated themselves to the predominant Polish-American culture that was evolving in Detroit rather than accept U.S. substitutes for things that their own group could not provide. Polish, as it was spoken in Detroit, had also developed into a lingua franca for Detroit's Slavs. The relative closeness of the Slavic languages made Polish intelligible for other Slavic groups with a little effort and many of Detroit's Slavs-Rusyns, Ukrainians, Belorussians—as well as the non-Slavic Lithuanians came from areas in Europe in which the influence of Polish language and culture had been strong for centuries. Thus the appeals on Polish radio attracted not only Poles but members of other, smaller ethnic groups who were also regular listeners to popular Polish shows.

The size of the Polish-American group in Detroit and its preponderance and political power in Hamtramck, in which such key plants as Dodge Main and Chevrolet Gear and Axle were located, made it the focus of Nowak's efforts. The militant mood of the community as well as his wide contacts and considerable skill in bringing diverse groups into alliance allowed him to build a coalition in the Polish community that covered the entire political spectrum from right to left. The culmination of those efforts came during the Ford drive in 1941, when a meeting of the leaders of the Polish community at the Dom Polski (Polish Home) produced a manifesto pledging support for the unionization of the Ford Motor Company and characterizing it as necessary for the preservation of democracy in the United States. Henry Ford was described as a Fascist sympathizer and friend of Adolph Hitler. The document was signed by presidents of lodges of the Polish Roman Catholic Union, Polish National Alliance, and Polish Women's Alliance; by leaders of professional groups such as the Polish Lawyers Society and of university clubs; and by individual judges, elected officials, journalists, and radio and stage personalities.[13]

The Ford drive marks the height of union influence in the ethnic communities of Detroit. Both the unions and the ethnic groups were soon distracted by other events, especially the war. The unions, now with their own buildings and new bureaucracies and preoccupied with the work of consolidating their hard-won positions, no longer found close ties with ethnic organizations as necessary as earlier and had neither the resources nor the willingness to continue to develop those ties. As a result, the bonds that had been forged during the struggles of the thirties began to attenuate after 1941.

Margaret Nowak's story of the thirties gives pride of place to actions of the immigrant and U.S. southern women with whom she and her husband worked. The involvement of immigrant women in the organizing drives reflected the militancy of the communities from which they came—a militancy they themselves had been central to fostering. The cigarworkers and Ternstedt women came out of the same neighborhoods the meat boycotts had originated from. Mary Zuk, whose political career had been launched by the boycott, worked with Stanley Nowak during the cigarworkers strike. The courageous support neighborhood women gave to the strikers, as in the Federal Screw strike described in the book, bears witness to the role of community militance in mobilizing women as well as men. Margaret Nowak's women yield to no one in their daring and imagination. They prove false the belief that women are always harder to organize than men and act less militantly.

Black Americans play a less central role in the Nowak story than the immigrants and their children, but it is not an unimportant one. The racial situation in Detroit had begun to deteriorate during the thirties. Beginning with the First World War, white Southerners had begun to come north and to compete with immigrants for work in the auto plants. They brought their nativism and racial attitudes with them. The parallel stream of black migrants also began to threaten the immigrants' access to jobs. Ethnic workers started to identify as "white" in reaction, in order to get a leg up in the competition. Blacks, in turn, seeing desirable jobs held by immigrants who had arrived only shortly before them became increasingly nativist, arguing that work should be reserved for U.S.-born citizens and denied to foreign-born. The hunger, unemployment, and insecurity of the Great Depression exacerbated the grievances and sharpened the antagonism of the three groups at the bottom of Detroit's society.

During the organizing drives many employers used blacks as strikebreakers. In many such strikes, such as the 1939 sit-down at Dodge Main, they were pitted against a largely East European work force. The most serious clash came during the 1941 Ford strike when several hundred black men attacked the UAW picket lines. Just two years before the Detroit race riot, immigrant workers and their sons and blacks battled each other with clubs and iron bars over jobs at the instigation of the Ford Motor Company. Cynical company policies combined with the depression to create an explosive situation in Detroit by the early forties and left a legacy of deep antagonisms that still plague the city.[14]

The clash over jobs began to translate itself by the end of the thirties into a struggle over housing and neighborhoods. Up to that point blacks and immigrants had lived in relative harmony in the Detroit area. In the largely Polish city of Hamtramck, for example, blacks and immigrants had shared the same neighborhoods since the first decade of the century. The infamous 1926 attempt by a mob to prevent Dr. Ossian Sweet from moving into a new home in a white neighborhood had taken place several miles from the nearest East European neighborhood and had little effect on conditions there. But by 1941 the situation had changed for the worst. Housing was in short supply for all but especially for new black immigrants. In the wake of Dodge and Ford strikes and in the midst of a massive layoff of over 250 thousand workers to shift factories over to war production, which brought misery unseen since the early depression and desperate pleas for emergency federal assistance, a clash took place between East Europeans, mainly Poles, and blacks over the ownership of the Sojourner Truth housing project. This first major contest over neighborhoods broke into violence in early 1942 before being resolved in favor of the black claimants.[15]

Government studies of the impact of the Sojourner Truth housing project incident on war production clearly tied the housing clash to the struggle for jobs. They reported,

> The conflict dramatizes all of the insecurity and displaced aggression of the immigrant in northern cities. . . . The conflict could better be called a Polish-Negro conflict . . . than a Black-White conflict.
>
> In Detroit, the Poles are the biggest cultural minority and the Negroes the second. . . . During the past depression and to a certain extent even during the lush pre-war boom, and now again . . . there have never been enough jobs to go around.
>
> The immigrant class is a working class. The Negro class is a working class. Due to a competitive set up they both compete with each other for jobs. Due to the many things both groups have suffered, both tend to look for substitute targets for their aggression and feelings of resentment against injustice and oppression, because they are afraid to make a direct attack upon the authors of their misery, or because they haven't the education or the patience under strain to sit down and figure out by social analysis why their living standards are low and why they must compete against each other for jobs.
>
> Under such a condition one always wonders why he does not get a job when someone else does and begins to devise rationalizations why he should have a job and the other fellow not.
>
> The important facts in this case are that immigrants say white men should have jobs before Negroes and Negroes say that people who have been in this country the longest should have jobs first.[16]

It was against this background that the Nowaks courageously chose to run a joint campaign in Stanley's bid for a seat on the Detroit City Council with his black colleague from the Michigan Senate, Charles Diggs, Sr. Their efforts were significant in winning considerable support for Diggs from Stanley Nowak's ethnic constituencies during a time of deteriorating racial relations. He later ran for the city council with Rev. Charles Hill, a black community leader, as a running mate.[17] As a result of his influence, Hill got 60 percent of Nowak's vote in the most heavily Polish precincts of the city in the 1949 election.

In the course of his effort in organizing workers Nowak also devoted considerable effort to winning crucial support of black workers and building coalitions between them and white workers. In the face of the aggressive, racially divisive policies of Detroit's major employers and the accumulated anger of the city's racial and ethnic groups, the efforts of the Nowaks and others like them in the union movement were critical in keeping the situation from sinking into anarchy. The race riot of 1943 was a terrible event, but Margaret Nowak's story reminds us how tragic indeed the situation in Detroit would have become by the mid-1940s if the union movement had gone down to defeat.

Stanley Nowak's two indictments came during periods of repression and antiradical and antiforeign hysteria, the first during early days of World War II and the second at the height of the McCarthy era. The internment of Japanese Americans was only the most outrageous and shameful act of a general development of hostility to foreigners during that first period. Although the repression against European foreigners did not reach the same intensity then that it did during World War I, it was sufficiently threatening to force the Nowaks to devote considerable effort and time to defend their foreign-born friends and constituents. Even some liberals hoped to save foreign-born or ethnic U.S. citizens from harm and humiliation by massive government programs of "Americanization," to remove their "foreign" characteristics.[18] Sensing a favorable climate, Nowak's enemies brought charges against him in order to destroy his influence with his ethnic and working-class constituency and remove him from the Michigan Senate and the political scene entirely. The move to discredit and jail him failed utterly.

By 1943 the nativist and antiradical feelings began to weaken. The turning tide of war, the lingering effects of the New Deal and struggles of the thirties, and the alliance with the Soviet Union helped to dissipate them. After the war, however, they returned with a vengeance as the nation became obsessed with the perceived threat of the Soviet Union abroad and Communist subversion at home. For the Right, the cold war climate offered the ideal opportunity to settle old scores. The Nowaks were again victims of the hysteria. This time escape was not so easy. The repression was more intense, and Stanley was more vulnerable as he no longer held a political office. It would be almost six years before they would again be free of the fear of deportation.

The war had complicated the Nowaks' political world. Stanley had made his reputation in the Michigan Senate as a spokesman for the cause of working people, labor unions, and consumer interests. On the basis of that work he had won a deep loyalty from his constituents. Domestic problems, however, were increasingly being ushered aside by world events. During the war, he and Margaret were pushed into the wider arena of foreign policy and world politics. He became a national officer of the American Slav Congress, which sought to rally U.S. Slavic groups behind the war effort and to strengthen the alliance of the United States and their respective homelands with the USSR. The positions of the American Slav Congress were supported by many of those with whom they had worked in organizing ethnic workers in the Midwest. After the war that support was to cost left-wing ethnic leaders much of their influence. This was especially true in the Polish community.

It is ironic that again, as in the case of the First World War, the Left in the Polish-American community was condemned because of its foreign policy stance.[19] The events in Eastern Europe caused Polish and other East European workers to see the Soviet presence in their homelands not only as the imposition of atheistic communism but also as a renewal of traditional Russian imperialism. The Catholic and Orthodox churches and most of the ethnic leadership supported that position militantly. Those who advocated acceptance of pro-Soviet governments in Eastern Europe were accused of being agents of a dangerous foreign power. To support the American Slav Congress, which ended up on the attorney general's list of subversive organizations, was to appear both un-American—a fear made all the more powerful by the patriotic pressure cooker of World War II—and an enemy of one's people in the old homeland. The position of the Nowaks and others like them became, as a result of the cold war, increasingly marginal in communities in which they had exercised great influence only a few years before.

The legacy of the militance of the thirties and of the work of people like Stanley and Margaret Nowak among the ethnic workers of Detroit was, however, never completely engulfed by postwar developments. Detroit's ethnic workers combined a strong anticommunism in foreign policy with a continuing support of New Deal progressivism in domestic affairs. The significant difference made by the Cold War climate in that support was that after 1945 the Democratic party became the sole, rather than only the major, agency for articulating it in the public arena. Despite the curious myth of the hard-hatted ethnic working-class reactionary that developed during the sixties, most of Detroit's ethnic workers did not deviate markedly from the political faith they had learned in the years of struggle.

They were less likely than most other groups to support a George Wallace or a Joseph McCarthy and they continued to vote for national and local Democratic party candidates identified with the party's progressive wing even when those candidates paid little attention to them.[20] For example, Hamtramck workers voted for George McGovern in greater numbers in 1972 than did college professors (59 percent vs. 57 percent).[21] Despite the gradual drift of their children in the suburbs to the Republican party in the 1980s, at least at the level of presidential politics the older workers in the ethnic neighborhoods were still likely to give their votes to the Democrats.[22] In the precinct around St. Florian's Church in Hamtramck—an area still more than 85 percent Polish—the Mondale-Ferraro ticket got more than 56 percent of the vote in 1984 and the Democratic incumbent Senator Carl Levin did even better.[23]

Nowak's old constituency was also not conspicuous among the supporters of the Vietnam War. In fact, as national and local surveys showed consistently, blue-collar workers opposed the war earlier and in greater numbers than did middle-class people in the city and the nation. In the referendum of November 1968 in Dearborn, Michigan, an area that was part of Stanley Nowak's old senatorial district, 57 percent of the people voted against the war.[24] Again as in the thirties, attitudes about the need to change the United States' course may have "percolated up" from the working class rather than "trickled down" from the middle class, in the words of one observer.[25]

Margaret Nowak tells us a story of the lives of two people whose work and commitment markedly affected our times. These are not lives that can be understood separate from each other—the life work and accomplishment of each was clearly impossible without the other—nor can they be understood apart from the events of their time. In the course of telling her story she has given us a new look at a period of U.S. history that has been unjustly neglected. She has reminded us in the process that at a difficult time in our history when descendants of the founding fathers would have denied basic rights to many of their fellow citizens to preserve their own wealth and power, immigrant men and women and their children fought with courage and imagination, suffered, and even died to widen the meaning of justice and democracy in the United States. It is a story worth remembering and recounting. We are all in her debt for it.

NOTES

1. On the Communist Party and the UAW, see Roger Keeran, *The Communist Party and the Auto Workers Union* (Bloomington: Indiana University Press, 1980).

2. On the origins of the Proletarian party and its position, see Theodore Draper, *The Roots of American Communism* (New York: Viking Press, 1963), 158, 160–61, 182–84, 210–12; Irving Howe and Lewis Coser, *The American Communist Party: A Critical History,*

1919–1957 (Boston: Beacon Press, 1957), 35–38. The Party continued an organized existence in Detroit into the 1940s.

3. See City of Detroit, *Annual Report of the Department of Public Welfare,* 1922. The report concluded that the city "was faced with a situation more serious than that which confronted other large cities. Unemployment extended over a longer period in Detroit and affected largely a recent population who had not been able to achieve that degree of economic security which comes with thrift exercised over a long period of time." See also Helen Wendell, "Conditions in Hamtramck," *Pipps Weekly* 2, no. 23 (24 September 1921): 10–11.

4. On conditions in immigrant areas of Detroit during the depression, see Marian Tarkowski, "Sytuacja robotników Polskich i Polskiego pochodzenia w Okresie międzywojennym" (The situation of Polish and Polish-descent workers in the United States of North America during the interwar period), in *Problemy dziejów Polonii,* ed. Marian M. Drozdowski (Warsaw: Państwowe Wydawnictwo Naukowe, 1979), 88–93. Also see T. Radzilowski, with Don Binkowski, "Polish Politics in Detroit" in *Ethnic Politics in Urban America,* ed. Angela Pienkos (Chicago: Polish-American Historical Assn., 1978), 54–58; and Steve Babson et al., *Working Detroit* (New York: Adama Books, 1984), 52–110.

5. *Florianowo,* 4 March 1934, St. Florian Parish, Hamtramck, MI.

6. Stanley Nowak, speech, Nowak Collection, Box 3-6, File 3, Walter Reuther Library of Labor and Urban Affairs, Wayne State University, Detroit, MI.

7. Stanley Nowak, "Udzial Polakow w organizowaniu Związku Zawodowego Robotników Automobilowych w USA" (The role of Poles in the organization of the United Automobile Workers Union in the USA), *Problemy Polonii zagranicznej* 6–8(1971): 165–70.

8. Thaddeus Radzilowski, "Klasowość, etniczność a spoleczność lokalna: Polonia w Detroit i jej wklad w organizację CIO" (Class, ethnicity and local community: Polonia in Detroit and its contribution to the organization of the CIO), *Przęglad Polonijny* 12, no. 2(1987): 58–59; George Schrode, "Mary Zuk and the Detroit Meat Strike of 1935," *Polish American Studies* 43, no. 2(Autumn 1986): 5–39. See also my comments on Schrode's article in *Polish-American Studies,* 44, no. 2(Autumn 1987):.

9. Boleslaw Gebert, "Polacy w Amerykańskich zwiazkach zawodnych: Notatki i wspomnienia" (Poles in American industrial unions: Notes and reminiscences), *Przęglad Polonijny* 2, no. 1(1976): 151. See also Frank Renkiewicz, "The Polish American Workers, 1880–1980," in *Pastor of the Poles,* ed. S. Blejwas (New Britain: Central Connecticut State University, 1982), 130.

10. Radzilowski, "Klasowość, etniczność a spoleczność lokalna," 60–62.

11. Keernan, *Communist Party,* 56, 69.

12. Stanislaw Nowak, "Proba zlamania Strajków w zakladach McCormicka" (The attempt to break the strike at the McCormick plants) *Glos Ludowy* (Detroit), 17 November 1977. This article was one of a series of autobiographical reminiscences published by Stanley Nowak between 1974 and 1978 in *Glos ludowy.*

13. Stanislaw Nowak, "Wklad Polonii Detroickiej w organizowani robotników Fordowskich" (The contribution of Detroit's Polonia to the organization of the Ford workers) *Glos ludowy,* 8 October 1977.

14. Thaddeus C. Radzilowski, "Ethnic Conflict and the Polish Americans of Detroit, 1921–1942, "*The Polish Presence in Canada and America,* ed. F. Renkiewicz (Toronto: Multicultural History Society of Ontario, 1982), 196–207.

15. Ibid. See also Dominic J. Capeci, Jr., *Race Relations in Wartime Detroit: The Sojourner Truth Controversy of 1942* (Philadelphia: Temple, 1984). Capeci's study is a competent survey of the events, but it doesn't put the incident in its broader context and does not use foreign language sources.

16. Quoted in *P.M.* (New York), 27 June 1943.

17. Neither Nowak nor his black running mates ever got enough votes to be elected. The Electoral Reform of 1919, which came when Poles had become almost a quarter of Detroit's population, substituted at-large council elections for the system of an alderman elected from each ward. This effectively wiped out Polish-American political influence in the city. Since that date only three Polish Americans were ever elected to city council, two of whom had only minimal ties to the Polish community. David Greenstone (*Labor in American Politics* [New York: A. A. Knopf, 1969]) concludes about the 1919 reform engineered by Detroit's Protestant elite, "By comparison with other American cities, Detroit presents an extreme case of both the economic grievances that Marx emphasized and the sins of exclusion that concerned Bendix" (pp. 137–38).

18. One such plan was prepared by Alan Cranston, U.S. senator from California. Mr. Cranston was then a young bureaucrat in the Office of Facts and Figures. Cranston concluded that "a mounting discrimination is slowly dividing Americans, segregating them, turning them against one another and against America. This smoldering suspicion against all peoples of recent foreign backgrounds is an increasingly serious threat to American Unity and the success of the war effort." See "A Program for American Unity" Alan Cranston to Allen Grover, memorandum, 13 January 1942, Office of War Information, Office of Facts and Figures 1941–1942: Racial and Alien Questions, RG 208, Box 66, National Archives.

19. I am indebted to Mary Cygan of Northwestern University for this insight comparing the experience of the Polish Left in the U.S. after the two world wars.

20. Richard Hamilton, "Liberal Intelligentsia and White Backlash," in *The World of the Blue Collar Worker,* edited with introduction by Irving Howe (New York: Quadrangle Books, 1972), 227–38; and Michael Rogin, "Wallace and the Middle Class: The White Backlash in Wisconsin" *Public Opinion Quarterly* (Spring 1966): 98–108. Both conclude that blue-collar ethnic voters were among the least likely to support George Wallace. Rogin concluded that the "higher the percentage of Polish stock, the *lower* the Wallace vote" (emphasis in original). Donald F. Crosby, Jr., S. J., *God, Church, and Flag: Senator McCarthy and the Catholic Church, 1950–1957* (Chapel Hill: University of North Carolina Press, 1978) notes that McCarthy ran at least ten points behind every other Republican in East European areas in 1952. In the heavily Polish precincts of Milwaukee he got only 28% of the vote. His main support was rural (pp. 96–97).

21. *Hamtramck Citizen,* 9 November 1972.

22. National polls such as the ABC–*Washington Post* poll show that East Europeans continue to give 55%–60% of their votes to Democratic-party candidates in senatorial, congressional, state, and local elections consistently.

23. *Hamtramck Citizen,* 8 November 1984. The St. Florian neighborhood, near the site of the Dodge Main and Chevrolet plants, has been designated a historic area as an excellent example of a "well preserved immigrant working class neighborhood built at the beginning of the century." The national East European vote in the 1984 election was approximately 54% for Reagan-Bush and 46% for Mondale-Ferraro according to the ABC–*Washington Post* survey. In 1980, the national Polish-American vote was 44%–46% for Carter, 40%–42% for Reagan, and 13%–15% for Anderson. The vote for the Democratic ticket was higher than the national average in both cases in Polish and other East European working-class areas of Detroit.

24. See Harlan Hahn, "Correlates of Public Sentiments about the War: Local Referenda on the Vietnam Issue," *American Political Science Review* (1970): 1186–88; and "Dove Sentiments among Blue Collar Workers," *Dissent* (May–June 1970): 202–5. A. Greeley, "Civil Religion and Ethnic Americans," *Worldview* (February 1973): 21–27. Gallup polls between 1964 and 1974 consistently show white working-class people more opposed to war and escalation than the middle class.

25. Harlan Hahn, "Dove Sentiments among Blue Collar Workers," 204.

1 Women on the March

In 1936 Stanley Nowak was thirty-three years old. Since the age of ten he had lived and worked in one working-class Polish community or another in the United States and used the Polish language at work, at home, and in his social life.

In June 1936 he had joined the international organizing staff of the United Auto Workers and had been assigned to organize the thousands of Polish and Slavic workers in Detroit area shops. To help in this task he had established the UAW Polish Trade Union Committee, and twice weekly he was heard on the radio by thousands of Poles and Slavs from every industry in the Detroit area as he spoke in Polish on the advantages of a union. Employees in other industries began to emulate the autoworkers, sitting down on the job on the spur of the moment without a union or any idea of how to proceed, then frantically calling the UAW for help.

One such group, women in the cigar factories of Detroit, mostly of Polish or Slavic background, fought hard for and obtained Stanley's help in their struggle, where they set an outstanding example to Detroit workers by their courage, determination, and discipline.

In December 1936 women began to realize that the sit-down could be a woman's game, too. While Madame Galli Curci, the noted opera singer, was in Detroit preparing for the "Ford Sunday Radio Hour," women sitting down in the Gordon Baking Company were singing a different tune, and their strike made the front pages of the papers on the eighth.

The great General Motors sit-down in Flint, Michigan opened the year of 1937. Through January, February, March, April, and later sit-downs occurred in rapid succession in many Detroit plants, among them the Packard Motor Car Company, Midland Steel, Briggs, Aluminum Company of America, Chrysler, Kelsey-Hayes, Bohn Aluminum, and Kelvinator.

While this domestic war flared, the war in Spain was in full swing, with daily reports from Ernest Hemingway in the *Detroit News*, and Wallis Simpson's romance with the Duke of Windsor splashed all over the front pages.

The Polish paper, *Glos ludowy* (People's Voice), reported on 7 January 1937 that twenty-five women had been fired by the Bernard Schwartz Company, makers of the R. G. Dunn cigars. At management's request, disgruntled women had elected a committee of twenty-five to present their demands, and after the Christmas holidays all twenty-five were fired.

This provocative act enraged workers in every cigar shop in the city. There were six, employing over four thousand women, in a four-mile-square area from Milwaukee to Warren Avenue at the north and south and from St. Aubin to Grandy in the east and west. Trouble was brewing in every cigar shop in the area, as almost all cigarworkers knew each other from having worked together at different times in one or another of the shops. Many were related – mothers and daughters, sisters, aunts, nieces, cousins – working sometimes in the same shop, sometimes each in a different one.

Most were Polish and constantly brought their seething anger to the attention of the UAW Polish Trade Union Committee; but since its members were all overwhelmed by the monumental efforts of the UAW to organize the autoworkers and since there was thus a shortage of organizers, committee members could only offer sympathy and advice.

On the morning of 17 February a phone call summoned Stanley to UAW Secretary-Treasurer George Addes's office, where a group of women from the cigar factories had assembled. Before Stanley could learn why they were there, Addes waved him into his office: "Stanley, these women came early this morning demanding your help in organizing the cigar shops. Women have been sitting down in one of the shops since yesterday noon, and they don't know how to proceed. I told them we don't have enough organizers to handle calls for help from auto shops alone and that you are working on the Ternstedt drive, which is already too long delayed."

"I know," agreed Stanley. "These same women have talked to me at Polish meetings and affairs, and I've told them the same thing."

"Well, you should have seen them this morning!" said Addes. "When I said we couldn't spare you, they all exploded at once and reminded me that the UAW has helped others besides autoworkers. Since the cigarworkers are probably the lowest-paid workers in the city, with the worst working conditions, they don't see why you can't help them.

"I asked, 'Why Nowak?' and all said the cigarworkers mostly speak Polish and need someone who speaks their language. They listen to you on the UAW Polish radio program and they want you. I asked why they didn't go to the AFL Cigar Workers Union, and they said they had, several times, but without results. They feel that the AFL is not interested in such low-paid workers. At that point I phoned you. See what you can do with them, Stanley."

Addes and Stanley went out to face the women, who stood up expectantly. "I realize your problems," Stanley began in Polish, "but it is true we have more calls for help than we can handle. You know that I am assigned to organize the foreign-born autoworkers. Also, Reuther asked me weeks ago to work on the Ternstedt drive, but the General Motors Flint strike intervened. Now if I go with you, it means the twelve hundred Ternstedt workers, mostly women, must still wait for an organizer."

The women were unimpressed. Helen Nowak (no relation, now Piwkowski) a tall, slim, attractive blond, turned to Stanley, her blue eyes smiling but her words pointed and sharp: "What is it, Nowak? Are the Ternstedt women more important than we are? *They* are not on strike. We *are.* And we need you."

"Ternstedt's is a GM shop," Stanley explained. "We must get the workers signed into the union so management will comply with the GM master contract and bargain with us. The situation is critical."

"All right!" Frances Niewiadomska, tall, big-boned, heavy, and blond, eyes flashing indignation, spoke up. "We hear about the UAW sit-down strikes. Until Addes sends you with us we will have our own sit-down right here! We're not leaving without you!" With that, she sat down in one of the chairs. The other women quickly followed her example and turned angry, accusing eyes upon Addes.

"Now what?" he asked, since the woman had spoken in Polish.

"They're staging their own sit-down right here," laughed Stanley. "They say they're staying until you send me with them."

"Are they serious?" Addes asked.

"Judge for yourself," replied Stanley.

Sophie Myszka, small and soft-spoken, stood before Addes. "You think we're kidding?" she said in English. "We mean it!" She waved a warning finger under Addes's nose. "We'll show you!"

Addes quickly took Stanley back into his office. "Stanley, you know Reuther will be sore if you don't get on with the Ternstedt drive, and yet we can't have these women cluttering our lobby and disrupting work here.

Besides, the publicity might be bad for the UAW. Do you think if you helped them for a few days, they might be able to carry on without you?"

"I don't know, George. It might be possible."

"Well, I don't know what else to do," sighed Addes, "but only for a few days, mind you!"

He and Stanley returned to the lobby to find the women phoning their families and preparing for a prolonged stay. They had not expected victory so soon.

"Nowak can go with you a few days to get you started," announced Addes, "then he will have to go to Ternstedt's."

"Hurray!" chorused the women. All talking at once, they took Stanley by each arm and propelled him out of the office, leaving Addes shaking his head. Little did he or anyone know how those "few" days were to stretch.

Stanley took some of the women in his car, and Helen Nowak took some in hers, and all headed for the Webster Eisenlohr Cigar Shop at 5545 Grandy, where their strike was under way. On the way, the women related what had led to the sit-down. This was corroborated by news articles that day.

With no experience to guide them, a large number of the women had decided to do something about their deplorable working conditions. They had put a notice on the bulletin board announcing a sit-down and warning the women not to leave the plant. The newly won Kelvinator sit-down was mentioned with the words, "they're getting sixty-five cents an hour out there."

The women then asked the manager for a 10 percent raise and a change in hours. He told them to select a committee, then said he had no authority to negotiate but would contact the company president, who had agreed to meet with the committee Sunday morning. Temporarily pacified, the women returned to work, but their indignation grew until they again stopped and demanded immediate action. Some had heard Stanley on the Polish radio program and had met him at Polish meetings, picnics, and affairs. They proposed a delegation visit the UAW to demand his help. A group was quickly chosen, and these were the women who had been in Addes's office.

Before reaching the Webster Eisenlohr shop, the women described their working conditions, which they said were typical of cigar factories. The most highly skilled workers found it difficult to earn more than twelve to eighteen dollars a week, working six and sometimes seven days a week. Such hours were hard on women with families, yet their wages were desperately needed.

The women said there was hardly any ventilation in the shops because the air had to be kept humid to prevent the drying out of the tobacco, and workers often fainted from the fumes. They also told of inadequate and unsanitary toilet facilities. The only place to eat lunch was at the machines or on a few benches in another room. Management begrudged even lunch time and allowed only ten minutes.

When Stanley and his escorts arrived at the Webster Eisenlohr shop, the strikers were trying to organize themselves and had already chosen Cecilia Krygowski as chair. With the delegation's arrival, the women stopped to hear what had happened in Addes's office.

The manager approached Stanley in some agitation. "What's going to happen to the tobacco?" he asked. "It must be kept humid, you know; and the machines, what about them?"

"Don't worry," Stanley assured him, "no damage will be done, and your cooperation will speed the strike settlement."

Stanley mounted a bench to speak, and several hundred women gathered around. "The CIO is not trying to organize you but is only offering its help," he said. "Do not damage the property, and organize committees if you want the strike to be a success. There is a cigarmakers union in the AFL, but they are not here, and somebody's got to help."

Under Stanley's guidance, the necessary committees were elected to conduct strike affairs and formulate demands, to provide sleeping accommodations, to see to the care of strikers' children, to establish a kitchen, and set up strike headquarters in the Polish Club at Palmer and Mitchell avenues. Within less than six hours, committees were functioning, the kitchen was going in the club, and food was prepared.

The phone rang frequently as husbands called to ask, "What's keeping my wife?" A number of husbands were reported as coming to the shop, and some arguments ensued about "cutting out this stuff"; but in the main, the husbands were supportive.

Hamtramck council member Mary Zuk, a former Dodge worker and member of the UAW Polish Trade Union Committee, was alerted and came to help. The UAW furnished some cots and blankets as the GM strike was concluded and the Flint plants were being evacuated. Families and community people sent in cots, bedding, and food.

News of the strike spread quickly to every cigar shop in the city. No sooner were the Webster Eisenlohr women organized and their committees functioning than a delegation appeared from the Mazer-Cressman Cigar Shop at 5031 Grandy, where 400 women had just sat down. While Stanley was there, another committee came from Essex Cigar Company at 5247 Grandy. There, another group came for him from the Tegge-Jackson shop at 4771 Dubois. Before he could finish there, a delegation came for him from the Bernard Schwartz Corporation, makers of the

R. G. Dunn cigar, at 2180 Milwaukee. Still fuming over the January firings there, a total of 1,000 women were on strike, and around 350 of them had spent the night in the factory. Before Stanley could get their strike apparatus functioning, another committee came from the General Cigar Company at 2682 Forest, where 70 women had sat down around noon.

From the morning of 17 February in Addes's office to early afternoon of the 19th, Stanley had been on the run, snatching a bowl of soup and sandwich from the strike kitchen wherever he might be and going with each new delegation to find a situation similar to the one he had just left. He had caught an hour or two of sleep on a table or bench in whatever shop he found himself when exhaustion overtook him. He had also phoned me in between all this to tell me what was happening. By now, he was so tired, dirty, and rumpled he felt he must go home, bathe, and get some rest. He agreed to meet the General Cigar strikers the next morning, the twentieth, at their shop; then he came home. When I got home from work that evening, he was sound asleep and never stirred until the next morning when I got up to go to work. Over breakfast he filled me in on the details of what was happening.

The Polish paper *Glos ludowy* reported that after Stanley had left the Bernard Schwartz shop the afternoon before (the 19th), to come home and rest, the cigarworkers had visited Waclaw Golanski, the popular Polish radio commentator, to ask him to announce the cigarworkers meetings on his nightly program. He enthusiastically agreed and contributed five dollars to the strike fund. He began to relate the story of the cigar strikers in humorous rhymes on his program, in the character of Antek Cwaniak (Polish for *smart-aleck* or *joker*), which he had created. Detroit's Polish community chuckled over the antics of Antek Cwaniak, and the cigarworkers listened with delight.

That same evening, workers from all the cigar shops had a mass meeting at Dom Polski (Polish Home) on Forest and Chene to rally support and raise funds, after which they paraded around every cigar shop in the area.

By this time the strikes involved twenty-five hundred women, according to *Glos ludowy* of 19 February. They held frequent meetings, each plant individually or several jointly, at Dom Polski. Mary Zuk, John Zaremba of Dodge Local No. 3, and other members of the UAW Polish Trade Union Committee visited the cigar shops regularly to give needed help. Joining them in their rounds were Helen Nowak, Sophie Myszka, Frances Niewiadomska, and others.

On the morning of the twentieth, after a night's rest, Stanley went to the General Cigar Company as promised. There he found Hamtramck councilwoman Zuk and members of the language and labor press waiting as well as reporters from the regular daily papers. From open windows on the second floor, women called and beckoned Stanley. A committee escorted him and Mary Zuk down a long hall to a stairway leading to the second floor.

In the cafeteria, women gathered around as Stanley mounted a table to speak. While guiding them in the election of committees, he saw a group of men enter through the rear door and station themselves in front of metal lockers lining the walls. Each time he tried to speak, they pounded on the lockers with their fists so he could hardly be heard. Angry shouts from the women had no effect. Obviously, management had prepared for Stanley's arrival. Speaking as loudly as he could against the din, he said, "We have opposition here and may have to change to a conventional strike with picket lines."

"No! No! Don't let us down!" pleaded the women.

"Don't worry," he reassured them, "your strike is not being abandoned, but we may have to work from the outside."

Mary Zuk also tried to reassure the women, but her voice could hardly be heard. As she spoke, Stanley saw several men, bearing clubs, enter from the rear and slowly advance toward him and Mary. If they stood their ground, Stanley knew they would be defended by these unarmed women, many of them in their middle years, who would surely be injured. He and Mary would have to leave, and the only way out was through the open windows behind them.

"Come on, Mary, we'll have to jump for it." Stanley hurriedly took her arm and headed for the windows. Shouting hasty reassurances to the strikers, he and Mary leaped to the ground. Mary landed on a police sergeant, according to the *Detroit Times* of that day, 20 February, without harm to either; but Stanley landed on his heels on the sidewalk, lost his balance, and fell. A couple of officers helped him to his feet. Although he felt no pain, his left foot would not bear his weight.

"Can we take you to a doctor, or would you prefer a hospital?" the officers asked.

"Please take me to Dr. Eugene Shafarman on John R. near the Art Institute," Stanley requested. The officers helped him into the squad car. As the numbness wore off, Stanley became aware of pain. At the doctor's office, he was unable to get out of the car. One officer went to fetch the doctor, and together they pulled Stanley from the car. Dr. Shafarman lifted him as if he were a child and carried him to the examining table.

Suddenly realizing that unless I were told what had happened before the afternoon paper came out, I would be shocked and alarmed, Stanley asked if he could call me. The doctor brought the phone to the examining table, and Stanley called me at my office to say he had been hurt, "a little—nothing serious."

The X ray disclosed a cracked heel bone and arch, much to Stanley's dismay; for his Ternstedt assignment still waited, and he was worried about how the cigarworkers were faring in the shop from which he had leaped. He explained this anxiously to Dr. Shafarman, whose keen, blue eyes under heavy, dark brows and hair regarded him quizzically, then smiled sympathetically. "I'm afraid I can't give you a new foot, and we can't argue with a broken bone," he said.

Eugene Shafarman realized full well what a critical time it was and how desperately Stanley and other organizers were needed. He was one of a handful of doctors who took medical equipment to picket lines where blood was expected to flow and who set up first-aid stations. Wherever trouble was anticipated, he was there.

Stanley's worries about the women he had left at the strike scene were needless. The women remained in the shop to deal with the antiunion disrupters, some of whom they knew. They continued their sit-down but sent a large delegation that night to a meeting at Dom Polski of strikers from all the cigar shops and received the needed help in electing committees and continuing the strike.

Stanley was forbidden to participate further in strike activities until his foot began to heal. Women, bringing flowers and small gifts of appreciation, came from various cigar shops to our apartment for advice. Night after night, I came home wilted and drooping after my day of work and a meeting or two to find the women discussing strike problems with Stanley, full of life and fun. They were a constant wonder.

I was busy with my own activities. As educational director for the citywide committee of the UAW women's auxiliary, I had to provide teachers for classes for that committee and the auxiliary locals. Frances Comfort, head of the AFL Teachers Union, was a great help. I also went with women from our citywide committee to meetings of UAW locals to offer help in establishing women's auxiliary locals. Among those coworkers were June Dinkfelt and Babe Gilles.

During this period we launched a short-lived mimeographed publication, "The Women's Auxiliary UAW." I often went after work to the Hoffman Building, where our city-wide committee met in the UAW International Offices, to help Anna Ganley and Helen Goldman cut stencils, write articles, and mimeograph the first few issues.

Stanley insisted my activities should not be interrupted, as he was well cared for. People dropped in at all hours to consult him on union problems or just to keep him posted on union matters.

Before leaving for work each morning, I brought him breakfast on a tray. The phone and crutches were beside him, and books and magazines within easy reach. A neighborhood restaurant brought his lunch. The door was left unlocked so people could come and go without Stanley's having to get up. If I could not get home for supper, the same restaurant brought him supper and later picked up the tray.

When the cigar women found that I sometimes did not get home for dinner, they brought food. Thus Stanley enjoyed many Polish dishes that I did not know how to prepare even if I had had the time, and he certainly thrived on the attention.

An article in the *Detroit News* of 28 February featured the strike at the General Cigar plant where Stanley had been injured. According to the article, the strikers called their establishment the "Hotel de General Cigar Corporation" and set up strict "hotel" regulations. Visitors were admitted by a "clerk," who took the names of the strikers wanted and sent a "bellhop" to page them. Volunteer cooks served meals in the cafeteria. Cots were lined up along the walls on both floors. "Chambermaids" saw that beds were made, and people designated as "detectives" patrolled the building day and night. Men had their own quarters and served as "porters," their mops and brooms busy most of the day. Troubles were reported to the designated "manager." One woman volunteered as a beauty operator for a time, and appointments were registered as in any beauty salon. Committees ran everything.

Other cigar shops had neither the facilities nor the forces to manage so well. According to Cecilia Chromecki from the Bernard Schwartz plant, there was a kitchen in the basement and a supply of dishes so that food could be prepared and served there. The rest of the shops depended upon the strike kitchens. Some women brought small electric grills from home or borrowed from friends.

Since not all shops were able to obtain sufficient cots, many women slept on the floor on quilts or mattresses from home. Some slept on benches. Helen Nowak reported she and others at Essex had to sleep at their work benches, heads cradled in their arms on the work tables. She reported each woman there brought her own dishes and flatware and washed them herself. Without a dining room, they ate at their work tables.

In most shops, each striker went home every third day to bathe and change clothes, do the family laundry, prepare food for her family, get medical aid for herself or family members, and perhaps go to mass. In case of illness or unusual problems at home, a striker was released from duty.

Grandparents, husbands, or other realtives or neighbors looked after the strikers' children, who often visited their mothers in the shops and sometimes ate with them if there were kitchen and dining facilities.

Every other day, according to both Helen Nowak and Cecilia Chromecki, a striker was required to participate in the committee in charge of soliciting food and help from community stores and business places. Scrounging pennies for gas for her little Model-T Ford, Helen and her helpers picked up huge metal containers of milk from the dairies; pillowcases stuffed with day-old bread, hot-dog and hamburger buns, and cakes from bakeries; cartons of sausage and hot dogs from such stores as Jackiewicz and Kowalski; ground beef and other meat from the butcher shops; and other items from different stores. Helen and her crew delivered all this to the strike kitchens and to those shops having kitchen facilities.

On 25 February Judge Nicholas E. Gronkowski in Hamtramck called together a citizens committee and chaired hearings in his courtroom on the working conditions and wages of the cigar workers. Prominent citizens on this committee were Dr. F. Henik, Wladyslaw Drozdowski; W. Franczak; attorney Jan Kaminski; Ernest Lilian, Polish journalist; attorneys Stanley Majewski and Jan J. Poleski; Dr. W. Pawlowski; J. Sobieski, Chairman of the Polish National Alliance; and Clara Swieczkowska, prominent Catholic activist and head of the women's league.

Out of the hearings came a permanent fact-finding committee, composed of Judge Gronkowski, attorney Poleski, Dr. Henik, and Miss Swieczkowska. According to *Glos ludowy* 26 February, Judge Gronkowski stated that the owners of the cigar factories had refused his invitation to attend the hearings.

The hearings continued from 25 February through 8 March with daily reports published in *Glos ludowy*. Judge Gronkowski's committee members expressed surprise at the appalling revelations. Testimony was given by forty-eight people employed in five factories as to the dirty, unsanitary, unhealthy working conditions and the extremely low wages in spite of the skill and speed demanded, which could only be acquired by years of experience. The women testified they were usually paid one dollar for one thousand cigars and had to work very fast to make twelve to eighteen dollars a week. Almost always, some of the cigars were put aside as "rejects" because of so-called imperfections, and the women were not paid for these even though the companies sold them as "seconds" and profited on them. Women told of having constantly to fend off unwanted attentions of inspectors or foremen and that when such attentions were refused, the number of "rejects" was higher.

At the conclusion of the hearings, the records were presented to the Commissioner of Labor in Lansing and to Governor Murphy.

The AFL cigar union now began to show interest in the cigarworkers, and AFL officials began appearing at strike meetings. On 2 March *Glos ludowy* reported that Local No. 155 of the AFL Cigarworkers Union was formed and officers elected. Among those named as honorary members were Hamtramck council member Mary Zuk and organizer Stanley Nowak.

On the fourth, *Glos ludowy* announced the first strike victory at Mazer-Cressman and on the fifth another at Essex. That day, a parade of over a thousand strikers began at 1:00 P.M. at Dom Polski on Chene and Forest and proceeded on Chene to Joseph Campau past the Dodge factory, ending in Hamtramck. As they marched past the Dodge plant, workers there gathered at open windows to sing, "The Union Makes Us Strong" and to wave such signs as "Smoke Only Union Cigars." The demonstrators carried signs, one of which said "*Glos ludowy* Is the Only Paper Supporting Us."

On the tenth, *Glos ludowy* reported a mass meeting called by the UAW Polish Trade Union Committee at Yemans Hall to inform the public on the situation in the cigar industry. Nowak, on crutches, was the main speaker, his first public appearance since his injury.

On the eighteenth, a conference on the cigar strikes was held at Dom Polski, with representatives from labor, political, church, and civic groups, including the YMCA and YWCA. Delegates heard a report from Judge Gronkowski's fact-finding committee, and Bill Carney of the Rubber Workers CIO in Akron, Ohio appeared. Many expressions of wide support were given.

Glos ludowy of 20 March reported that eight cigar strikers from three plants met in the Hotel Statler with plant executives and the mayor's mediation board, consisting of Father Frederick Siedenburg, Rabbi Leon Fram, and Rev. Benjamin J. Bush. There were no results.

On the twentieth, the whole city was rocked when Mayor Couzens and Police Commissioner Pickert cracked down on sit-downers in several establishments, including the cigar shops. The *Detroit News* reported that forty mounted police battled a crowd of five hundred men and women, mostly strike sympathizers from the UAW, at Milwaukee and Dubois next to the Bernard Schwartz plant, where women had been sitting in since the nineteenth. Six men and women went to Receiving Hospital and others received minor injuries.

According to statements of strikers and witnesses and articles and photos in the press, the police broke down the doors and pulled women out of the shop by their arms, twisting them painfully; or by their hair or their clothing, almost tearing off both in the struggle to drag the women out of the building.

At a protest meeting on 22 March Viola Wojcik, chair of the new AFL Cigar Workers Local No. 155, reported that police had beaten not only sit-downers but also neighborhood women sympathetic to the strike, even chasing them up on their own porches to club them.

One such woman was Mrs. Anna Rzemkowska, mother of an eight-year-old child and expecting a baby. She lived next door to the plant and was quoted in both *Glos ludowy* and the *Detroit News* of 21 March: "I went out on the porch to observe what was going on and saw two policemen clubbing a man lying on the pavement. I shouted at them to stop. . . . One of them came up on my porch, grabbed me and threw me off, breaking the porch railing. As I fell, another policeman hit me with a club and left me on the ground, . . . blood streaming from my head. The doctor said if the blow had been a little harder it would have caused a skull fracture. All my right side and leg are covered with bruises."

Protest meetings were held in the community. The *Detroit News* of 21 March quoted UAW president, Homer Martin, as follows:

> The UAW is prepared to call a general strike in the automobile industry in Detroit Monday unless the brutal eviction of sit-down strikers and the ruthless clubbing of workers by Detroit Police is stopped immediately. . . . Commissioner Pickert is going to have to learn that the legitimate labor movement in this city is a force whose right he cannot violate.
>
> He is going to have to learn that his men are not going to attack defenseless women sitting peaceably on their own front porches. This was done Saturday evening in the attack on the Bernard Schwartz cigar factory. Automobile workers are determined that strikers in these smaller plants shall not be the victims of police brutality.

A rally of 200 thousand unionists took place on the twenty-fourth in Cadillac Square, with speakers from labor, civic, political, and church groups, all decrying the recent show of police brutality and demanding the firing of Police Commissioner Pickert and the removal of Mayor Couzens. Workers from all over town marched to Cadillac Square from all directions, over twenty thousand from the west side alone. A huge contingent of cigarworkers carried signs.

On the thirtieth, a delegation of Bernard Schwartz strikers went to Lansing to see Governor Murphy. Helen Nowak (Piwkowski) crowded five women into her small car (Bernice Toler, Victoria Lesinski, Stella Remenek, Theresa Kurzawy, and Gertrude Everett) for the trip. They were received in the governor's office by James F. Dewey, a federal mediator, who informed them that Murphy was in Detroit that day but was expected back the next day. The women had no money for a room or hotel, so they bedded down in the gallery around the balcony of the capitol building. The guards did not disturb them, perhaps realizing that these were very determined women.

The next day, Dewey informed the women that he had talked to Murphy by phone, and although he was not returning to Lansing that day, he gave his word that he would help the cigar strikers as soon as the Chrysler strike was ended. The disappointed women returned to Detroit, but Helen Nowak learned that the governor was staying at the Whittier Hotel and immediately took the women to visit him. She and her delegation were courteously received, and Murphy listened with interest to their description of their working conditions and the strike impasse.

The Chrysler strike ended 7 April and, true to his word, Governor Murphy issued a public statement on the tenth, expressing dissatisfaction with the lack of action by management in the cigar shops. He appealed for a federal mediator in the matter, and on the twenty-second, in Lansing, a conference of the striking cigar workers and their employers took place in Murphy's office. Judge Gronkowski and Clara Swieczkowska were present. The governor announced the end of the cigar strikes on the twenty-third, and the agreement was signed in his office in his presence.

Very early in the cigar strikes, the UAW had advised the strikers to join the AFL when the strikes were concluded; but later the UAW executive board reversed its stand, and on 17 May *Glos ludowy* announced that the CIO had issued a charter for Cigar Workers Local No. 24, with Sophie Myszka as chair; Cecelia Lewandowska, vice-chair; Bertha Theis, recording secretary; Mary Cebula, financial secretary; and Elsie Lamparska, treasurer. Those previously signed up by the AFL now transferred to the CIO local.

There were continued contract violations by some of the cigar factories. Workers held protest meetings and threatened strikes as late as 19 June, but conditions in the shops improved.

The cigarworkers had been part of the upsurge of women that year to claim for themselves the gains being made by men sit-downers in the auto industry. On 18 February, the day after Stanley became involved in the struggle of the cigar women, the Farmcrest Bakery and Frigid Foods workers sat down. On the twenty-seventh, the women in Woolworth's downtown store sat down. On 8 March, women sit-downers in the office of the WPA won a victory hailed by *Glos ludowy* as the means of saving fifty thousand families from hunger.

The *Detroit News* published a daily list of firms on strike. The list grew, week by week, naming more and more establishments employing largely women—the National Biscuit Company; American Lady Corset Company; Yale and Town Manufacturing Company; and prominent shoe stores, drugstores, department stores, and hotels.

At first, feeling alone, rejected, and abandoned, the valiant cigar women were encouraged by the victories of other women all over Detroit and by the growing support of the Polish community, the entire city, and finally state and federal officials. It took a very special brand of courage and determination to wage such a long, wearisome battle from February through June with such tenacity in the face of such odds. And they did it with unequaled grace and spirit.

Eventually, all the cigar factories would leave Detroit for Florida, where they could exploit unorganized, defenseless women. In early 1937, however, the fighting spirit, energy, and vitality of these Detroit women amazed and inspired people all over the city and state.

Many people have asked why the cigarworkers had been so adamant about having Stanley, and no one else, as their organizer and champion. If we go back to his childhood and see where he came from and the forces that shaped him we shall find the answer. The women knew that Stanley was strongly rooted in organized labor and the Polish community and could bring them widespread support in their fight.

2 Growing Up in Chicago's Polish Community

"Hey, Stasiu," called brother Joe from his front porch one evening in the summer of 1914. "Would you go to the store and bring my paper, *Dziennik ludowy* [People's Daily]?"

"You can bring me one, too," a neighbor called from his porch. Thus began what would become a sizable paper route, as neighbors for blocks around put in requests for this socialist paper in the Polish language.

The boy picked up the papers at the neighborhood variety store for a penny each and sold them for two cents. He noticed bundles of three other Polish papers in the store, *Dziennik zwiazkowy* (Alliance Daily), *Dziennik narodowy* (National Daily), and *Dziennik Chicagoski* (Chicago Daily). As he made his daily rounds he received requests for some of these papers and obligingly picked them up and delivered them on his route along with *Dziennik ludowy.*

As events in Europe developed, many who were not regular customers bought papers, so the boy began to carry extra copies. As the world moved step by step toward war, eleven-year-old Stanley Nowak called out the increasingly ominous headlines. The one of 6 August announcing Austria-Hungary's declaration of war on czarist Russia threw the community into an uproar. Most of its residents had come from the same part of Austrian Poland as Stanley and his family, and all along the route people rushed out to buy a paper and talk excitedly in small groups.

"Well, it finally happened, just as we expected!"

"Yeah! We got out just in time."

"Russia will march right through Ujkowica on the way to Przemysl."

"Those mock battles we saw every year will be real ones now." The boy's heart thudded as the full impact of the comments hit him, and he had trouble making the right change for customers.

He thought of that night in Poland, only a little over a year before, when he had slipped out of bed in the dirt-floor, thatch-roofed cottage where he had been born and where his family lay sleeping to see what the flashing lights outside the windows were all about. Giant searchlights had played over the village and fields, making it almost as bright as day, while soldiers had rushed around in all directions. Divided into "attackers" and "defenders," they had struggled for possession of the fortress in the nearby woods and for the stores of grain and supplies hidden away. As long as he could remember, these military maneuvers had taken place annually following the harvest, with regiment after regiment of soldiers from all over Austria marching past the Nowak cottage, sometimes for three days and nights. Only now could he begin to realize the import of those events. His mind was troubled by visions of invading armies trampling the fields where he had played with his dog, Bobus, and taken the family cows to pasture each day since he was seven. "Where is Bobus now?" he wondered. Thoughts of horse-drawn cannon blowing cottages to bits and toppling trees flew through his mind. From the comments around him he knew such things were happening in Ujkowica and the other fortress villages ringing the ancient town of Przemysl, to which he had walked with his father to fetch the village mail.

The unusual demand for his paper brought the boy back to the present moment, but his mind was still in a whirl as he listened to the conversation around him and frequently brushed the blond curls from his perspiring forehead.

At home that night there were more of the same comments from his father, Jan Nowak, son of a former serf on the estate of Count Potocki in the town of Lancut not far from Przemysl. By the time Jan had reached young manhood, serfdom had been abolished by Franz Jozef in the Austrian empire, but the constant threat of war and the lack of any economic future had driven Jan and thousands like him to the United States with their families in 1913.

The Nowak family had settled in Chicago, where the eldest son, Joseph, had lived for eight years and had married and established a home. They lived at the edge of the packinghouse complex, where thousands of illiterate peasants from Poland and other Slavic nations lived and worked. Without any education, hardly able to read or write even their own language, these families could do only the least-skilled and lowest-paid work, such as existed in the packing industry.

Shortly after his arrival in Chicago in late October 1913, ten-year-old Stanley had been enrolled in the neighborhood parochial school, Sacred Heart, at Forty-sixth and Honor streets, where he began to learn the English language. At home the family spoke Polish, and the earliest English words and expressions he learned were those used in the street games of neighborhood children.

By the time of the 6 August 1914 declaration of war on czarist Russia by Austria-Hungary, which had thrown the community into such turmoil, fighting was already under way on the western front and soon began in the east, when, for the first time, U.S. citizens heard of the town of Przemysl in news reports. The town was an ancient center of commerce, and in the struggle for its possession that raged back and forth for about six months the chain of fortress-villages surrounding it, such as the Nowaks' village of Ujkowica, became one vast battlefield. Przemysl was eventually surrounded and seized by Russia and later recaptured by Austria-Hungary and Germany and held until their defeat. All mail from Poland had stopped with the onset of the war, and people with friends or loved ones still there awaited the daily papers with fear and anxiety.

Stanley's daily paper route took him through a park at Forty-fifth and Paulina, where workers gathered in the late afternoon for a breath of air and some relaxation after the long hours in the packing plants. As the boy passed through the park, they called out, "Hey, Stasiu, what's the headline today? Come read it to us and we'll buy your paper."

Obligingly, he sat down among them to read the latest reports. Most of these men had come from Poland when peasants did not have even the limited educational opportunities of Stanley's generation and could neither read nor write. They frequently interrupted his reading to comment or debate among themselves. Their remarks and those of his family stimulated the boy's interest in reading for himself. He followed the news about his birthplace and began to read editorials and other items, forming what would become a lifelong habit of regular and systematic reading of current events. He listened with heightened awareness to discussions swirling around him. His horizons were expanding.

The twelve-year-old's interest was also stimulated in another direction. On a street corner near his home one day in 1915, a stranger handed him a leaflet about a play in the Polish language in a neighborhood theatre. Stanley read it several times. Noting his interest, the stranger said, "Would you like to earn a little money by passing some of these from house to house?"

"Sure!" agreed the boy. After distributing the leaflets, he returned to the corner to ask the stranger more about the play. Sensing that the boy had never seen a performance, the man handed him a ticket. "Just give this to the man at the door and tell me later how you liked the play," he said. After the Sunday matinee, Stanley saw the stranger in the theatre lobby and delighted him with his enthusiasm.

Members of the Polish drama group drew the youngster into their activities, paying him small sums for distributing leaflets, doing odd jobs, selling copies of their songs between acts, and even playing minor roles. Some took a more personal interest in the lad, particularly Waclaw Golanski, the matinee idol, a handsome man with a vibrant speaking voice and dashing manner. For about two years, he and others gave the boy books in the Polish language, introducing him to the great classics, among them the novels of Henryk Sienkiewicz and Wladyslaw Remont and the poetry of Adam Mickiewicz and Maria Konopnicka.

Years later, during the General Motors strike in Flint, Michigan in 1936–37, Golanski's radio program and his popular rhyming monologs in the Polish language would play an important role in creating a favorable climate for the United Auto Workers Union drive among Slavic nationalities in the Detroit area.

Chicago's Polish community was the largest in the United States, second only to Poland's city of Warsaw as a center of Polish population and culture. Here were the national headquarters of the major Polish organizations. Stanley knew of thirteen Polish theatres operating seven days a week. Four daily papers in the Polish language were published in Chicago. There were several Polish libraries, and Stanley borrowed from the one at Division and Noble streets.

During World War I, U.S. Poles reflected the thinking of the major political currents in Poland. All of them carried on intensive activity and propaganda in the Polish community where Stanley lived.

At public meetings and in the pages of *Dziennik zwiazkowy* Paderewski, the great pianist-turned-statesman, issued appeals for Poles to enlist in the Polish Army in France to fight on the side of the Allies against Germany and Austria for Poland's liberation. Stanley's brother, Walter, was an early volunteer.

In the fall of 1917, at the age of fourteen, Stanley obeyed a nagging sense of responsibility and dropped out of school. He found a job as office boy for the Polish paper, *Dziennik zwiazkowy,* where he spent three years, at first delivering messages and serving as errand boy, later escorting notables about town. Here he was surrounded by conservative Polish intellectuals opposed to Germany and Austria. He attended staff and public meetings and often heard Paderewski speak.

The war was the constant topic of discussion among family and friends, who frequently invited Stanley to public meetings, some arranged by the Socialist party. The union and its organizing drive among the packinghouse workers were also frequently discussed. Sometimes Stanley was a guest of neighbors or family members at union meetings. His mind was often in a whirl from so many differing points of view, attracted first to one and then another. He listened, observed, and read everything that came to hand, in both Polish and English. It was a period of intensive learning and thinking.

On reporting to work at the Polish paper one morning late in 1919, he was jolted by his greeting from a coworker: "Stanley, they want to see you in the editorial office." At these words, Stanley's heart beat a little faster, as he had just turned in an article about the growing dissatisfaction and strike sentiment among packinghouse workers and had been expecting an unfavorable reaction. He knew it meant another confrontation, as they had called him before them not too long ago. At that time they said, "Stanley, your articles severely criticize the packers. As you well know, they are our biggest advertisers. Can't you write anything good about them?"

"I write only what I know to be true," he had replied. "My family and neighbors all work for the packers, and while the workers' wages are being drastically slashed, more and more demands are being made upon them."

"That may be," said one of the editors, "but can't you be a little more diplomatic, tone it down a bit, be more objective?"

"I will try," the boy had agreed, and he did. But as the struggle sharpened he saw more and more people bitter and angry over wage cuts and speedup. In spite of the warning from the editorial board, he continued to write as factually as he could, and now today he faced what he knew would be an unpleasant showdown. Maybe he would be fired. He squared his shoulders, took a deep breath, and headed for the editorial room. This time he took issue openly with the staff as they took him to task for his recent article, relating incidents affecting his family, neighbors, and friends. Staff members showed surprise at his able defense of his position.

"You can go back to work now, but Mr. Zychlinski will probably want to see you," they said as they dismissed him. Sure enough, the boy had hardly got back to his post when the summons came from Zychlinski.

Kaziemierz Zychlinski was president of the Polish National Alliance, which owned *Dziennik zwiazkowy* and the building it occupied and maintained offices on the top floor. The boy wondered what to expect, and many things went through his mind as he went to answer the summons. Zychlinski had often called him to his office to run errands or to escort visitors about town and sometimes had taken time to chat about various things and offer friendly advice. It was Zychlinski who had originally suggested that Stanley report on the packing disputes.

As the youth entered his office, Zychlinski regarded him thoughtfully for a moment; "Stanley how can you write such trash?" he demanded, throwing the boy's latest effort on his desk. Stanley faced him resolutely, quietly, describing things he had witnessed, pointing out that if the workers won their strikes, their victory would be reflected in greater support for the paper, provided it supported their struggles.

Zychlinski interrupted him. "I don't know what has happened to you, Stanley, but you no longer fit into this organization. I am much disappointed in you. Here you had a chance to become somebody, to get somewhere; but apparently you prefer to throw it all away on the nobodies. I am sorry, but we must let you go."

"Can this really be happening to me?" Stanley wondered as he went to get his final paycheck. He was deeply wounded that those whom he had held in such high esteem and who had been his friendly associates, counselors, and sponsors should now turn from him because of his honest convictions. He did not know how to resolve his hurt; and for days he brooded and took long, solitary walks, turning over in his mind the events of the past year that had led up to this situation.

During the union organizing campaign and periodic strikes in packing, only one of Chicago's four Polish papers, *Dziennik ludowy*, had supported the strikers. The others were openly hostile, carrying on antiunion propaganda while seeking the support of Polish workers for Polish newspapers, businesses, and professional people.

Dziennik zwiazkowy, where Stanley worked, had ignored the packinghouse ferment until the pressure of readers became uncomfortable. Then the editorial staff, at Zychlinski's request, had assigned Stanley rather than one of the more experienced reporters to report on the matter, which they apparently felt was not that important. The boy had fulfilled his assignment as honestly as he could and had written some good articles.

Now he was filled with disappointment. He had come to the paper a naive but promising boy, eager to learn and to please and greatly impressed with the editors and officials. Their present attitude he found confusing. Why couldn't they understand what to him was so clear, especially when he had provided evidence that he thought should convince anybody as to the justice of the workers' demands?

No sooner had the war ended, in November 1918, than business interests locally and nationally had launched a vigorous antiunion campaign and began drastically cutting wages. An answering wave of strikes swept the nation throughout 1919, involving every major industry and reaching into the Polish community. The packinghouse ferment was part of this national turmoil. Statistics showed that the cost of living had doubled since 1914, but wages were 14 percent less.

Stanley often went with family members to their union meetings. There he heard Joseph Kikulski, heading the organizing drive in the two Polish locals of the packinghouse workers, where meetings were conducted in the Polish language. The boy listened to debates on local and national issues.

Still hurting over his firing by the Polish paper but as yet undecided on what to do next, he was approached by a friend, Peter Mojsiewicz, a member of one of the neighborhood reading circles flourishing then: "Why don't you come to work in the clothing shop where I work? I can get you a job there and you could share my apartment and split expenses?"

"But I've had no experience in that kind of work and might not really like it."

"Nonsense!" Peter urged. "You will learn! And if you don't like it, we'll find something else."

"Thanks, Pete. Let me think about it a little while."

The wave of strikes would continue throughout the nation as organized labor struggled for its very existence. This would be spelled out to sixteen-year-old Stanley in terms of the Polish community, the matrix that he had come from and that formed and shaped his ideals and goals. The struggles to come would take him beyond the Polish community to the national arena and would bring him leadership not only in the Polish community but in the national fields of labor and political life, always with close ties to that ethnic group from which he came and with which he would work all his life.

3 Learning Experiences

On his way home, New Year's Day 1920, after an all-night celebration, Nowak noticed a commotion in front of a hall on Forty-eighth Street near Hermitage. A Russian educational club held meetings and social affairs there and allowed other nationality groups to use the hall for similar purposes. A police wagon loaded with people drove away from the curb leaving bystanders crying and talking excitedly as Nowak ran toward them. "What's the trouble?" he asked. "Why have the police taken the people away? What have they done?"

"Nothing! The police have been in the hall all night," someone volunteered. "Anyone entering was arrested and taken to jail as soon as the wagon was filled. This is their third trip and they are still in there arresting anyone coming in. They won't even tell us where they're taking the people."

"But why are they doing this?" Stanley pursued. No one had an answer. He walked to other ethnic clubs in the area and found the same things happening. At dinner he talked with his family, but no one had an explanation. Disturbed, he returned to the Russian Hall. Again the police were there, and the youth watched as officers unceremoniously shoved people out of the hall and into the waiting vehicle. Tearful families and angry neighbors stood helplessly by.

"This is America!" someone shouted. "You're not supposed to do things like this!"

"Never mind!" snapped the officer. "Stand back! If you get in our way or try to interfere, we'll take you, too!" and with this he brandished his club menacingly.

Stanley stood unbelieving, puzzled. These were neighbors, some from his village in Poland. He had never known them to say or do anything against the government. Why were they treated in this manner? This and other questions kept him awake much of that night.

The morning papers announced similar raids in seventy cities to seize aliens for deportation. Six thousand people, both aliens and citizens, mostly trade union members and officials, had reportedly been seized at meetings, in their homes (even in their beds), and on the streets and thrown into jail by order of Attorney General A. Mitchell Palmer and his aide, J. Edgar Hoover.

Before Nowak could finish breakfast, a neighbor came in, her eyes swollen from weeping. Her husband had gone to the Russian Hall on New Year's Eve to exchange greetings with friends and had failed to return. He had undoubtedly been arrested, but the woman could not find where he had been taken.

"Please, Stasiu!" she pleaded, "Help me! You smart boy. You speak good English. Help me find my husband!"

He was relieved to be able to do anything in this troubling situation. As a reporter, he had learned the location of most police precincts. He made the rounds with the woman, using the press card he still carried to identify himself. He found the man, but the police released him only after questioning both him and his wife, with Nowak serving as interpreter. This incident was repeated many times as others sought his help.

The majority of those arrested nationally were released, their arrests called "mistakes." Of the thirty-five hundred held on charges or for deportation, most were acquitted and freed. Nationwide, it was reported that exactly three pistols and no explosives were found on these supposedly "dangerous" aliens.

Like thousands of others, Stanley asked how such things could happen in a country symbolizing freedom and hope to all the world. To find answers, he listened to discussions in community and union groups whose members had been victims. He visited cultural clubs that had been raided. At last, the picture became clear to him.

The foreign-born constituted one of the most aggressive and militant elements in the organized labor movement all over the nation, just as in the Chicago stockyards and Gary's steel mills. It appeared the Palmer raids, directed against the foreign-born, were launched to quell the rising tide of labor struggles in the postwar period.

Without income since losing his job, Stanley felt he was placing an unfair burden on the family. He accepted Peter Mojsiewicz's offer to share his apartment and work in the clothing shop. Thus in early 1920 he moved to another Polish working-class neighborhood near Division and Ashland, not far from his new place of work.

His frequent family visits and encounters with them and former neighbors at union meetings kept him in touch with events in the packing industry. The local strikes he had witnessed and written about now developed nationally. At union meetings he often heard Joseph Kikulski address the workers in the Polish language. When Kikulski learned of Nowak's dismissal from the paper because of articles about the strikers, he took time to explain the issues and problems to the youth personally.

On 18 May Stanley's sister phoned that Kikulski was hospitalized following an attack by two men the night before. The papers reported that as he had walked home from putting his car in a rented garage a few blocks away, he was followed by a taxi. Two men had leaped from the vehicle and clubbed and shot him.

Within twenty-four hours, police arrested the driver. He stated two men had hailed him and asked him to drive them around the neighborhood, and when they spotted Kikulski they left the cab, crept up behind him and attacked. Then they reentered the taxi and were dropped off several blocks away. The driver was released but again arrested and interrogated following Kikulski's death on the twenty-first. The assailants were never identified. The Polish community, including Nowak and his family, were stunned by the tragedy. An estimated ten thousand attended the funeral, and Nowak marched with his family in the long funeral cortege. Once again he was puzzled and troubled. He had regarded Kikulski as a friend and was deeply saddened.

The organizing drive in packing limped along without a director for weeks until John Rokosz, a well-known official of the Polish National Alliance was persuaded to accept the job. Almost a year after Kikulski's death, Rokosz was killed in the same manner on South Ashland Avenue near West Thirty-fifth Street in broad daylight. There were witnesses, one a police officer a block from the scene, who commandeered a car and gave chase, firing several shots after the fleeing taxi bearing the killers.

For some time, no one would even consider the dangerous job of strike director. Finally, Joseph Krassowski, a man of courage and some trade union experience, accepted the post. He guided the organizing drive with militance and determination. A vote in December 1921 launched the strike in the teeth of continued threats.

The packers successfully divided the union on racial lines by importing Black workers from the South with promises of jobs and good pay. They were unaware of what they were getting into and were brought directly into the plant by elevated railway, thus making it impossible to picket them. Wherever streetcars were used to bring strikebreakers, white or Black, to the plant, the packinghouse strikers took out their frustration and anger by dragging people from the cars and beating them. Shocked by the anger and violence he witnessed, Nowak talked to his eldest brother, Joe.

"Remember, Stanley," Joe said, "the strikers are fighting desperately for their jobs, and whether the scabs are Black or white, they are hated by the men whose jobs they replace. You will continue to see such things until the packers quit importing workers to replace the strikers. Men will battle for their livelihood and families."

Further division was created between native and foreign-born union members by the withdrawal from the union of one local composed of native-born workers and some foreign-born members who were more Americanized. When the strike ended, the packing union was wiped out.

Greatly affected by all these events touching his family and friends, Stanley emerged with a deep commitment to the organized labor movement, not only among Polish workers but among all workers everywhere in their struggles for a better life.

He had left school at the age of fourteen to find a job. Now, at eighteen, employed and contributing to the expenses of the apartment shared with Mojsiewicz, he began attending classes at Hofmann Preparatory School on Damon near Milwaukee to get a high school diploma. The subjects seemed unrelated to the real world around him, and he began to look for other avenues of learning.

Half the workers from Poland he knew could not read or write their own language, not to mention English. Many U.S.-born workers had been compelled to leave school at an early age because of economic necessity. There was a widespread and growing desire for self-education. To answer this need, workers educational groups, known as *educational clubs* or *reading circles,* sprang up all over the country to provide lectures, classes, forums, debates, and discussions.

One such group, known as the Polish People's University, was a national organization sponsored by rightist elements in the Socialist party. It provided Sunday morning lectures by educators and authorities in various fields, as well as weekday evening classes in elementary subjects, all in the Polish language.

Nowak and his brothers and sisters had received a very rudimentary education in Poland, but his father's generation and those before him were given no education whatever under serfdom. Therefore, they had to be taught to read and write in their own language. Such classes and lectures were offered by the Polish People's University in Schoenhoffen Hall on

Ashland Avenue near Milwaukee. Here there were meeting rooms, large or small, to accommodate numerous activities.

Another Polish group, the Pilsudski Circle, also held Sunday morning lectures in Schoenhoffen Hall with audiences frequently numbering two hundred or more. This was a purely local group supported by Chicago residents who greatly admired Marshal Jozef Pilsudski, a former Socialist who had become a prominent military man and statesman in Poland. He had been active in the Socialist party until Poland gained its independence at the end of World War I, at which time he withdrew because of political ambitions of his own.

From all these sources, from 1921 to 1924, Stanley met some outstanding individuals who influenced him greatly and contributed to his education in no small measure.

One of these was Arthur Morrow Lewis from England, a scholar of note, who had trained for the ministry but had become one of the Socialist party's outstanding educators in the United States. Instead of the current propaganda approach, he used a more basic and scientific manner to persuade by argument and reason.

Week after week, Nowak heard Lewis lecture on political topics, natural science, and sociology at the Garrick Theatre at Randolph and Clark streets. Slight, silver-haired, the perfect gentleman in dress and bearing, Lewis was a teacher rather than an orator, but he intrigued and held his audience with his easy, interesting manner of presentation.

After one of the lectures, Nowak stood at a table display of books for sale, many authored by Lewis. A voice beside him said, "Young man, I have seen you every week at my lectures, and have wanted to talk to you and know more about you. I notice you always buy a book. Have you found them helpful?" It was Lewis. Stanley told of his background and interests, and Lewis suggested additional reading material.

In this same Garrick Theatre, Nowak heard Clarence Darrow debate both Arthur Morrow Lewis and Scott Nearing, another socialist lecturer who came every year to speak on world topics in private halls or hotel lecture rooms. Nearing had lost his teaching post in 1917 because of his antiwar stance. Then he began visiting some foreign country each year and writing and speaking about his travels. He was tall and spare, with sandy hair and piercing blue eyes. He punctuated his points with a wry and very telling sense of humor. Nowak always heard him when he came to town.

Another important influence entered Nowak's life sometime in 1921, providing exactly the kind of information he was seeking.

Walking on Milwaukee Avenue one Saturday evening, he noticed on the corner of Paulina Street an attractive young woman speaking on a soapbox and attracting quite a crowd. He had often seen men soapboxing on this corner, but never a woman; and his curiosity brought him to hear what she had to say. She was a dynamic speaker, with dark hair and eyes and a magnetic personality that drew a response from her audience. She spoke of the growing unemployment and the injustices in the economic and social world and invited people to enroll in classes on labor history and economics conducted by the Proletarian party at its headquarters and to attend lectures held in various halls around Chicago.

When she dismounted from the soapbox, Nowak went to introduce himself and to inquire about the classes. She was Sarraine Loewe, a colorful and flamboyant personality, married to Carl Bareiter of an old German socialist family. Both were active in the Proletarian party.

Nowak visited the Proletarian party headquarters, located, as nearly as he can remember, on Randolph near Lake Street. It consisted of one very large room with office equipment, chairs, and tables, providing ample room for classes.

Books by various authors were offered at reasonable prices for use in the classes, and he saw quite a few by Arthur Morrow Lewis with which he was already familiar. In the classes he studied *Shop Talks on Economics* by Mary Marcy, a U.S. socialist; *Value, Price, and Profit* by Karl Marx; *The Theoretical System of Karl Marx* by Louis Boudin; *Origin of the Family* by Friedrich Engels; *Social Forces in American History* by U.S. historian A. M. Simons; and *The Economic Interpretation of the Constitution* by Charles A. Beard, another U.S. historian of considerable stature. Nowak was finding explanations for many long-unanswered questions.

He also read with interest *The Proletarian* (later to be known as *The Proletarian News*), published by the Proletarian party and edited by the party's secretary, John Keracher, former secretary of the Socialist party of Michigan.

It was Keracher more than anyone else in this group who influenced Nowak. He owned an interest in the Charles H. Kerr Publishing Company, which published English translations of most of the works of Karl Marx as well as many of the books used in the classes.

In physical appearance, Keracher was the very image of the "John Bull" (signifying England just as "Uncle Sam" signifies the United States). He spoke in precise, proper English and was a man of great intelligence with considerable education. He took much interest in and helped foster Nowak's socialist education.

For the next two years, in between his other activities, Nowak attended one or two classes weekly at the Proletarian party headquarters and participated in its social affairs.

The clothing shop where Nowak worked also exposed him to forces and personalities that helped shape his thinking. The shop employed about three hundred people, with Jewish workers forming the largest ethnic group and the Poles ranking second. Up to this time, Stanley had had very little contact with Jewish people. At union meetings he learned that the sewing and tailoring skills of many Jewish immigrants had drawn them into the clothing industry, where they constituted its most aggressive and militant segment. In 1922, at the age of nineteen, he became the youngest shop chairman in the local's history and would be unanimously reelected in 1923.

During his years in the clothing shop, Nowak met some outstanding trade union personalities. One of these was Leo Krzycki, newly elected vice-president of the Amalgamated Clothing Workers, who spoke at a local meeting. Already middle-aged, tall, well-built, with a short, brush haircut and a little bald spot on the top of his head, Krzycki was an eloquent speaker. His shrewd, gray eyes twinkled with humor. With perhaps twenty-five years in the union and the socialist movement already behind him, Krzycki had ahead an even more colorful future and would play a vital role in organizing the mass industries of the United States under the CIO banner—steel, packing, rubber, farm equipment, and auto, where Nowak would work with him.

Another person Nowak admired at a respectful distance was Sidney Hillman, international president of the Almagamated Clothing Workers. When the union's yearly contract with each clothing manufacturer in the area expired, Hillman came to negotiate a new agreement. Each clothing shop held an individual ratification meeting. The Hart, Shaffner, and Marx shop where Nowak worked always rented a hall across the street and as employees left for the meeting, union guards at the door directed them across the street to the hall where other guards saw that the employees entered and participated in the debate. Sidney Hillman was a skilled negotiator rather than orator, and Nowak admired his presentation of issues, his logic, and persuasive powers. During Nowak's ten years in clothing, this annual ratification meeting was the extent of his contact with Hillman, whom he never met personally.

Histories of the Amalgamated Clothing Workers show that its founders were socialist-oriented. Both Krzycki and Hillman reflected this ideology in their comments, which helped radicalize Nowak in his union beginnings. Thus he was not surprised years later when Hillman and Krzycki joined John L. Lewis in founding the CIO and fostering the organizing efforts of the UAW. Both Hillman and Krzycki contributed much to the UAW's growth and success. Kryzcki had at one time been national chairman of the Socialist party.

Nowak's reputation as a speaker, in both Polish and English, grew and he was invited to speak in Detroit, Michigan on May Day 1924, by the International Educational Association, a group of Poles publishing *Glos robotniczy* (Voice of the Workers). The paper, originally a daily founded by the left wing of the Socialist party, had become a weekly and was independent of any political affiliations. It was rapidly losing circulation and heavily in debt. In the autumn of 1924, its staff asked Nowak to come to Detroit and help put the paper back on its feet. He agreed and took a leave of absence from the clothing shop.

He worked hard as editor, wrote many of the articles and did the proofreading. By hard effort and long hours, he and the staff revived the circulation. However, they learned that an ethnic paper needs advertisers and a loyal group of sustainers and fund raisers to survive. At that moment, prosperity was prevalent and labor was not in a mood to exert itself. The paper fell victim to the temper of the times, and at the end of two years the print shop was sold and the paper folded. Nowak returned to Chicago in December 1926, to his old job in clothing. He delivered lectures in both Polish and English and resumed his union activity.

In 1927, a quick tour of the Field Museum of Natural History intrigued him. Selecting one subject at a time, he found books on it, then went to the museum with notebook and pencil to examine and compare the exhibits with what he had read. He soon became a "fixture," receiving special attention and help from the guards, attendants, and office staff. They directed him to exhibits not yet ready for display and provided pamphlets and other material.

While describing some exhibits to several of his older friends, one eagerly interrupted, "How about taking us with you to the museum?" He hesitated, feeling unprepared for such a thing, but the eagerness of his friends touched him, and so it began. The first time, he took only three people along. They were so delighted, they spread the word, and soon he had twenty volunteers for a tour. At this point he sought help from the museum staff.

"We could furnish a guide," they offered.

"Do you have someone who speaks Polish?" asked Nowak.

"Sorry, no."

"My group consists of Poles with limited knowledge of English. They need someone who speaks Polish."

"Then why don't you do it?" he was asked.

"Because I don't know enough about the exhibits to answer the many questions that will be raised."

A middle-aged woman with graying hair had been listening from a chair nearby. She rose and approached Nowak.

"Excuse me, young man. I couldn't help hearing your conversation, and I may be of some help. My name is Rowena Morse Mann."

"Do you speak Polish?" Stanley asked, not imagining how else she could aid him.

"No," she said, "but I am knowledgeable in the field of natural history and sociology. I think I could help you prepare yourself to show and explain the exhibits to your friends in the Polish language."

Nowak learned she was a Unitarian minister and recalls vaguely that she was doing some teaching, perhaps at Meadowdale Theological College, which had some affiliation with the Chicago University. Mrs. Mann gave him her address and invited him to call. He visited her spacious home near the university and remembers book-lined walls, paintings, and art objects on shelves and tables. The two set to work mapping the tours.

"I would suggest," said Mrs. Mann, "that you take the group once a month and cover only one section on each visit. It would be difficult and perhaps confusing to do more. In addition to the books I will lend you, I will be happy to accompany your group and help answer any questions that may be difficult for you."

She drew up a schedule of exhibits each month. Stanley studied the books, and she accompanied the tours, keeping in the background unless Stanley turned to her for an explanation at some point. He then introduced her as a resource person and translated her remarks into Polish.

At the museum one day, the woman at the desk said, "You're a very lucky fellow, did you know that?"

"Why?" asked Nowak.

"Because you have the services of such a competent person as Mrs. Mann. She has a brilliant academic background and is the first woman ever to receive a Ph.D. degree from the University of Jena, Germany. Also, she happens to be the granddaughter of Samuel Morse, inventor of the telegraph."

"Well! I really *am* a lucky guy!" Nowak agreed. When he next saw Mrs. Mann he told her what he had learned and asked what motivated her to give so much time and effort to his project.

"Well, you see, Stanley, through you I am reaching people who never had the chance to learn such things, yet are eager to know. It gives me real pleasure to be able to do this."

Nowak was deeply touched by the generous spirit of this great and kindly woman, and they worked together on the tours for about a year until he was drawn into other activities. The tours proved as valuable to him as to his friends, for he was compelled to study intensively for each trip. The eagerness with which his friends absorbed information and their intelligent, probing questions, made it rewarding and satisfying.

By 1929 very few orders were coming into the clothing shop and production dropped. In accordance with a long-standing union-management policy, all members in good standing remained on the payroll and the work was shared equally. A little work was better than none, since unemployment compensation did not as yet exist. In Nowak's department, half the employees worked one week and the rest the following week, until finally there were only two or three days of work every other week.

Older workers in the shop recalled similar drops in production over the years, but no one knew why. Nowak's desire to find the reasons drove him to the Crerar Library on Randolph and Michigan, where he asked for books on political economy. This was not a circulating library, so he spent every free day there from about 10:00 A.M. to 5:00 P.M., with time out to take a walk in nearby Grant Park, eat a sandwich he had brought with him, and perhaps have coffee at a nearby restaurant.

He went through so many volumes that the librarian stopped her daily practice of bringing him books she felt would be of interest and gave him access to the stacks to select what he wished. One of the books he found was an English translation of Karl Marx's *Capital* in which he found the answers he was seeking regarding the nature of capitalist economy, with its "boom" and "bust" cycles.

Stanley thus pursued various subjects until the economic situation worsened and his life took another turn, setting him in a different direction.

4 A Near Frame-Up

Following the stock market crash of 24 October 1929, mass layoffs began in all industries, and bank closings occurred. Nowak was now working only a few hours every other week. On his way to the shop one morning, he came across a crowd of people on the corner of Division and Milwaukee streets, shouting, crying hysterically, and pounding on the doors of a bank owned by Jan Smulski, publisher of the *Dziennik narodowy*. This was where Nowak did his banking and he rushed to investigate. The sign on the door announced the bank's closing.

"How can a bank just close like this?" people demanded. "Open up! Open up! Give us our money!"

These were Nowak's friends and neighbors, many of them unemployed and still paying on homes. Nowak's savings were also wiped out by the closing of this bank.

The widespread and growing layoffs, bank closings, and the difficulty of obtaining welfare all produced scenes of stark destitution and tragedy, which Nowak observed. One of the most heart-rending was seen along Michigan Boulevard and Wacker Drive circling the Loop in Chicago. Under two miles of the boulevard, in the heart of downtown, lies a lower level with entrances and exits for daytime delivery of goods and produce to stores, hotels, and business enterprises. It is hardly visible from the upper level, and is empty of traffic at night. Here from all over town came hundreds of homeless men of every nationality every evening, carrying bundles of newspapers. They built fires in the center of the street, around which they placed several thicknesses of papers to lie on, covered themselves with more papers, and huddled together for warmth.

The Proletarian party assigned Nowak to report on these men for its paper, *The Proletarian,* and he came repeatedly to watch them assemble for the night and listen to their stories. These were not bums and drifters. They were simply unemployed workers, unable to obtain welfare, struggling to exist from day to day. They foraged through garbage cans for food, stole when necessary, sometimes doing odd jobs or running errands for a few pennies which they pooled with others to buy and prepare food over the night fires.

As they emerged from this lower level every morning, penniless, cold, hungry, often in rags, they were confronted by the words *Buy and Bring Prosperity* on huge billboards everywhere. This slogan was plastered all over the country and became the butt of frequent jokes.

In various places around the country, the unemployed banded together in Unemployed Councils or Unemployed Leagues to obtain food and welfare and to fight evictions. Nowak was approached by such groups in Chicago to ask for his help and was often asked to speak at their meetings, in English. People of different political persuasions were active in these groups.

The Proletarian party had branches or subscribers in Illinois, Indiana, Ohio, and in the East in New York, New Jersey, and Massachusetts. Someone proposed that Nowak go where the party had such contacts and help them organize the unemployed in their localities. He was only working a few hours every other week, unable to contribute much to the household he shared with Peter Mojsiewicz, and was becoming increasingly uncomfortable in spite of Peter's reassurances. As he thought about it, Stanley decided that for what little he was earning, he might as well undertake the work with the unemployed. It would give him a chance to see something of the country. He would have bus fare and a place to stay in each of the towns he would visit.

His first trip in 1930 from Chicago to Boston and back, with many stops in between, lasted three months. He rode the cheapest bus line, carrying only a couple of changes of clothing and money for coffee and a snack along the way and for streetcar fare and phone calls to locate the people he was to stay with. Sometimes he ran out of funds before locating the right parties and had to walk long distances to reach them.

The Unemployed groups met in churches, vacant stores or dwellings, garages, barns, empty lots, and so on. In each town, people found accommodations for Nowak—a couch in someone's living room or even a place on the floor with a blanket and pillow. Food was provided, and his hostess washed his clothes and pressed his one suit.

Farm produce wasted while city folk went hungry. One function of the Unemployed Councils was to find transportation and visit the local farmers, who gladly let the unemployed have the produce rather than see it rot in the fields. Food thus obtained was divided among members of the council.

Nowak made another tour in 1931, sometimes remaining several weeks or months in one locality. The summer of 1932 he spent with his eldest brother, Joseph, in South Bend, Indiana, home of the Bendix and Studebaker corporations. What happened here is a good example of how the Unemployed Councils got under way in many places.

Joseph Nowak owned a home and a car, both fully paid for, but he had been laid off by the Studebaker Company along with hundreds of others, and the bank closings had left him without money for groceries or gas. Nowak suggested he canvass his neighbors for pennies and nickels to get gas and visit the farmers in the area to get some produce they could not sell. Joe found his neighbors only too happy to cooperate. Together they brought several loads of vegetables and fruit, dividing it among the neighbors. The news spread and more people came from surrounding areas to participate. Before long a thriving Unemployed Council of over a thousand members was established.

Nowak was experienced in conducting meetings; and there were others in the group, members of socialist organizations, with some experience. Together they worked on problems of the unemployed. Sometimes they obtained an empty store in town for little or nothing, brought their "fiddles" or accordions, and invited people to a fund-raiser. No one had much money but they managed in this way to raise enough to cover expenses and buy food for members, such as meat, milk, butter, and cereals. Also they were able to help people who had been evicted from their homes or apartments.

In cities where he had stayed, some Unemployed groups had been initiated by Communists and some by socialists; but usually people of varying political ideologies simply came together out of mutual need. In the South Bend group, a well-known chiropractic doctor, who was a socialist, helped initiate and augment the group with friends and patients and there were others from several socialist groups. Whether workers or intellectuals, all were unemployed and without funds because of the layoffs and bank closings and all were trying to survive and willing to work with anyone else for their mutual benefit. Each Council that Nowak worked with was purely local in character. There were no funds to finance a national group or to affiliate with such a group and contribute to it if one had existed.

Sunday morning, 5 June 1932, Nowak was shocked fully awake by the banner headline of the *South Bend Tribune:* "Reds Bomb Bendix Factory." The article reported that a bomb had shattered over a hundred windows in the carburetor division of the Bendix plant Saturday night. That night Nowak had attended a fund-raiser dance for the Unemployed Council, and everyone there had heard the fire sirens and wondered where the fire might be.

On Monday, the sixth, the *Tribune* named Wallace Woodward as one of the suspects and stated he was in police custody. Woodward had worked on the arrangements committee for the Saturday night dance and had worked with Nowak and other council members until 2:00 A.M. Obviously, he could not have been in two places at the same time. Something was very wrong. The Monday *Tribune* article also stated that Woodward had made a partial confession, implicating himself in a plot to bomb another plant. The article contended that radical activities were behind the bombing of both the Bendix and Studebaker plants, the latter explosion occurring an hour or two before the one at Bendix.

Nowak and other council members tried to visit Woodward at the jail but were not permitted to see him. A committee tried to obtain an attorney for Woodward, but not one would take the case because of its nature and the group's limited funds.

"Why not try to persuade some professional or business people to join our defense committee and contribute funds or help raise money?" Nowak suggested.

At first no one would listen because of the newspaper publicity, but finally one businessman showed interest. He owned a furniture and upholstering establishment and was well known. He joined the defense group, and within a day or two the prisoner was allowed to see his defense committee.

"They have questioned me over and over," he said, "about the activities of the Unemployed Council, especially about you, Stanley, and your views."

"Did you tell them where you were the night of the bombing and that you have witnesses?" Nowak asked.

"Yes, but they still pressured me to confess. I told them repeatedly that I know nothing about the bombing."

The committee members had seemingly exhausted all possibilities and the case came to a standstill. Another meeting failed to bring any new ideas until the businessman spoke up: "There is one more thing worth trying. I have a friend, a retired police detective, who might be persuaded to help. He is a decent, honest person and has the necessary contacts. I'll go with you to see him."

With the businessman, the committee members visited the retired detective, who showed increasing interest as Nowak related the facts concerning Woodward's whereabouts the night of the explosions.

"Give me a few days, gentlemen," he said. "I want to check some facts, and I have some ideas. As a retired detective, I cannot be officially identified with the case, but I have connections and know where to get information. I will do all I can to get to the bottom of this. I will get in touch as soon as I come up with anything."

Soon, things began to happen. Of special interest to council members was an article on the front page of the *South Bend Tribune* of 8 June with the headline, "Bendix Sleuth under Arrest for Bombing." The article revealed that a special investigator employed by the Bendix Corporation was a participant in the bomb plot; his purpose was to "mak[e] his job good." The investigator named was Gordon (Bud) Miller, a former member of the Mishawaka police and fire departments, and the article stated that in his work of investigating "radical activities" for the Bendix Corporation, Miller had contacted Wallace Woodward. In fear of losing his job as undercover man in the Bendix plant due to an economy program, Miller had tried to make his job secure by pretending to discover plots against the plant and officials.

The news article caused some excitement among members of the Unemployed Council because, some time before, Gordon Miller had suddenly appeared at council meetings, exhibiting unusual interest in council activities. He had attended every meeting and volunteered to work on committees and had taken special interest in Nowak.

"Let me drive you home," he would offer, or "I'll take you to your appointment tomorrow" or "Why can't I pick you up at your home and bring you to the meeting?"

From the first, Nowak was suspicious of Miller's expensive car and clothes and the ample money supply he always had on his person. He was a smooth talker and much too eager to be in the midst of the council's affairs. In spite of Nowak's constant rebuffs, Miller persisted, until Nowak finally resorted to ignoring him. Finally Miller transferred his attentions to Wallace Woodward, the young farmer and former Bendix employee now in police custody.

Apparently the retired police detective who had agreed to help had kept his promise, for both Miller and Woodward were released (see *South Bend Tribune*, 10 June). Woodward immediately met with the council members and related what had actually happened when Miller had transferred his attentions to him from Nowak.

Miller had become most friendly and helpful and one day asked Woodward to accompany him to Mishawaka, a small town nearby, to buy some dynamite that Miller said he needed on his farm. All unsuspecting, Woodward took Miller's money into a hardware store, purchased the dynamite and signed for it, then came out and turned it over to Miller. From this dynamite the bomb at the Bendix plant had been fashioned.

Police investigations of recent purchases of explosives had turned up the name of Wallace Woodward, and he had been immediately arrested. He freely admitted buying the dynamite for Miller and thus became implicated in Miller's plan to throw suspicion on the Unemployed Council and to scare his superiors into "making his job good."

The *South Bend Tribune* of 2 July announced that William Vernon, chief of the Bendix private police and Miller's superior, had participated with Gordon Miller "to make their jobs look necessary" in the face of economy moves at Bendix. Vernon was fired, and the entire matter was to be turned over to the county's grand jury in the circuit court for action in September.

Nowak was not concerned about the fate of either Vernon or Miller now that Woodward had been cleared and released. Since this had been accomplished, he decided to return to Chicago and other activities, and to resume the Unemployed tours. It was on one of these tours, later that year, that we met. But the story of how two people of such widely divergent backgrounds came together belongs in another chapter.

5 Margaret's Story

Could I have known thro' all the groping past
  What was decreed beyond the shadows cast;
That somewhere in a strange and distant land
  Was one whose soul my soul could understand,
There would have been a light upon the days,
  A rainbow-gleam athwart the darksome ways.

Could I have known that your dear hands would bless
  My own, with tender, comforting caress,
And that your answering spirit, kind and wise,
  Would share my dreams, be swift to sympathise,
I should have pressed more bravely through the night,
  Led by an unseen beacon on the height.

"Could I have known!"—a dolorous refrain
  Time has transmuted to a gladder strain;
At last I know, and merge the quick regret
  For what was not, in joy that we have met;
All the old haunting sorrow disappears,
  Now you have come to crown the yearning years.

—author unknown

My older brother was waving a leaflet in front of my nose, and I was doing my best to ignore him. He was always spouting off about one social injustice or another, damning his bosses, complaining, complaining, complaining!

"Aw c'mon, Sis," he urged. "Our friend, the barber down the street, gave me this. It's about a debate between William Lovett, president of the Michigan Manufacturers Association, and Al Renner, of the Proletarian party. There'll be some fireworks. You know you like a good debate. Let's go and hear what they have to say!"

"What is this Proletarian party?" I demanded, "and who is Al Renner?"

"The barber says it's a labor party of some kind and Renner is one of its officers and spokesmen."

I read the leaflet through. It was sharply critical of the government and the administration.

"Are you sure this is not some kind of Communist propaganda we're going to hear?" I said skeptically.

"I don't know. Anyhow, the Michigan Manufacturers Association is going to present its side, too!"

So, the following Sunday afternoon I found myself in the auditorium of Northern High School on Clairmount at Woodward, where I had graduated earlier that year.

Mr. Renner impressed me enormously, every inch the gentleman in his dark suit and glasses. Tall and self-assured, he paced back and forth behind the lectern like a restless lion as he hurled facts from government data or other respected sources. I learned that millions of people were unemployed through no fault of their own; that banks were closing, leaving people without money; that people were being evicted from their homes for nonpayment of rent or mortgage installments; that many babies were dying every minute from malnutrition while New York dairies dumped unsold milk into the harbor. He cited many examples of food being destroyed while people went hungry.

I might have been aware of some of this had I been a regular newspaper reader, but I wasn't. I shriveled inside as a new, unpleasant world opened before me. "Where have I been all my life that I've been ignorant of these things?" I asked myself. "The dairies should distribute the unsold milk to starving children. And why isn't such food given to people on relief instead of being destroyed?"

William Lovett, speaker for the Michigan Manufacturers Association, made no attempt to dispute Renner's facts. They were unassailable. Lovett's weak attempts to wave them away as of no consequence only brought boos and jeers from the audience.

I was deeply shaken by the revelations of that late summer afternoon of 1931. Up to this time I had known very little about organized labor and the unemployed movement in which Nowak was so deeply involved. These were just things mentioned in the press, where strikers and activists were depicted as agitators, troublemakers, largely Communists.

My father, Orlando Bird Collingwood, was born on a farm near Jackson, Nebraska in 1859. His parents, one of English and the other of Pennsylvania Dutch origin, had come from Pennsylvania in a covered wagon. As an adult, he had worked on farms as a handyman or in the towns as an unskilled laborer on railroads or in factories, or he worked as a rough carpenter.

My mother, Elizabeth Leslie, also of English and Pennsylvania Dutch parentage, was born on a farm near Decatur, Illinois in 1875, and grew up on farms or in small towns in Illinois and Missouri, later working as a waitress or housekeeper. My parents met in Missouri and later moved to Washington near Seattle. I was born in Hartford, not far from Seattle, on 3 May 1908, in a cabin made by my father. He had obtained the lumber from the mill where he worked a short distance away. The doctor came from Seattle on a handcar to a railroad siding not far from our cabin to deliver me "just in time for lunch," my mother said.

Wherever we lived, we attended the Church of the Brethren, a Protestant denomination originating in Germany. The women wore little net caps in church (called *prayer veils*), to obey St. Paul's admonition to cover their heads in worship. Most Brethren women also wore the simple Brethren bonnet instead of a hat. Men were not supposed to wear neckties, and my father always resisted our attempts to get him to wear a collar and tie even for special nonchurch occasions. He would "lose" his collar button or find other reasons.

He read the Bible to us daily, often quoting scripture and heatedly debating its meaning. Mother was more interested in putting her beliefs into action by helping neighbors and friends who were ill or who needed comfort in trouble or sorrow. She was impatient with dogmatism and the wearing of distinctive garments to signify one's beliefs.

My father was forty-nine years old when I was born and by the time I was in high school, his earning power had shrunk. At that time we lived in South Bend, Indiana, where we had moved some time before, and there my mother kept boarders and rented out rooms to supplement our income. When she became ill and could not continue to do this, my brothers and sister helped pay for my books and school clothes; but it was still not enough.

It was decided that I should leave school and seek employment. This was a disappointment, as I was in my third year of high school and had hoped to go to college. I had taken college preparatory courses; but thanks to my sister I had also taken typing, shorthand, and bookkeeping, which enabled me to obtain work as a stenographer at the age of seventeen. In each successive job I gained experience and skills, and by 1929 in Detroit, where we had moved, I was supporting myself and contributing to the family.

I worked for a small manufacturer who produced parts for the automobile industry. As the depression developed, my employer proposed that I work every other week. I suggested instead that I take morning classes to complete my high school work and come to work each afternoon. He was delighted, as this enabled him to keep up with correspondence and whatever orders might come in.

By completing the evening courses in which I was already enrolled, attending morning classes, and working afternoons, I graduated from Northern High School in June 1931. I continued to read a great deal but was still insulated from the world of economic and political struggle in which Nowak was involved until I attended that (for me) world-shaking debate in late summer or early fall of 1931 at Northern High School.

After the debate I obtained the address of the Proletarian party and some information about the classes that had been announced. Somewhat frightened but determined, I climbed a dark stairway on Woodward Avenue near Elizabeth Street the next evening. I had lain awake much of the night, disturbed and troubled by all that I had learned and feeling certain that divine guidance had led me to the debate to learn of the injustices related by Mr. Renner. I was sure that God was directing me into a new pathway of service in keeping with my Brethren traditions.

At the top of the stairs I found ordinary people of all ages playing chess, checkers, or card games, reading or talking. Someone welcomed me and I asked about the classes. I was introduced to several people and conducted to another room where a labor economics class was in progress. I enrolled in this and another class on labor history and received a list of books available at any library or book store. Government publications were also listed.

From the books and classes I learned the violent, bloody history of labor struggles in the United States, and about child labor. It was all there in the books and statistics, yet none of this had come to my attention in my school years. I felt cheated and angry that only now, at the age of twenty-three, I was learning this part of my country's history, which every person in the United States was entitled to know.

Some of the teachers in our classes were from England's socialist movement, some from similar movements in the United States. All were knowledgeable, able people, volunteering their services to make available the true history of our nation's people.

I volunteered for office work and to serve on committees. In my association with members, I learned that several had rented a vacant house jointly, pooling their meager and uncertain resources to pay rent and utilities and buy food. Each person took his turn at all household tasks. They sometimes borrowed a truck and managed to find money for gasoline to go to the contry and solicit free food from farmers, harvesting the produce themselves. They even shared items of clothing if one had a job interview or some business requiring presentable garments. Groups were pooling their resources in this manner all over the city.

I stood at the window in the headquarters one day, overlooking an alley across Woodward Avenue and watched a couple of men forage through garbage cans for food. I saw this happen in a number of places and found it frightening.

Often after an evening class I walked on Woodward Avenue past Grand Circus Park on my way to the Gratiot streetcar. This is a small park in the center of town, where men slept on benches or on the grass, some lying on newspapers or covered by them. The press occasionally reported a man picked up unconscious or dead in the park, a victim of starvation or exposure or both.

Deeply troubled by all that I was witnessing and learning, I talked to my church people about it, but most of them felt helpless to do anything but pray about the situation. There was so much human need under our noses and so many ways to reach out and work with other concerned people, but the fear of being labeled *radical* or *Communist* kept many from doing anything. I suggested that Jesus had been called a few names for associating with the "undesirables" of His day. Some said that these unfortunates must have sinned somehow or God would not allow such calamities to come upon them. "What a convenient way to avoid responsibility for one's fellow human beings," I thought.

I turned away from my church and what I felt was a mockery of religion and became more involved in the activities of unemployed groups and the Proletarian party. Here, I felt, was religion in action; here I belonged.

There were individuals in Brethren churches around the country who shared my concerns and were speaking out, but as yet I was unaware of them. I felt very much alone, convinced that I had left religion behind. Working for a better world here and now was far more satisfying than the idea of a distant and problematical Heaven. I believed that if there really were a God, He would be with the people in their battles against poverty, hunger, disease, and ignorance and in their demand for justice. I also believed that instead of seeking God in the ceremonies and rituals of the church, one would find what we call God in a dynamic way in the struggle for human needs and dignity, which, to me, was the truest form of worship.

Few of my labor friends understood what I felt, and none of my fellow church members. So I continued on my own way with increasing satisfaction in the expansion of my intellectual horizons and in the growing conviction that I was doing what was right for me. My father questioned and challenged my views. He feared for my soul but later came to see that I was merely putting into action the values I had acquired from my religious faith. I have never forgotten that my political and social values and concerns grew out of that faith.

In our labor classes were were assigned to find news articles and then seek data to either substantiate or disprove them, and then to stand before the class to express our ideas. We were introduced to the *Communist Manifesto* by Karl Marx and Friedrich Engels, also Engels's *Origin of the Family* and *Socialism, Utopian and Scientific,* in addition to studies in economics and history generally.

There were our regular Sunday forums at Northern High School with speakers such as Scott Nearing and Anna Louise Strong. There were debates between teams of our young members against teams from high schools and colleges. We were encouraged to speak before various groups. My maiden speech was made in the city hall in Jackson, Michigan: "Women, Religion, and Socialism."

Most of us, I think, were interested in the fun aspects of learning, debating, speaking, and socializing together. We participated in the unemployed movement and some demonstrations, such as the one to free Tom Mooney, a West Coast labor leader imprisoned on a frame-up. We donned prison garb and held signs urging Mooney's pardon as we stood on the old city hall steps where Kennedy Square now is, or we carried petitions for people to sign and talked to curious passersby. We joined the widespread campaign to free the Scottsboro Boys and attended forums of other radical groups. I even chaired a meeting for Nearing at one such forum.

The Proletarian party was like a labor college or an educational society rather than a political party. It was the seedbed out of which came numbers of young people who would play important roles in labor organizations in later years. Among these were the Mazey brothers—Ernest, who would head the Detroit chapter of the American Civil Liberties Union, and Emil, who would become the treasurer and financial secretary of the UAW and hold that office for many years—;Myra Wolfgang, who headed the Hotel, Motel, and Restaurant Workers for years; and Elizabeth Yochim who served with several unions as an international representative (organizer).

As I continued my studies, I found ample evidence in the life around me of the truths I was learning. At age seventy, my father wore out shoes looking for work. To aid him in this difficult period, my brothers obtained and set up cutting, grinding, and polishing tools in our basement, and there Dad made very good butcher and paring knives that he sold from door to door. My two older brothers and my sister, all in Detroit, had families; and their sporadic and uncertain employment barely enabled them to get by, with little to contribute to my parents. Another brother in the U.S. Coast Guard allotted half his modest service pay to Mother and Dad. I worked part-time and went to school but helped as much as I could, while Dad trudged from house to house to sell his knives. Yet there was still not enough money for rent, utilities, food, and necessities.

After some sleepless nights, Dad said to Mother, "Well, Lizzie, I guess I'll have to go to the welfare office for help." His steps were slow and reluctant as he left the house, for this act branded him a failure in his eyes. The word *relief* held unpleasant connotations for a proud man who had always made his own way. Hours later he returned, his face white, his whole body drooping with fatigue from standing in the long lines. He slumped, wordless, into a chair at the kitchen table; put his head in his big, work-worn hands; and burst into sobs, something we had never before seen him do.

"But Dad," I protested, "you've raised a big family and given them some education. You've made your contribution to society. Now if society has to help you, it is no more than is due."

He raised his tear-streaked face and wiped his eyes but just shook his head. He couldn't see it that way. However, as the weeks passed and more and more younger people registered for help, he came to realize that he was not the only one who might be classed a "failure," if that is what it meant to seek help.

At the Proletarian party headquarters one Saturday night early in 1932, at one of our weekly social affairs, I was standing at the edge of the dance floor talking to someone when a voice at my elbow asked, "May I have this dance?" I turned to find a stranger, stockily built, with wide, gray eyes and wavy, brown hair, smiling and holding out his arms in invitation. "Of course," I replied, and off we went.

We introduced ourselves, and while his courtly manners and charming accent were enchanting, his dancing had no relation whatever to the music and, adding insult to injury, he carried on a political discussion as we struggled through the dance. This was too much! It isn't that I don't enjoy political discussions, but I like to give them my undivided attention; and when I dance I like to listen to the music and feel the delight of moving in harmony with it. I could hardly wait for this most unenjoyable dance to end, and I avoided the stranger the rest of the evening. I didn't even remember his name.

The next morning at what we called our "Sunday school," a class in labor economics, the instructor announced we had a visitor who was touring the country on behalf of the Unemployed Councils. To my surprise, the guest was the miserable dancer of the previous evening; and he was introduced as Stanley Nowak. He spoke extemporaneously and interestingly about his work, and I was fascinated. I turned to my companion, to whom I had described the unhappy dance, and said, "That man may not have much in his feet, but he certainly has a lot in his head."

After class I went up to talk to the speaker. He was courteous and friendly but seemed completely unaware of me as a woman, a response quite different from that to which I was accustomed. Perhaps our dance had been as unenjoyable to him as to me. I did not see him again before he left town, but he came through Detroit several times on subsequent Unemployment tours. Each time I was more favorably impressed. Although I was not romantically attracted to him, my respect for his intellect and integrity grew, and I remember telling someone, "Now *that* is the kind of man I should marry—if I ever do."

Sometimes when Stanley visited Detroit, I thought I detected a glimmer of personal interest, but nothing developed. Things might have continued in this manner indefinitely but for a mutual friend. She often saw Stanley on her visits with friends in Chicago, and talked to him about me (she later told me). On her return to Detroit she talked to me about him. I had begun to think that he was perhaps capable only of a beautiful friendship or perhaps that he really was not very much interested in women.

Then on one of his later trips through Detroit, I found him watching me repeatedly at our weekly social. Before the evening was over we shared another dance, almost as bad as the first one had been. Yet I accepted when he asked for a date. "There *are* other things in life besides dancing," I told myself—with some disappointment, for dancing was one of the loves of my life.

From the beginning I felt that our relationship might become serious, and before allowing that to happen I had to be sure that we shared similar views on things of importance to me as a person. During that first and subsequent dates, we held long, searching conversations. He was the first man I had ever dated who showed interest in my ideas and attitudes and who shared with me the goals I had set for myself—to learn, to grow, to take part in activities that might bring social changes of benefit to the little people of our country.

Many men in the Proletarian party did not encourage their wives to attend classes with them or become too active, except to accompany them to forums and meetings and to perform cooking and serving chores at our social affairs. Yet these same men complained that their wives did not understand labor or political issues and were not in sympathy with their ideas and activities.

I knew that my happiness lay in learning and growing, trying to make it a better world for everyone and that I would always be part of this in some manner. If I married, it would have to be to someone willing to share mutual responsibilities and help me make my own contribution so that

I would not be a prisoner of domesticity while my partner would go about his own interests.

Stanley and I found that we were both concerned about the same things. He soon came to Detroit to seek work so that he could buy some clothes, as those he had were literally falling apart. He also confided to me that one reason he had been so diffident with me at first was his reluctance to become involved and make a commitment when he was unemployed, without funds, and had no idea where or when he might find a job and be able to establish a relationship.

In Detroit he formed a partnership with a mutual friend to buy old gold and sell it to agencies, which in turn sold it to the government. This was a depression-born occupation. People having gold jewelry or even loose dental fillings or caps could dispose of them for needed cash. With a small kit for testing metals, Stanley solicited from house to house, turning over each day's finds to the agency in order to have money for carfare, food, and lodging. He often knocked on many doors before finding any gold, and people naturally tried to get as much as possible for it. Sometimes he found it heart-breaking to bargain for treasured keepsakes.

By early 1934 the city had been solicited by hundreds of other men and women, and my oldest brother found a job for Stanley in a small auto parts factory where he worked. Stanley worked the afternoon shift, soliciting in the morning for a few hours. This left Saturday and Sunday for political and social activities.

The weekend passes issued by the Detroit street railway for twenty-five cents enabled us to get around to meetings or parties or to Belle Isle to bike around the island or picnic with our crowd from the Proletarian party or with my family.

Stanley soon abandoned the soliciting to spend that time in the library, where I frequently joined him, as I was still working only part-time and had much reading to do for my labor classes.

In the shop where he worked, Stanley helped establish a small UAW nucleus. The company learned of it and fired all members, who became UAW members-at-large until a local could be formed in their shop.

In Hamtramck Stanley found a job as salesman in a paint store where his knowledge of Polish was an asset. He worked ten hours a day, five days a week, and twelve on Saturday. Sundays he attended union or political affairs with me.

We had talked of marriage for some time, but our combined income was only forty dollars a week, and I was contributing to expenses at home while Stanley was replenishing his very sketchy and worn wardrobe. We had known each other three years, dating steadily the last eighteen months.

Late in 1934 or early 1935 I had been called back to work full-time. When Memorial Day of 1935 came around, the factory where I worked closed down for a week, and I phoned Stanley from my office before I left for home:

"How would you like to marry me this weekend?"

"Fine! But what would we use for money? I deposited most of my pay before the bank closed."

My sister came to the rescue. She knew I did not want to marry in Detroit, as the newspapers published daily lists of marriage licenses. My employer, opposed to married women working, might see my name and fire me. My sister suggested that Stanley and I share expenses and ride with her and her husband to South Bend, Indiana, where they were to spend the holiday with his relatives. South Bend's city hall was closed for the weekend, so friends took us to Plymouth, Indiana, where we got our license and found a justice of the peace. I wore an old suit and a borrowed ring for the ceremony.

By the time we got back to South Bend, it was late and we were all hungry. Our friends Bryce and Freda Weaver took us to dinner to celebrate. Later we drove around the town to see many of the beautiful places I remembered from my high school days with Freda. On Lake Shore Drive, Bryce stopped the car with no explanation and Freda got out. "Wait just a minute," she said. In a few moments she returned with an armful of bridal wreath blossoms she had taken from a bush in bloom beside the car. "No bride should be without a bridal bouquet," she said with an impish grin as she handed the bouquet to me. She had always been ready for a lark, and now, with two sons and a household on her hands, she still had the old sparkle and sense of fun. I treasured that bouquet more than any I have ever received.

On our return to Detroit, Stanley and I began married life by living with my parents, sharing household expenses and tasks, but life was not to remain peaceful and serene for long. The growing union movement in Detroit would soon engulf us in the tremendous upsurge of the people of our city and nation in their struggle for a better life.

6 A New Venture

Our first wedding anniversary, 31 May 1936, found us in the country at a Polish picnic. The sound of the band drew us to the pavilion; and as we circled the floor in the Polish polkas, obereks, and waltzes, Stanley's friends sitting on benches along the walls smiled and nodded approval. He was still not good at regular ballroom dancing, but he did the Polish dances well and we both enjoyed them.

Stanley's old friend from his youth in Chicago, Leo Krzycki, vice-president of the Amalgamated Clothing Workers, was at the picnic, sent by the CIO to help organize the autoworkers. He, UAW president Homer Martin, and Stanley were the scheduled speakers.

Later, Stanley introduced me to Martin, and to Krzycki, who greeted me with flowery language and courtly manners. With blue eyes twinkling, he referred to Stanley as a mere "youth" and praised him extravagantly to Homer Martin. The reason for this became apparent when he led Martin, Stanley, and me a short distance from the noise of the band and the food booths to the shade and quiet of a big tree. There Krzycki raised the question of organizing Poles and other foreign-born workers. He pointed out that Poles constituted a large segment of the autoworkers; and unless they and other foreign-born groups were brought into the union, it could not be successfully organized. Their limited knowledge of the English language made it necessary to approach them in their own tongue. Krzyski urged Martin to assign Stanley to head the organizing drive among such groups, and outlined Stanley's experience in the Amalgamated Clothing Workers and his many ties to labor generally.

Martin, of medium height and build, with abundant light brown hair, listened quietly, his rather pleasant features thoughtful, glancing at Stanley and me occasionally through his steel-rimmed glasses, sometimes commenting, flashing his famous smile, or asking a question. "Sounds like a good idea," he finally agreed. "Stanley, come to the executive board meeting next week and bring your plans for carrying out such a program." With this, he left.

Stanley took a day off from his job at the paint store in Hamtramck to attend the board meeting. Martin first introduced him to the UAW's first vice-president, Wyndham Mortimer, fiftyish, tall, slim, with the look of an intellectual. "I've heard of you," he said. "We had many Poles in the Pennsylvania mines where I began work at the age of twelve. I was one of the first to join the United Mine Workers there."

George Addes, secretary-treasurer of the UAW, came to be introduced. He was in his thirties, of medium height, dark of hair and eyes, with a swarthy complexion. Stanley felt a quiet warmth and steadiness about him.

The room came alive when the UAW's second vice-president, Ed Hall, came in and was introduced. "How are you, Stanley?" he boomed in his gravelly voice. "I've heard of you from Leo Krzycki in Milwaukee." Stout, boisterous, genial, he shook Stanley's hand vigorously. "So, you are coming to work with us?"

"I hope so. Martin asked me to come today to meet everyone and said it would be decided at the meeting."

"Well, we have lots of good Polish unionists in Milwaukee, where Leo and I come from. If you're like them, you'll make a good addition to our staff."

When Dick Frankensteen came in, he towered over Stanley, with the build of a football player. A former follower of Father Coughlin and his National Union for Social Justice, Frankensteen had organized a company union at Dodge and brought it with him into the UAW when he became disillusioned with what he considered Coughlin's betrayal of the workers in their time of crisis. "Glad to see you, Nowak," he said heartily. "Are you sitting in on the board meeting?"

"Yes, I'm to outline a plan for organizing the foreign-born, particularly Poles."

"That should be interesting. We need all the help we can get. Good luck to you!"

Slim, red-headed Walter Reuther came in and was introduced to Stanley just before the meeting, so they had no chance to talk much at that point.

Martin opened the meeting, relating how he had met Stanley at the

Polish picnic and how Leo Krzycki had suggested putting Stanley on the international organizing staff to bring Poles and other foreign-born groups into the UAW. "Nowak is here," said Martin, "to lay before you his plans for this. Stanley, will you tell us your proposals?"

Stanley's presentation went something like this: "Poles constitute the largest ethnic group in almost every factory. Thus, we cannot concentrate on any one shop but must carry on general prounion agitation in the Polish community as a whole. First, I would suggest that we buy time from Waclaw Golanski's radio program in the Polish language on station WEXL in Royal Oak. He is a former Polish actor and has a one-hour daily program on which he presents commentaries, humorous monologs, rhymes, and pointed observations on social and economic issues. He is a very popular radio personality and his program has a tremendous audience among Poles and other Slavic groups in the Detroit area, including Czechs, Slovaks, Russians, and Ukrainians, all of whom understand Polish.

"Second, we should hold meetings in Polish halls and clubs. Printed material in Polish should be distributed at Polish churches, clubs, and factory gates. We could arrange outdoor meetings in parks and on empty lots in Polish neighborhoods, after leafletting the area. UAW representatives could appear at such meetings, picnics, and other affairs. The Polish paper *Glos ludowy* carries announcements of union affairs and news about the organizing drive. We should see that such material gets to that paper regularly. This kind of campaign would bring to the UAW a huge segment of Detroit's autoworkers."

Discussion of the proposals followed, and Walter Reuther took the floor: "What Stanley says is true. I have worked in a number of shops and found that there is a language problem with many of the foreign-born. I support Stanley's proposals to reach the large number of Polish and Slavic workers. This seems the logical way to reach many foreign-born groups."Further discussion followed, and Stanley was put on the international organizing staff by unanimous vote. After the meeting, Walter approached him: "That was a splendid program you outlined. It certainly should bring results."

Stanley was only too happy to leave the paint store to do the work he loved and for which he was fitted by experience. The other members of the organizing staff with whom he would be working were organizational director Dick Frankensteen; John Anderson, the Scotsman from Tool and Die Local No. 155 UAW; Joseph Kennedy, an old-timer from the AFL; and Arthur Greer, president of Hudson Local.

Stanley began his new assignment at once. He called together Poles from shops throughout the city and established the UAW Polish Trade Union Committee to head the drive in Polish and Slavic communities.

Among those contributing enthusiastically and selflessly to this work were Hamtramck council member Mary Zuk, a former Dodge worker; Vincent Klein, secretary-treasurer of Chrysler Local No. 7, who became secretary-treasurer of the new Polish Trade Union Committee and would later be elected to the Michigan State Legislature; Anthony Plezia of Dodge Truck; John Rusak and Adam Poplawski of Packard; Edward Danielewski and Frank Danowski of Dodge Local No. 3; William Sylvestrowicz of Chevrolet; and John Zaremba, recording secretary of Dodge Local No. 3, who became recording secretary for the new UAW Polish Committee. Nowak was elected chairman. These were all key people in the Polish community.

The UAW purchased from Waclaw Golanski's radio program fifteen minutes twice weekly for presenting union issues in Polish. On the remainder of his daily programs throughout the week, Golanski commented favorably about the union and developed humorous monologs about events in the organizing drive. He also composed and recited amusing rhymes about all this. Soon the union was the talk of the Polish and Slavic communities.

To test how widely the program was being heard, the Polish Committee sent some of its members out on summer evenings to walk in Polish communities. Windows were wide open in the warm weather, and both John Zaremba and Anthony Plezia reported that as they walked up and down the streets of various Polish areas, they heard the entire program without missing a word. This was also reported in Ukrainian and other Slavic neighborhoods.

The UAW Polish Trade Union Committee arranged meetings in clubs and meeting halls of Polish and Slavic groups and distributed leaflets in Polish and English at factory gates, churches, clubs, and in neighborhoods. Meetings were small at first, but soon Stanley was speaking before sick-and-death benefit organizations such as the Polish National Alliance, the Polish Roman Catholic Union, and the Polonia Society of the International Workers Order. He was asked to speak at Polish and Slavic social affairs, picnics, banquets, and political meetings. One of the international officers or organizers usually appeared with Stanley at these meetings and was enthusiastically received.

The Polish Catholic clergy, business people, and professionals wielded a powerful influence in the community. Stanley visited them to win their support, pointing out that their welfare was bound up with that of the autoworkers in their battle for higher wages and better working conditions. While some listened, most showed little interest or understanding, and some were openly hostile, making little or no distinction between communism and unionism, particularly CIO unions.

Two Polish papers were published in Detroit, *Glos ludowy*, a weekly, and *Dziennik Polski* (Polish Daily). *Glos ludowy* carried articles and announcements about the union drive and its meetings or affairs of interest to Polish workers. A weekly column in Polish by Waclaw Golanski, similar to his radio monologs, became a regular feature. Frank Winn, head of the UAW publicity department, contributed a weekly column in English, "Auto Union News," carrying statements by Wyndham Mortimer, first vice-president of the UAW, and by UAW president Homer Martin and other officials. This English material always appeared either on the front page or in the English section of the paper.

The other Polish paper, *Dziennik Polski*, while not openly antagonistic, carried no announcements or news about the union. Stanley took a delegation of Polish UAW members to call on Frank Januszewski, the owner and publisher, a member of the state committee of the Republican party and known as a Republican leader. He received Nowak with chilling courtesy. "Yes, Mr. Nowak, you wished to talk to me about the UAW and the Polish autoworkers? Now what is this all about?" His silky-smooth, slightly nasal syllables fell like drops of ice and the atmosphere was as cold.

"You realize, Mr. Januszewski," began Stanley, "that vast numbers of Poles work in Detroit's auto shops and many read your paper. You might carry announcements of union meetings and affairs, or perhaps do a series on the organizing drive among Polish workers. You surely must be aware that the more your paper supports the union, the more the Polish workers will support your paper and its advertisers."

"You may be right, Mr. Nowak, but I fear there are too many Communists in the UAW; and before our paper could support the union it would have to expel all Communists."

"But, Mr. Januszewski, a union local consists of all workers in a particular shop, regardless of political beliefs, religion, or race. If differences of this kind were raised, the organizing drive would not succeed."

"That well may be, Mr. Nowak, but we cannot offer any assistance to the UAW except on the basis that I have stated."

Realizing that no cooperation was to be forthcoming, Stanley ended the interview. Some weeks later, Leo Krzycki came to Detroit. Thinking that perhaps this persuasive old charmer might help, Stanley took him along on another visit to the *Dziennik Polski*.

Januszewski was out of town, but Editor-in-Chief Janusz Ostrowski received them cordially and took them through the plant. He introduced them to the editorial staff, one of whom was Waclaw Soyda. Stanley and Krzycki discussed with them the UAW organizing drive, suggesting that the paper carry announcements and articles of interest to Polish autoworkers. Ostrowski regretted, he said, that he could not change the paper's policy. Only the owner, Januszewski, could do that. Afterward, Mr. Soyda came to Nowak privately.

"Send any material to me," he invited, "and I will see that it gets into the paper."

Soyda kept his word until his dismissal from the staff about six weeks later, when he began to work with Golanski on his daily radio program, on which Stanley spoke twice weekly. I helped prepare the English text of Stanley's speech for the files of the radio station, and Soyda made the Polish translation for the program.

Thus began a warm friendship and pleasant working association with Waclaw Soyda, lasting until his death in 1954. He was one of the ablest and best-informed of the old-time Polish journalists in the United States, with a record of over forty years in the newspaper field.

Polish and Slavic workers from shops all over the city flocked to the meetings of the UAW Polish Trade Union Committee and signed UAW membership cards. Applications from workers in shops where UAW locals had already been established were sent to those locals. Applications from those workers in shops having no UAW members would provide the nuclei out of which UAW locals could later be set up.

Some old friends came to Stanley in the Hofmann Building to renew friendships, and others came to meet this new Polish organizer. Two whom Stanley had never met but had heard about came to him within a couple of weeks after he was settled in the UAW international office. They were Dave Miller and Bill McKie, both of Scottish origin, both veterans of many years in the labor movement. Both had been fired some time earlier by the Ford Motor Company for establishing a nucleus of a local for the AFL at Ford's.

Miller, tall and deliberate of speech, had a pronounced Scottish burr. His rugged, homely face broke into a warm smile as he talked. Bill McKie was slight, delicate of feature with a shock of snowy hair above blue eyes and a pink-and-white complexion. Stanley and I would come to know them well in the union work. Stanley would also work with Dave Miller later at West-Side Local No. 174.

Early that summer (1936) a young man who said his name was Miller frequently came for union literature and membership applications. "My name is really Zygmund Dobrzynski," he confided one day, "but I used the name *Miller* to get a job at Automotive Fiber Company. My mother knows you, and I would like you to visit her and meet my brother."

When Stanley came to call, the mother recalled him as editor of the Polish paper, *Glos robotniczy* in Detroit from 1924 to 1926. "My husband and I were readers and supporters of that paper," she said, "and now I read *Glos ludowy.*" She was now a widow of limited means. The house was run down and sparsely furnished but immaculate, and she was still interested in the progressive Polish community and organized labor. Ziggie, in his early twenties, seemed to share her interests and appeared able and likable.

One afternoon a call came for Stanley in the UAW office. "This is Ben Allen," said the caller. "I represent the LaFollette Committee and would like to see you in my office as soon as possible on an urgent matter." With considerable curiosity, Stanley kept the appointment the next morning. The La Follette Committee had been established by Congress to investigate antilabor spying and other antiunion practices by large firms. The committee was headed by Robert M. LaFollette, Jr., a Republican senator from Wisconsin. Its Detroit office was in the old First National Building downtown. There, a tall, thin man with features suggestive of Sherlock Holmes introduced himself as Ben Allen, took Stanley to the inner office, and motioned him to a chair.

"Mr. Nowak," he said, "we have made a very interesting discovery concerning someone in your office." With this, he presented a report from an employee of the Pinkerton Detective Agency, a verbatim record of a conversation between Stanley and a Briggs worker in the UAW office.

"I can't imagine who might have recorded this," Nowak said as he read the report. "I recall the conversation because this was the first Briggs worker to come to the office. As the report says, he was suffering from metal poisoning and wanted to know what we could do for him."

"Was anyone else in the office with you when you talked to this man?" questioned Allen.

"The only other person I can remember was Arthur Greer, a fellow organizer."

Allen's face lit up. "Aha! Now we're getting somewhere. Don't say a word about this to anyone. This man has been under suspicion for some time but we haven't been able to get anything on him. We'll keep checking. Keep an eye on him and let us know of anything unusual; and if we come up with something, you will hear from us."

After that, Stanley was careful about his comments on the phone in the office or when interviewing a worker; especially if Greer happened to be sitting opposite him at the big flat-topped double desk they shared.

Greer had been appointed an international representative by Homer Martin after the South Bend convention of 1936, to which Greer had been a delegate from Hudson Local, of which he was president. Workers had frequently complained of his red-baiting at meetings, and they had indicated distrust of him because of his general behavior, which seemed strange to them in a union man and local officer.

It turned out that Arthur Greer was, indeed, the stoolpigeon in the international office and a captain in the Pinkerton Detective Agency. Through the efforts of Ben Allen and the LaFollette Committee, Greer was exposed and fired from the UAW.

Another visitor in those first few weeks after Stanley joined the UAW international staff was Emil Mazey, an old friend of ours from the Proletarian party. He was working at Briggs and asked for union literature and membership applications. He returned several times for more material and advice, then he came in one day with a problem: "I've been fired for union activity, Stanley. The organizing is going well and I would like to continue what I started, but how can I if I'm out of the shop? Is there anything you can do to help?"

"Let's go see Addes," said Stanley. He introduced Mazey to Addes, pointing out the importance of what Mazey was doing at Briggs and asking that the UAW give him some help.

"Why not put him on the international payroll, give him a new leaflet each day and what other help he might need to continue?"

Addes started Mazey out with ten or fifteen dollars a week and all the material and assistance available, and this was Mazey's beginning with the UAW. He later became the official UAW international representative in the Briggs organizing drive, which culminated in the famous Briggs strike in January 1937.

The first president of Briggs Local, Ralph Knox, was a racist and redbaiter, branding as Communist all who opposed him. He launched such a campaign against Mazey that the latter's position became jeopardized and Mazey again came to Stanley for further help. Again they went to Addes.

"We can't permit this situation to continue," Stanley urged. "If you, as an International officer, could speak at the next local meeting and point out the danger that Knox's red-baiting could divide the local, it would help." Addes did just that. Things quieted down and Mazey's job was saved. Knox's conduct had so discredited him among the local's membership that he would lose the presidency to Mazey in the next election and eventually drop out of sight.

Still another person coming to Stanley's attention early that hectic summer of 1936 in the UAW office was Billy Allan, reporter for the Communist paper, the *Daily Worker.* He was a likable fellow with a slight Scottish accent, sandy hair and blue eyes. When Stanley began organizing the Polish workers into the UAW, Allan began following him and other organizers from one meeting or strike to another. He was everywhere, brimming with wry humor, writing colorful stories of the sit-downs.

In November 1936 Dave Miller of Cadillac Local again came to Nowak, this time with a problem: "Stanley, we have Cadillac completely organized except for the foundry, where workers are about evenly divided between Poles and Negroes. The Poles have joined the UAW to a man, but the Negroes refuse. Would you meet with the Poles in that department and see if you can help them persuade the Negro workers to join?"

Meeting with the Poles from Cadillac's foundry, Stanley asked, "Have you tried to organize the Negroes working with you?"

"Yes, many times," one answered, "but they hardly talk to us. They have a social club and baseball team for which Cadillac provides uniforms. They don't feel they need a union."

"Is there any one person with some influence among them?" asked Stanley.

"Yes, Percy Keyes is their spokesman and leader. The men are solidly behind him."

Stanley called at Keyes's home, and the door was opened by a slim, very dark man of medium height, apparently in his middle years.

"Are you Percy Keyes?" asked Stanley.

"Yes, and you must be Stanley Nowak. One of the fellows in the foundry said you might be coming to see me. Come in, Mr. Nowak." He took Stanley's coat and pointed to a chair. "Please sit down, and may I offer you a drink?"

The home was simple but comfortable, and several small children played about as the men talked over their drinks. After some small talk, Stanley became serious: "You know, I am sure, that the union at Cadillac is organized in every department except the foundry, where I understand the Negro workers refuse to join. Can you tell me what their objections are?"

"Well, first, Mr. Nowak, we have a social club and a baseball team. Our uniforms are paid for by the company, and we have some small benefits."

"Don't you think your members have earned whatever concessions you have received? After all, the company name on your uniforms is an advertisement for Cadillac wherever you appear in public to play another team."

"Yes, that is true," conceded Keyes.

"Have you ever asked for raises or requested that Negroes be allowed to work in departments other than the foundry?"

"Yes, but they always say that, as an athletic club, we should not be concerned with such matters."

"What about seniority, paid vacations, that sort of thing?"

"We have talked about these things among ourselves but haven't dared raise them with management since they turned us down on the other matters."

"I don't know if you fully realize, Mr. Keyes, what the union could mean to you and your friends. Other union members would certainly support your demands. The UAW is struggling to gain improved working conditions, safety measures, pay increases, and seniority for all members, black or white. Divisions in the union weaken its approach to management. I hope you and your fellow club members will think about joining the union so we can all work together."

The two conversed for some time, and when Stanley left Keyes shook his hand warmly. On subsequent visits, Keyes asked questions and was always friendly but wary and noncommittal. At length, he asked for application cards for himself and his friends. By this time he and Stanley were on a first-name basis.

Keyes very soon had the foundry 100-percent organized and proved to be a loyal, dependable, and vigorous defender and supporter of the union. He not only took an active role in Cadillac Local, but also went with West Side Local members to help other locals where mass picketing was needed.

With many interruptions of this kind, Stanley continued his long-range task of bringing the UAW message to Poles and Slavs by his radio speeches, outdoor meetings, appearances before Polish clubs, and at political gatherings. Articles by him also appeared in the Polish paper, *Glos ludowy.* He always dictated them in English to me, and the editorial staff at the paper translated them into Polish.

I was still working full-time; and between my job, the work in the UAW women's auxiliary, the household, and working with Stanley in preparing his radio speeches and articles for the Polish paper, not to mention going with him to union meetings and affairs, it was a busy time for me as well as for him.

Other members of the UAW Polish Trade Committee kept the Polish work going whenever some plea for help elsewhere diverted Stanley temporarily or when he was assigned to head the organizing drive in a specific shop or handle a strike that had erupted. The first of such assignments came in early December 1936 and was typical of what was happening throughout Detroit.

7 The Pot Boils Over

When the phone rang in the UAW international office on the morning of 11 December 1936, Frankensteen picked up the receiver.

"Send us an organizer, we're on strike!" a man's voice urgently demanded.

"Who's on strike? Where?"

"Send someone to American Aluminum [ALCOA] in Hamtramck!" came the agitated reply. "Hurry! We're all sitting down!" and the receiver banged in Frankensteen's ear.

"Stanley, you go see what this is all about," said Frankensteen. "I have a meeting this morning."

On Joseph Campau at the corner of Dunn Road in Hamtramck, Stanley found two buildings surrounded by a big yard and high wire fence. Almost two hundred men and women were milling around in the cold. Nowak stood close to the fence and beckoned everyone to him. "Did someone here phone the UAW?" he shouted. Several people came to the fence and he repeated the question.

"I don't know," answered one, turning to his companions. "Did any of you call the UAW?" All shook their heads.

"Why do you want to know?" someone asked.

"I'm from the UAW," said Nowak, showing his credentials. "Someone phoned us for an organizer and I'm here to help."

"Oh! That's different. Yeah, we know who called. Just a minute."

A slender, young man, apparently in his early twenties, was pushed forward by his companions. "Here's Walter Pupka. He knows all about it," they said.

"I don't know too much about it," said Pupka, obviously ill at ease at thus being thrust into the spotlight. "We talked about it and someone must have called you."

"Do you have a union of any kind?" Stanley asked.

"No, that's why we called the UAW."

"Have you elected a strike committee?"

"Is that what we're supposed to do?" Pupka's brow furrowed beneath his dark hair, and his brown eyes grew unsure as he nervously took off his cap to scratch his head.

"How did you call a strike without a committee or organization of any kind?" asked Stanley.

"I don't know. It just happened. Things are pretty rough around here, and we've all been talking about it. They speed us up so that sometimes we can't even eat our lunches, and our wages are only forty-one cents to fifty cents an hour. Then the other day, the company said some of our work will be sent out to other factories. That was the last straw, as it will mean layoffs here. We've all been reading about the UAW and sit-downs all over the country, and we figured if others can do that, we can, too."

"So what happened?" Stanley urged.

"Well, when I came in this morning I heard a lot of commotion in the foundry; and the foreman said 'Don't go in there! That's a bunch of Communists sitting down.' I went in anyhow and found about 40 night shift workers from the extrusion department who had become so disgusted they just sat down about 5:30 A.M. and spread the word. Probably 150 more joined them, so about 200 are there now."

"How many shifts are there?" asked Stanley.

"Three."

"Do they know about the strike?"

"A lot of the day-shift workers do," answered Pupka, "because, like myself, they were warned by the foremen not to join the sit-downers. It looks like some are working in some departments, but others went home. A few, like me, joined the strike. But I'm coming out. I think I can help more on the outside."

"Good! Now, who is in charge of the entrances?"

"The plant protection men."

Nowak's heart plummeted at this news. Here was a strike against a national and powerful company owned by the Andrew Mellon Enterprises and known to be strongly antiunion. Moreover, the strikers were without union experience or organization and all entrances in the hands of company police. Nowak climbed to the top of his car at the curb and waved everyone to the fence where he outlined the necessary tasks: "You will need food, bedding, and personal items. You need a food committee to receive and serve the food that will be brought in from the outside; a clean-up committee to protect the factory, machinery, and equipment; a strike committee to see that all other committees function and that discipline and order are maintained. Okay. Now let's get these things done as soon as possible."

All this was carried out right there at the fence. Armand Maurice of the Straighteners, one of the instigators of the sit-down, was elected strike chairman for those inside the plant. Others elected to the strike committee were H. Marshall of the foundry mold trip department; Fred Jarna of Runout; Gilbert Blondin of the stretcher department; L. Isralin of Aluminum Lite; Edward Grobbell of Strighteners; W. Golding of Millwright; S. Schuman, inspector; Henry Voorhees of dies, machines, permanent mold; and Howard of the foundry.

There were volunteers for the other committees. Then Stanley rushed to Dodge Local nearby to get the use of its hall for meetings of the afternoon and evening shifts and to phone Frankensteen about what was happening. Then Stanley dashed to the international, where the office staff prepared leaflets for the afternoon and midnight shifts when they reported to work at ALCOA.

The international had already alerted the women's auxiliary and Dorothy Kraus, wife of Henry Kraus, who edited the UAW paper, the *Auto Worker.* Dorothy had just finished supervising the strike kitchen at Midland Steel where a bitter sit-down had been successfully concluded. She immediately set up a strike kitchen in Dodge Local for ALCOA strikers. UAW women rallied from all over town.

On his return to the ALCOA plant around 1:00 P.M. Stanley was joined by Walter Pupka on the outside, who said about six hundred more day-shift workers had joined the sit-down. Stanley and Pupka handed leaflets to members of the afternoon shift as they came to work. Their reactions were spontaneous and vocal.

"Hey! What's going on?"

"You mean we have a sit-down right here?"

"Hurray! It's about time!"

"In their enthusiasm some wanted to climb over the fence and join the sit-down, but Stanley restrained them. As their numbers grew, he mounted the top of his car to be heard and addressed them: "About eight hundred sit-downers are already in there. Only a short while ago six hundred from the day shift joined the two hundred in the foundry. You are all needed out here. When food comes from the strike kitchen at

Dodge Local, people have to get it over the fence to the sit-downers. We need you to visit the families of the inside strikers and let them know what is happening and to bring bedding, clothing, personal items, and food for the strike kitchen. We also need some of you for a twenty-four-hour vigil and liaison force between those inside and those outside the plant. Dorothy Kraus says they need help in the strike kitchen."

Cars were already arriving with food from the kitchen. Men stood on benches at the fence to lift over huge pots of hot food to waiting hands on the other side. In the same manner, large baskets and cartons of bread, milk, salad, fruit, and enormous pots of coffee went over the fence, along with aluminum dishes, flatware, and so on. Later, the empty containers would go out over the fence in the same way. The strikers in the plant announced that the company had turned on the steam, so they were now warm and comfortable.

When the number of afternoon workers in the yard had grown to five or six hundred, Stanley again climbed atop his car to ask them to go to Dodge Local for a meeting and to elect committees for the work to be done. Glad to escape the cold, they went eagerly, and the business was soon accomplished.

The visiting committee began calling on families to describe what was happening in the plant; and by nightfall cigarettes, blankets, cots, and personal items were coming from families, friends, and the community as the news spread. Great quantities of bread came from Hamtramck bakeries, and many kinds of meat from the area's meat markets.

Stanley and some afternoon workers greeted the night shift with leaflets announcing the strike. Their reactions were the same as those of the afternoon workers. They went with Staney to Dodge Local to elect committees to work with those of the afternoon shift.

According to Edward Grobbel, there were not enough cots, mats, or mattresses, and many had to put down layers of cardboard from the packing boxes to sleep on, covering themselves with quilts, blankets, or coats.

That same night, according to *Glos ludowy*, following a meeting of Dodge Local No. 3 members, about one hundred cars full of Dodge workers surrounded the ALCOA plant to demonstrate their solidarity. They had collected twenty-five dollars among themselves to bring to the ALCOA strikers. Members of Tool and Die Local No. 155 of Midland Steel, which had just emerged from a long and difficult sit-down, also contributed twenty-five dollars. These evidences of support strengthened the morale of ALCOA workers and gave them courage.

The next morning, 12 December, workers outside the plant from all three shifts met at Dodge Local. A joint strike committee, with members from all three shifts and headed by Walter Pupka, was elected to operate outside the plant in collaboration with the inside strike committee, headed by Armand Maurice. All other committees of the afternoon and evening shifts were combined.

At this meeting it was announced that Packard Local employees had collected twenty-six dollars for the strikers, and employees of Dodge Local had donated fifty-nine dollars. It was also reported that the committee seeking food donations from neighborhood and community stores had been well received and had been given many things for the strikers. A dairy was sending twenty gallons of milk daily, and a local music store sent in some radios. Newspapers, magazines, books, and games were also coming in.

Glos ludowy distributed copies to all Polish workers at the meeting. Of the 1,000 ALCOA employees, 300 were Polish, about 150 Black, and the rest of various ethnic backgrounds, many of whom read the Polish paper. *Glos* had assigned a reporter to the strike from the beginning, and his daily articles appealed for help for the strike.

Reports came to this same meeting of 12 December that rumors were flying among strikers' families about immoralities supposedly being committed in the factory. The presence of women strikers gave an appearance of credibility to the rumors and, that very afternoon, follow the morning meeting, a crowd of irate wives stormed the shop gates. All attempts to reason with them failed.

"Bring our men out of the shop!" they shouted. "We know what's going on in there. If you don't pull the women out we'll call the police to get the strikers out!"

"All right! All right! We'll do something about it," Stanley promised; but the women were still shaking fists and muttering ominously as they left.

At an emergency meeting later that afternoon, the joint strike committee operating outside the plant decided to call out the women sitdowners. Having witnessed the fiery demonstration by the wives of the male strikers, the inside strike committee quickly agreed the women sitdowners should come out of the shop. Everyone came out of the building into the yard, and Stanley mounted his car to announce the decision, which was greeted with strenuous and vociferous objections by the women. Stanley held up his hands for silence, and said, "First of all, let me congratulate the women on their courage and enthusiasm. You have borne the discomforts of the strike with spirit and goodwill. But it is precisely because you are women that our enemies are able to spread rumors to alienate the wives of the men in the plant. You saw what happened this afternoon. These women are already threatening a court order to bring the men out of the plant, and the company has been looking for just such an excuse to oust the strikers. Moreover, there is much work out here for you to do. You can visit strikers' families to tell them what has really been happening in the plant. We need you to solicit and help prepare food for the strike kitchen, and to seek support from neighbors, friends, and the general community."

This put another light on the matter, and the women responded well. They had no wish to endanger the strike. They joined in the unanimous vote that the women sit-downers should come out of the shop, and went immediately with members of the women's auxiliary to talk to the strikers' families. This eased fears and suspicions and brought strikers' wives and other family members to help in the strike kitchen or on various committees and to participate in other strike activities.

Nat Ganley, a well known Communist activist, came to volunteer his help in the strike. Tall and thin, dark of hair and eyes, and with a raspy but kindly voice tinged with humor, Ganley quickly won friends with his wry jokes and gentle wisdom. He handled publicity for the strike. He was everywhere collecting material for a bulletin, mimeographed daily, to go to every striker inside or outside the plant. This kept workers and their families informed of all developments, squelched company rumors, and warned of dangers. It also helped build solidarity among the strikers and strengthened their morale. Two artists among them—D. Gadwell of the core room and Art Oliver—and Henry Marshall, a poet, livened the bulletin with cartoons and amusing rhymes.

Shortly after his election as chairman of the joint strike committee operating outside the plant, Walter Pupka was provided with a desk in Dodge Local's headquarters. A few men were assigned to him as "runners," to carry messages to strikers in the ALCOA plant, to bring information about items needed by the inside strikers, and to help round up people needed to provide them. Pupka soon learned to handle crises, and Stanley watched him grow with his responsibilities. It was well that he did, for no sooner was one problem solved than another came.

The morning after the demonstration by the angry wives of the sit-downers and the pulling out of women strikers from the plant, another difficulty appeared. At 2:00 A.M. on 13 December a liaison committee member rushed to Dodge Local where Stanley was sleeping on a bench to report that liquor had appeared in the shop and the men were drinking and making a lot of noise.

Stanley contacted Pupka, who had been given a telephone in his residence by the strike committee. He lived only a short distance away and appeared shortly to go with Stanley and the courier to find a worried Armand Maurice at the fence with members of his inside strike committee.

"What's going on?" Stanley and Pupka asked.

"So far, they're just having a good time."

"Where did the liquor come from?"

"We don't know. All of a sudden, bottles were found all over the place and the fellows began drinking."

"Didn't anyone see liquor being brought in?"

"No, and we've asked everyone. We think it may have been brought in by the foremen or plant protection men, maybe both. It wouldn't have come in over the fence without our knowing about it. If the men keep on drinking they may get into fights or do some damage, but we don't know what to do."

"I would suggest," said Stanley, "that you quietly remove the remaining liquor without antagonizing the men. We'll do something about it later today after they have sobered up and realize what they've done."

Stanley returned to Dodge Local to try to get some sleep, and Pupka went home. In the morning, Stanley called the joint strike committee together at the fence with the inside strike committee and pointed out the trap that had been set for the strikers by supplying liquor in the hope that quarrels and disturbances might bring in the police. Fortunately this had not happened.

Both strike committees collaborated in outlining resolutions to be presented for a vote by all the strikers. Stanley then went to have them typed at Dodge Local, then returned to the ALCOA plant, where all sitdowners were brought together in the yard. From the top of his car, Stanley prefaced the reading of the resolutions with some comments: "Now I have nothing against drinking itself, but there is a time and place for everything. It is dangerous to drink heavily in the midst of a battle, and that is right where we are at this moment—in a fight to win this strike. Anything that makes us unable to function efficiently is risky. Okay? Now I want to read the resolutions drawn up by your strike committees. Then you will vote on them." One resolution pledged to drink no liquor for the duration of the strike. Another authorized the election of a special committee to escort from the shop anyone caught drinking and compel him to remain outside for the rest of the strike. Still another authorized the new committee to pour down the drain any remaining liquor they might find on the premises. All resolutions were unanimously adopted and carried out to the letter.

In the middle of all this, Stanley was confronted with another strike. For several days, Zygmund Dobrzynski had been trying to reach Stanley at the UAW international office and finally caught up with him at Dodge Local, knee-deep in problems of the ALCOA strike. "I've been fired by Automotive Fibers for signing up union members on company time," announced Dobrzynski.

"How many members have you?" asked Nowak, harried and anxious to be on his way to the ALCOA plant.

"Only about forty out of approximately thirteen hundred workers, but they insist on striking, and I need help fast!"

"I can't get away from the ALCOA situation right now. Things are happening too fast. But I'll talk to Frankensteen tomorrow and see what can be done," Stanley promised as he ran out the door.

The international put Dobrzynski on the payroll at ten dollars a week and provided a new union leaflet every day to hand out in front of the plant. Many employees signed UAW membership cards, and Dobrzynski called a meeting. The news reached management, and on the eve of the meeting a dozen Automotive Fibers workers were fired. The remaining employees became so incensed that almost a hundred came to this first meeting, attended by Stanley who had managed to get away from ALCOA briefly. Still settling difficulties there and needing time to bring it to a conclusion, he suggested an organizing campaign be undertaken by Automotive Fibers UAW members.

"No! No! We want to strike *now*!" they chorused. "We already have enough members."

"But you're not prepared for a strike," warned Nowak as he outlined the problems and tasks involved.

"Okay! We'll do all that! Let's strike now!"

Reluctantly, Stanley helped them select the necessary committees. Now he had two strikes on his hands at the same time. How was he ever going to manage it?

The next morning, 14 December, Stanley picketed with the Automotive Fibers strikers at 6:30, with signs and leaflets. The rest of the work force had known nothing about the strike until confronted with the picket line, which they enthusiastically joined. Not a single worker went into the plant.

On his return from Automotive Fibers to the ALCOA plant, Stanley found another critical situation. While he had been away, management had inveigled the inside strike committee to negotiate—a plot to split them way from the joint strike committee on the outside and divide the union. Negotiations were going on inside at that very moment.

"We tried to warn the committee," said Armand Maurice, "but no one would listen. What can we do?"

"Good Lord, what next!" Nowak thought in alarm. "Only yesterday we rescued the strikers from the plot to get them drunk and ousted from the plant. And now this!"

"I guess there's no other way," he said. "I've got to get in there and stop the negotiations. I know it's illegal if I'm caught, but something has to be done. Help me over the fence! Hurry! We haven't a moment to lose!"

He ran to a bench beside the fence. A couple of husky fellows helped him over into the yard. In the office he found negotiations in progress, and his sudden and unexpected appearance created instant confusion.

"You've been tricked!" he shouted. "This is an attempt to divide you from the workers outside the plant so the company can break the strike. Do you want to lose all you've worked for? Come on! Get out of here! Hurry!" he urged as took a couple of the men by their arms and headed them for the door. The rest followed, pursued by furious countercommands by management.

"Nowak, you have no business on our property!" yelled the plant manager, John Collins. "You'll pay for this!"

Stanley knew Collins would call the police and there was little time. He raced to the fence to be lifted over, and quickly mounted his car to explain what had happened. He cautioned that all negotiations must be conducted jointly by both the inside and outside strike committees together with union representatives present. He hardly finished when sirens announced the arrival of the police. They took him from the top of his car amid boos and catcalls from the enraged and confused strikers.

"Phone the international," Stanley called out as the police led him away. They questioned him for about an hour. The company had charged him with trespassing.

"You didn't find me on company property, did you?" Nowak asked. "Wasn't I on top of my car at the curb? Is that trespassing?" Since they couldn't disprove his statement, he was released.

The *Detroit News* of 16 December announced that Edward C. McDonald and J. E. O'Conner, federal labor conciliators, were in Detroit to assist in ALCOA negotiations. That same day Ganley's strike bulletin announced that two CIO leaders, Leo Krzycki of the Amalgamated Clothing Workers and Allan Haywood of the United Mine Workers, were also in Detroit to work on the ALCOA negotiations.

The company never seemed to run out of tricks in its efforts to break the strike, one of which was to send men to strikers' homes with final pay slips to sign. If they did so, the company could claim technically that they were no longer on the payroll. News of this went out to strikers and their families immediately in the bulletin, warning them not to sign.

Three days after the inception of the Automotive Fibers strike Stanley phoned to ask the manager if he were ready to negotiate, and he readily agreed in light of the surprising turnout of pickets and the enthusiasm and solidarity of the workers.

On 18 December the *Detroit News* announced that after eight hours of negotiations at Automotive Fibers by Stanley, assisted by Allan Haywood and William Carney of the CIO, Automotive Fibers had agreed to union recognition, a temporary wage increase of five cents an hour for all workers making up to and including seventy cents an hour; the reinstatement of all discharged employees; and the negotiation of all demands, including larger wage increases. UAW Local No. 205 emerged from this strike with Zygmund Dobrzynski as president.

At ALCOA the approach of Christmas brought a new crisis. Families wanted their men home for the holidays. The sit-downers themselves were weary of makeshift accommodations and missed their families. It was feared the men might slip out one by one and go home. Moreover, there was difficulty in communications between the inside and outside strike committees and the sit-downers. The joint strike committee voted on Saturday the nineteenth to pull the men out of the shop the following Monday and establish conventional picket lines.

Monday morning, the twenty-first, the men came out to join their families in a huge demonstration. Carrying U.S. flags, they marched to a mass meeting at Dodge Local Hall to hear Stanley, Nat Ganley, and Hamtramck council member Mary Zuk. She promised to picket daily with the strikers, and she did, sometimes from 6:30 A.M. to 11:00 A.M.

There was a good picket line every day, and the strike kitchen furnished hot coffee and food. The UAW welfare department provided emergency relief for needy families. The strikers' solidarity and militance were strengthened by reports that the company was being pressured by customers to fulfill its contracts and that its national officers were urging the local officials to settle.

On Christmas Day, lookouts were posted to watch for company tricks, and the picket line was suspended for the day. Rumors came that the company had accepted the workers' demands; but they were taking no chances, since negotiations had not yet begun. The following morning, pickets appeared in greater numbers than before. This successful survival of the holidays by a united and confident union finally convinced management to negotiate in good faith.

Both strike committees, accompanied by Stanley, met with management in the same office from which he had led the sit-downers when they had been tricked into separate negotiations. Agreement was reached on most demands and the rest would be worked out by a negotiating committee. After scheduling a ratification meeting, Stanley drove home, half-asleep with fatigue, narrowly avoiding an accident when he momentarily drowsed at the wheel and ran a red traffic light. UAW Local No. 204 emerged from this strike and would later be transferred to the Aluminum

Workers of America CIO as Local No. 11. Still later it would become Local No. 339 of the Steel Workers of America.

Shortly after the conclusion of this and the Automotive Fibers strike, Stanley was again summoned by Ben Allen of the La Follette Committee. "I think we've found something at Automotive Fibers, which you recently organized," announced Ben Allen. "You may be surprised to learn there is a stoolpigeon there."

"Do you know who it is?"

"Not yet," said Allen, "unless you recognize this handwriting."

He handed Stanley a handwritten report to one of the antilabor spying agencies from an informer, without signature, and bearing only a number to identify the writer.

"The writing is not familiar to me," said Nowak. "How can this help us?"

"Take it with you and check it against membership applications on file at the local. If it matches the writing on any of them, this may uncover the spy."

Nowak took the report with him and headed for Automotive Fibers Local No. 205. On the way he reviewed in his mind the events of the recent strike there, searching for a clue to the informer's identity; but he could recall nothing to indicate such a person. At the local he checked the informer's report against every membership card in the files. With such a small local as Automotive Fibers, this was not such a monumental job as it would appear. The matching handwriting was found on all the applications of those workers fired at the inception of the strike. One person had filled out all of them as the recruiter and signed them, and that person turned out to be a man called "Frenchie," who had been sent by a spying agency at the beginning of the organizing drive.

Stanley took the informer's report and the matching union cards to Dobrzynski in the plant. They agreed to call together the local's officers the next day and go with them to the machine where Frenchie worked, confront him with the evidence and denounce and lead him out of the shop in the presence of the workers. Dobrzynski did not wait for the next day. As soon as Stanley had gone, Ziggie gathered a number of workers, told them he had discovered a stoolpigeon, and then took them to the machine where Frenchie worked.

"Here's our stoolpigeon," announced Ziggie proudly. Frenchie was escorted out of the shop, followed by boos and name calling, and Ziggie was hailed as a hero.

Dobrzynski's behavior puzzled Stanley. Later he learned that Dobrzynski had become involved with a factional group headed by Jay Lovestone, adviser to Homer Martin, and was trying to undermine Stanley's influence and discredit him politically and personally. However, at that moment, Stanley had other matters to be concerned about. Now that the ALCOA strike was settled, he could turn his attention again to the Polish work and to organizing Ternstedt's.

8 The Giant Crumbles

In June 1936, as part of his long-range assignment of organizing Polish and Slavic workers in the metropolitan Detroit area, Stanley began meeting in Flint at least once a week with small groups of Poles who worked for General Motors. At first, they met in the home of Frank and Lola Nowak (no relation to Stanley), and later in other homes or in the Polish Hall on Tillman Street. Flint was the key to the whole GM setup, and success there would be of strategic importance in organizing GM factories on Detroit's west side.

West Side Local No. 174, established in September with Walter Reuther as its president was made up of many small plants and such giants as Ford, Ternstedt, Cadillac, and Kelsey Hayes, all employing large numbers of Polish workers.

Late in December, Reuther requested the UAW to assign Stanley to work out of West Side Local No. 174 and concentrate his efforts on Detroit's west side, where only a few shops had been organized.

Ternstedt, a GM factory employing twelve thousand people, was to be Stanley's next target. He was already beginning the drive there when the Flint GM strike broke on 30 December, and all his efforts had to be directed there. Since the successful organizing of Detroit's GM plants would be predicated upon victory in the Flint GM strike, Stanley and his fellow organizers, Bob Kanter and George Edwards, had to drop other organizing assignments and concentrate on sending all available help to Flint.

In his book, *The Many and The Few,* Henry Kraus, first editor of the

UAW paper, the *Auto Worker*, tells how Bob Travis masterminded the takeover of Fisher Body Plants No. 1 and No. 2. Working with the strike committee headed by Bud Simons, Travis organized and planned their "home away from home" for the strikers. Liquor and women were banned. Great care was taken to protect the boilers, paint ventilators, supplies, machines, and the plant itself. Each person was assigned a definite responsibility, and patrols were maintained around the clock for the safety of both the men and the plants. Regular hours were scheduled for the required daily showers, clean-up time, and housekeeping chores. Strikers on the outside solicited or purchased and helped prepare food and took care of publicity, welfare and relief, picketing, defense, and organizing.

Aided by their experience in Detroit sit-downs, the UAW auxiliary women, expertly guided by Dorothy Kraus and Hazel Simons, fed enormous numbers of people at minimum cost. It was reported that from five hundred to a thousand sit-downers were fed three hot meals a day. The food committee used a restaurant across the street from the plant for its headquarters. Plant entrances were controlled by strikers, and food was carted across to the plant and received through doors and windows.

According to Kraus, GM made plans to recapture Fisher Body Plant No. 2, not because of its strategic or practical importance but because the resulting violence would provide an excuse to call in the National Guard. This was later admitted by several officials directly or indirectly involved. Their aim was to force Governor Murphy's hand and compel him to declare martial law and suspend all union meetings and other activities. The strikers could then be starved out and the plants repossessed at gunpoint. Thus it was not surprising that a meeting at noon on 11 January 1937 brought two hundred Flint business people to the Durant Hotel to discuss the "crisis"; and immediately after, things began to happen. For the first time, union people transporting food to Fisher No. 2 strikers were stopped at the gate by plant guards, who forcibly appropriated a ladder used to run food up through a window. Plant heat was shut off. All traffic approaches to the factory were closed, and owners of parked cars in the immediate vicinity were told to remove them.

Alarmed, the union gathered all available pickets at the plant, while a Chevrolet worker evaded a police cordon and drove the UAW sound car over a small, unpaved back road to the plant.

At Detroit's West Side Local No. 174, Stanley, Edwards, and Kanter worked ferverishly to mobilize all available workers and cars and get them to Flint. Union men, wearing special caps designating them as members of the union's flying squadrons, sped in fast cars to Flint from Detroit, Toledo, Gary, Chicago, Akron, and Cleveland. With them were members of the UAW women's auxiliary, wearing their emergency brigade berets, a different color for each region. The flying squadrons and emergency brigades were made up of volunteers on call to go anywhere at any time of day or night when a critical or dangerous situation needed their help.

On the evening of 11 January, following the moves of GM that afternoon against Fisher Plant No. 2, Stanley was addressing a meeting of Polish GM workers in Flint in the Polish Hall when the news came that Sheriff Tom Wilcox of Genesee County had deputized men and was headed for Fisher No. 2 to evict the sit-downers. Stanley and his audience immediately suspended their meeting and left in a body for Fisher No. 2, where they found the sheriff and his men, all wearing gas masks. Several squad cars were there. The scene was one vast turmoil of confusion, and the smell of tear gas hung in the air. The sheriff's men had thrown several gas grenades, but the wind had blown the fumes right back to them, much to their discomfiture and the delight of the pickets.

From the sound car, unnoticed until now in the confusion, Victor Reuther's voice encouraged pickets to stand their ground and urged the sit-downers to get the fire hoses going. Women picketers deposited their children in a nearby restaurant and returned. Inside the plant, men unwound fire hoses and poked them through windows. The streams of water were directed at the police and sheriff's men; but many spectators and pickets, including Stanley were thoroughly wetted. The police were blown back by the force of the stream. On the upper floor strikers unwound an additional hose and directed its torrent on the police below, who retreated unceremoniously toward the Flint River bridge, out of range of the hoses and the rain of hinges hurled from upper windows. Men on the ground floor brought out cases of empty milk and pop bottles for pickets to use in case of another attack, and the men upstairs threw down quantities of hinges for the same purpose.

The second police assault was larger than the first. Not wearing masks this time, the police and sheriff's forces lobbed tear gas grenades through the upper windows to force out the sit-downers. Anticipating this, the men inside seized the grenades with gloved hands and quickly doused them in pails of water readied beforehand. Water still gushed from the fire hoses in powerful streams; and again the police took to their heels, several drawing pistols as they ran, firing indiscriminately into the crowd and wounding a number of people.

The sound car was ringed by defenders and manned by Victor Reuther, his brother Roy, Bill Carney of the United Rubber Workers, and other organizers. At one point, the speaker of the sound car was seized by Genora Johnson (Dollinger), leader of the Flint Red Berets, for an impassioned plea to the women and the men to stand fast and carry on. Encouragement and directions to picketers and spectators came from the sound car all through the fight.

The wounded, fourteen in number, were taken by ambulance to Hurley Hospital. Among them was Bob Travis. In a letter to Stanley and me not long before his death in 1980, Bob wrote that as soon as hospital attendants had washed out his eyes to ease the discomfort from the tear gas, he managed to slip out because Adolph Germer had sent word that Governor Murphy wanted to meet with him.

This was the famous battle that went down in union history as the "Battle of Bulls' Run." After this second rout of the police and the sheriff's forces, Stanley noted the litter of broken glass, rocks, bottles, and hinges in front of the plant. Water from the hoses was freezing all into a sheet of ice in the sixteen-degree weather.

Women's auxiliary members, especially those of the Flint emergency brigade in their red berets, led by Genora Johnson, Hazel Simons, and Dorothy Kraus, were certainly tested under fire that night. Stanley saw them everywhere among the pickets, helping the wounded to the ambulances, standing beside the men and hurling bottles and hinges with the best of them, and getting drenched as the water hoses overshot their mark.

In spite of the rumored mobilization of the Flint Alliance (an organization of GM officials and prominent business people), none of the spectators had engaged in the fight on the side of the attackers. That their sympathies were with the strikers was clearly evidenced as some of them joined the pickets in response to a steady appeal from the sound car.

When it was all over, Stanley and others, soaked to the skin and shivering, left the scene. Rather than drive home in that condition, Stanley went to a hotel, took a hot bath, and let his clothing dry overnight. I had expected him home by midnight; and when I wakened at 4:00 A.M. to find him still absent, I became thoroughly alarmed. Further sleep was out of the question. He always phoned if he could. I knew something was amiss.

On my way to work that morning of 12 January, I picked up the morning paper at a stand near the streetcar stop. The front page was devoted to the Flint battle, and I fearfully scanned the list of wounded. Stanley's name was not there, but I still could not imagine why I had not heard from him. Later, his reassuring call to the office where I worked explained what had happened.

The Flint GM strike and the "Battle of Bulls' Run" received national attention. On 24 January Stanley and I were guests at a banquet arranged by the Polish National Alliance. At the speakers' table we heard everyone talking about the recent skirmish. One of the main speakers was Lieutenant Governor Leo Nowicki, a prominent Democrat, whose speech was an attack upon the Flint strikers for occupying company property, destroying machinery, and creating a riot.

The audience consisted mostly of autoworkers, either UAW members or sympathizers, some of whom served on the arrangements committee. One, who had wangled invitations for us, came to whisper a warning: "Nowak, you must answer the Lieutenant Governor and set the record straight. We hope you can do it without antagonizing him."

"Don't worry," Stanley reassured him, "it will be all right."

When Stanley was called to speak, everyone was all attention, fully expecting an attack on Nowicki. But Stanley surprised them: "I am very sorry that our lieutenant governor has fallen victim to the misinformation and propaganda of a hostile antilabor press. Since he has never been at the scene of a sit-down strike, he cannot be expected to know the extreme care taken to ensure the safety of the buildings, machinery, equipment, and other company property. I would like to give Lieutenant-Governor Nowicki an opportunity to see for himself the conditions in the shops during sit-downs. I will gladly escort him through the Flint auto plants now occupied by strikers. As the second highest official in our state, I think our lieutenant governor owes it to himself and to the people of Michigan to investigate this matter. I will take personal responsibility for his safety. What do you say, Lieutenant Governor?"

The storm of applause greeting this public invitation left Nowicki no alternative. Although taken by surprise and somewhat embarrassed, he accepted.

At 7:00 A.M. 28 January Nowicki picked Stanley up at our home and drove him to strike headquarters in Flint. The lieutenant governor's unexpected appearance created a sensation. Bob Travis, strike director, gave Stanley and Nowicki the required passes and an honor guard to take them to the gate of each plant, where a committee in charge of the particular shop escorted them through and pointed out the living arrangements and the conditions of the plant, machinery, and equipment. The tour lasted most of the day, with lunch at Chevrolet Plant No. 4. Nowick admitted surprise and satisfaction with what he saw. In later years we heard him speak on many occasions and worked with him in the Democratic party. Neither of us recalls hearing him attack organized labor again.

This strike in Flint GM served to show unorganized workers everywhere that even the most powerful corporation in the world could be defeated by a united and determined work force.

In this strike, as in others that followed, we observed that the great majority of workers had very limited labor experience. However, among them were always former or current members of the Socialist Labor party, Socialist party, Trotskyites, Industrial Workers of the World (IWW), Proletarian party, and Communist party. These people possessed some basic knowledge of trade union work. All were in favor of industrial, as opposed to craft, unions. They realized they faced a common enemy, the owners of industry. Whatever their ideological differences, they were united and worked together in the common struggles of the moment. Among these groups the Communists were the most numerous, having much influence in the ethnic groups making up the work force. They were disciplined and provided leadership. People from all these groups were present in every fight waged by the UAW. Perhaps this is what is commonly referred to as the *popular front,* and this is how it was manifested in every union struggle in which we participated. These groups came together not because someone told them to do so but spontaneously as they realized we were all waging a common battle against great odds, and that unity was essential for victory.

With the signing of the GM agreement on 11 February and the beginning of the evacuation of the Flint plants, Reuther pressed Stanley to concentrate on his long-postponed organizing assignment at Ternstedt's, the largest GM shop in Detroit. No sooner had he begun this task than the cigar women staged their sit-down in Addes's office and sidetracked Nowak to their cigar strikes. He broke his foot in the cigarworkers' strike, which postponed the Ternstedt drive still longer. However, once he was able to get about on crutches and had a driver to take him around for his organizing duties, Stanley began the Ternstedt work in earnest. Here he would work with another group of militant and very able women who helped make labor history.

Stanley in Chicago, 1919, at age sixteen.

Margaret in 1932, the year she and Stanley met.

Margaret and Stanley on their wedding day, 1935.

Helen (Nowak) Piwkowska, about 1927.

Helen Piwkowska (far right) with sister Lottie (left) and Cecelia Chromecki, 1978.

Irene (Young) Marinovich (left) during the Ternstedt slowdown, 1938.

Ternstedt apprentices have signed for these demands!
65¢
Minimum Hiring Rate.
Standard Curriculum.
Joint Representation.

Irene and Tony Marinovich in 1971. Photo courtesy of the Archives of Labor History and Urban Affairs, Wayne State University.

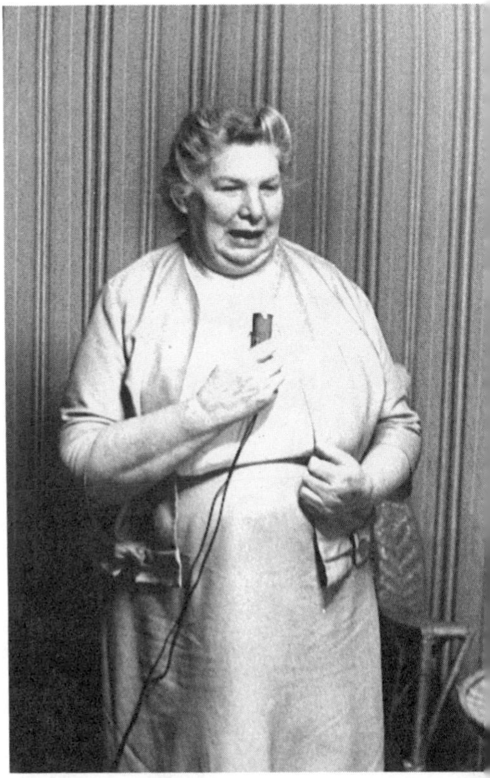

Martha Strong (Whisman) in 1971. Photo courtesy of the Archives of Labor History and Urban Affairs, Wayne State University.

Jack White in 1971. Photo courtesy of the Archives of Labor History and Urban Affairs, Wayne State University.

Tony Marinovich (left) with Stanley during the 1938 state senate campaign.

Stanley and poet Adam Kujtkowski during a radio broadcast, 1940.

The UAW Polish Trade Union Committee, 1941. From left: *John Zaremba, Stanley, and Frank Danowski.*

Speaking to factory workers during the 1941 city council campaign.

The city council campaign of 1941. Charles Diggs, Sr., and Stanley Nowak were the first black and white city council slate. From left: *Mamie Diggs, Charles Diggs, Sr., Stanley, and Margaret.*

Senator Chas. C. Diggs

TO ALL

Ford Workers

Negro and White

Senator Stanley Nowak

The eyes of the nation are upon you. You have done the "impossible." You have struck at and defeated the greatest enemy of the organized labor movement in this country. You have won the admiration of all working people.

On May 21 you will be asked to finish your task by casting your vote for the union of your choice. That date will mark one of the greatest steps in the history, not only of the Ford workers, but of the workers of the whole nation.

An overwhelming vote of the Ford workers for the CIO will put an end once and for all to the greatest speed-up, terrorism, and intimidation that has ever existed in any industry in the country. A CIO victory will pull out by its roots the most dangerous nest of reaction that has ever existed in our country. Your struggle with the Ford Motor Co., is part and parcel of the struggle that working people are carrying on throughout the world for democracy, peace, security, and for a higher standard of living. Your victory over the Ford Motor Co. will be the victory of democracy and progress over Fascism and reaction. Your vote for the CIO will be a vote for higher wages, job security, and freedom from the despised Service Dept.

As State Senators, elected by you and other workers, we have watched your progress with keen interest. We worked with you through all the stages of your organizational drive. Now when you are within reach of your victory, we want to add what we can to make that victory greater and more secure. We are aware that a barrage of charges will be blasted at the CIO on the eve of the Labor Board vote. Every effort will be made to divide you Ford workers on racial lines, to create a fight between Negro and White workers. As representatives of both Negro and White workers, we appeal to you again not to allow yourselves to be divided. Division among you spells doom to everything you have so far accomplished.

There will be attempts to frighten you with a barrage of charges of communism, foreign agents, subversive activity and attempts to turn White against Negro and Negro against White. Let nothing frighten you. Stand solidly together around the banner of the CIO. Do not permit the fruits of your long labor to be snatched from you now that you have it within your reach. Stand united and courageous and victory will be yours. This means higher wages, seniority rights, job security and better working conditions for all Ford workers.

ISSUED BY

SENATOR DIGGS ECONOMIC SOCIETY
and STANLEY NOWAK FEDERATION

37

Leaflet formulated by the Nowaks and circulated the Sunday before the 21 May 1941 NLRB election at Ford.

National Conference of Polish Trade Unionists, April 1942 in Cleveland. Among those present were Bill Gebert, Leo Krzycki, John Zaremba, Stanley, and Oscar Lange.

Reception for General Sikorski by the Polish Trade Unionists, December 1942. Vincent Klein, Leo Krzycki, John Zaremba, and Stanley were among those present.

Meeting of the Nowak Defense Committee, 1942.

Judge Patrick H. O'Brien swearing in the Nowak Defense Committee, 1942.

Margaret and Stanley after the 1942 arraignment. Photo courtesy of the Detroit Free Press.

Stanley speaking before the Polish SEJM *(parliament), Warsaw, December 1945.*

Elissa, Stanley, and Margaret, 1953.

Pioneers of the UAW in the mid-1970s. From left: *Emil Mazey, Bob Travis, Dave Miller, and Stanley.*

Margaret and Stanley Nowak with daughter Elissa and her husband, Dennis James, and grandchildren Kiley and Maya, May 1985.

9 UAW's First Slowdown

In December 1936 the UAW had granted Walter Reuther's request to have Stanley assigned to work out of West Side Local No. 174, of which Reuther was president. Shortly thereafter, the organizing staff of the local met with Reuther to discuss the organizing of Ternstedt's, the largest General Motors plant in Detroit.

Ternstedt's was one of the greatest aggregations of women workers in the automotive industry. The vast majority of the twelve thousand employees were women, and all previous organizing attempts had netted only about a dozen members. On some floors of Main Plant No. 18 hardly a man was to be seen, as men worked mainly in the tool and die section.

At the organizational meeting, considerable doubt was expressed as to whether women could be organized, especially since previous attempts had accomplished so little. Finally Stanley spoke up. "I disagree," he said, "that women are difficult to organize. In every shop I have organized, and in every activity in which women have participated with me, I have found them very dependable, vocal, and militant, often more so than men."

"Well, you can have it, Stanley," said the others, who willingly turned over to him the Ternstedt assignment. Bob Kanter had his hands full with small shops on Detroit's west side, and George Edwards was tied up with the Yale-Towne Strike.

Ternstedt's offices were located in Main Plant No. 18 on Fort Street at Livernois, and less than a half block away on Livernois was Plant No. 14. Since about 70 percent of the work force was employed in these two plants, Stanley concentrated his efforts there. He arranged for unemployed members of Local No. 174 to hand out leaflets at the entrances at the work shifts changed, while he spoke from the sound truck parked at the curb between both plant gates.

The office of Mr. S. E. Skinner, Ternstedt's general manager, overlooked the two gates, and he could see from his window all that went on. Because of this, many employees feared to be seen taking leaflets. Nevertheless, they were offered every day for weeks, with Stanley speaking from the sound truck. Gradually, workers began accepting leaflets as they passed by.

Stanley began stopping in at a neighborhood bar, where he learned of grievances in Ternstedt's different departments and featured them in the next day's leaflet. This caught the attention of the workers, and some of them began to stop for a word or two.

The tool and die men and some of the machine repair men began to stop at the sound truck to ask questions. Because of their skills they were less vulnerable than other workers, and soon they began to sign applications and hand out leaflets to fellow employees.

Stanley felt it was time to call meetings. The Slovenian Benefit Society owned the Slovene Hall on Livernois and South streets, about a block away. The sympathetic and cooperative manager permitted the hall's use as a temporary union headquarters and meeting place. Membership meetings grew until forty or fifty people were attending after each shift.

Stanley's day began with the 7:00 A.M. meeting; then he went to West Side Local to have leaflets mimeographed for the day's scheduled meetings. He returned to the Slovene Hall for the 4:00 P.M.-shift meeting, then back home for a few hours of rest, returning to the hall for the 11:00 P.M.-shift meeting. To cover the entire work force of twelve thousand people the meetings were held daily, and attendance grew.

On the morning of 5 January 1937, Stanley handed out leaflets announcing a meeting of Ternstedt workers the next afternoon at Martin Hall, on Martin near Michigan Ave. The hall was owned by a group of Ukrainians, but was located in the heart of the Polish community. The owners were friendly to the union drive and were happy to offer the use of their hall.

As Stanley handed out leaflets that morning, many workers who had been sent home earlier that week for lack of work due to the Flint GM sit-down, came for their pay. A man with clipboard and pencil was soliciting signatures on a GM back-to-work petition. A woman approached and began badgering the man. Her easy breezy manner and good-natured banter with workers standing nearby attracted attention.

"What are *you* collecting signatures for?" she asked. When the man explained, she said for the benefit of all within hearing, "Oh! In other words, you want us to help break the GM strike, is that it?" She followed with equally blunt but appropriate comments, and the man fled ignominiously as others gathered to heckle him. She then turned her attention to Stanley: "Who are *you*, and what are *you* handing out?"

"I'm the UAW organizer in charge of the Ternstedt drive," he answered, handing her a leaflet. As she read it her face lit up in a broad grin.

"Well, Halleluja!" she exclaimed. "It's about time somebody did something like this around here. I'm Irene Young. Let me have some leaflets and I'll help pass them out." They talked as they handed out the leaflets, and Stanley invited her to the next afternoon's meeting 6 January, at Martin Hall.

Another woman encountered that same morning during the leafletting was Martha Strong, who had been in the shop since 1925. Stanley invited her, too, to the next day's meeting.

Glos ludowy reported that almost two hundred Ternstedt workers attended that meeting, yet it had been publicized only by leaflets passed out at plant gates for a couple of days. Both Stanley and Frankensteen spoke. As Irene participated in the discussions, her crooked grin flashed and her brown eyes twinkled with humor or sparkled with anger. Small and short of stature, with brown hair fluffed about her face, she looked the essence of what is commonly called "femininity"; but she had the directness usually associated with a man, and she stood for no nonsense. She swore eloquently but without obscenity, and somehow her impish smile made it inoffensive. Irene was just what she was, like it or not, and most people liked. Stanley learned she was from a mining family in Illinois and had been conditioned early to unionism.

Irene's sense of humor, her energy, and her ability to debate issues had made her well liked and respected in the plant. That afternoon she was elected steward for her department. She would serve on the first bargaining committee, then as recording secretary for West Side Local No. 174, and still later as committeewoman in Fleetwood Plant of Ternstedt's.

Martha Strong also participated in discussions at that 6 January meeting. Taller than Irene, her broad, serene features framed by light brown hair, Martha had the soft speech associated with the South. Her wide, blue eyes were serious or smiling by turns; and in her quiet, almost tentative way, she could persuade and convince people to her point of view. She was elected that afternoon as steward for her department. Later she would be a delegate to the 1937 UAW convention, a member of Local No. 174's executive board and joint council. Both she and Irene would be stalwarts in the organizing drive and in general union affairs.

At that afternoon meeting the sixth a committee of ten was elected to prepare a list of grievances and arrange a mass meeting for the eighth at Martin Hall. Over three hundred attended the meeting of the eighth, where a committee of twenty was elected, consisting of representatives of the majority of Ternstedt departments. This committee scheduled a mass meeting for the afternoon of the tenth in Martin Hall to formulate demands to present to management. It was the very next day after that meeting of the tenth that Stanley spoke to Polish workers in Flint and got drenched at the strike scene.

Ternstedt meetings continued, department by department, shift by shift, and union membership grew. All doubts about organizing women had been dispelled as they joined in large numbers. Besides Irene Young and Martha Strong, some of those who came to prominence and played active roles were Irene Kotlarek, Lena Saline, Becky Lang (Kemsley), Mary Kaluszak, and Margaret Lupskin. A description of working conditions gleaned from Ternstedt workers explains their readiness to join the union and sign up new members and their steadfastness in fighting every step of the way.

Management's policy was reflected in the kind of workers hired, all from easily exploited groups—southerners, foreign-born, and women. According to Jack White, one of the very early unionists at Ternstedt's, there were only two Black workers in the whole establishment. One, in Plant No. 18, worked on a machine to bale metal and cardboard scrap; the other, in a garage beside the main plant, kept management's cars polished and in repair.

One reason for so many women employees was that the company manufactured small parts easily manipulated by women—door handles, chromium trim, and so on. Many women hired during World War I had been allowed to remain because they would work for less than men. Ternstedt's reputation for low wages was widely known. The bonus system was juggled so that it was almost impossible to earn more than the hourly rate, no matter how much production was turned in. This was one of Martha Strong's pet gripes. She described how on 7 January, after joining the union at the meeting the afternoon before, she proudly wore her union and steward buttons to work and signed up many new members. Since she was a veteran employee with considerable influence, her foreman grew disturbed and came to talk to her: "Why have you, of all people, joined the union?" "Well, I've been working on these door handles for five years now," she said in her soft voice. "When I started, I could make six hundred in a day and was paid five dollars. Now I make a thousand and still get only five dollars." The foreman had no answer; and although she had fully expected him to fire her, he did not.

In seeking an explanation for getting no bonus, Martha discovered and exposed the company policy of playing one group against another. In Plant No. 16, where she worked, the labor force was about equally divided between foreign- and native-born. Any U.S.-born worker was dubbed a "hillbilly," since southerners constituted the largest proportion of native-born workers in the shop. Similarly, a worker of any foreign nationality was automatically a "Polack," as Poles were the largest ethnic group there. Martha was sent by the "hillbillies" to see the boss about the bonus. Everyone had turned in heavy production, but no one received bonus pay. "I'm sorry," the boss said. "It couldn't be helped, because the Polacks turned in so much production this week."

Shortly after this Martha was recovering from a cold and sat near a radiator on the side of the room where the Poles usually gathered for lunch. A Polish woman sat next to her and they began to talk. Others gathered around. While they ate lunch together, someone suggested a delegation to see the boss about the bonus. Martha tagged along. This time, the boss said the darned "hillbillies" had turned in so much production that he could do nothing about it.

"How come?" spoke up Martha. "Last week you told my group the Polacks had turned in so much production that you couldn't give us a bonus. This time you blame the hillbillies. How do you explain that? This is your way of denying the bonus to either group!" Her outburst surprised everyone, including herself, and they turned indignantly to the boss for an explanation.

"What are you doing here with the Polacks anyhow?" he shouted at Martha. "You don't belong with them. You're a hillbilly."

Martha explained her presence. "And I'm glad I came!" she declared. "Now I know why there hasn't been any bonus. You were just playing the Polacks against the hillbillies to get a lot of production and not pay extra for it. I'm going to see that everyone knows about this!"

Another unfair practice was the "shape-up." Employees coming to work gathered around in a semicircle while the foreman selected workers for certain machines or tasks. After all the jobs for that shift were assigned, the remaining workers went home without pay, not even for carfare, since they were paid only for actual working time no matter how many hours they had waited for assignment.

Another complaint was that the more skilled workers were frequently shunted from one machine or job to another, often wasting hours of time from one machine or job to another, often wasting hours of time in the process for which they were not paid. They might spend ten hours in the shop and receive pay for only four or five hours of work, causing even the most skilled worker to wind up with little more pay than the production worker. Because of all these things, workers sometimes had no money for carfare. Martha Strong solved this problem by getting a Saturday job in a grocery store.

Both men and women were subject to these conditions. In choosing people for various jobs, the foreman selected those most cooperative in a personal sense. For men, this meant participating in lawn-cutting parties at the foreman's home on Saturdays or Sundays with no compensation other than sharing a barrel of beer. It might be a garage or summer cottage to be built or painted or a roofing job to be done. Those refusing such "privileges" were passed over in the next "shape-up" and got fewer assignments or even dismissal.

For women it meant dating the boss at his whim or accepting unwanted attentions. Refusal meant few assignments, sometimes a transfer to another department and less-desirable job, or even being fired. Pay for women was always less than for men, even for the same job and the same amount of production. This served as a whip over the men, who, if they complained, were told this particular operation could be given to a woman for less pay. The union promised release from such indignities and injustices and gave workers a sense of worth. No longer would the individual worker be at the mercy of the boss or foreman. This was illustrated early in the Ternstedt drive by an incident concerning Irene Young.

Like Martha, Irene had worn her union and steward buttons to work on 7 January after being elected department steward at the meeting of the afternoon before. She signed up members in her department and about two hours later was fired by Mr. Skinner. He did not say it was because of union activity. He got around that by a technicality: Irene had hired in as a single woman under her maiden name of Young instead of her husband's name, Marinovich. Nevertheless, Skinner's pointed questions about signing up union members on company time made it evident that this was the real reason.

Irene filed a grievance, and Walter Reuther informed Skinner that her case would furnish the basis for charges of unfair labor practices under the Wagner Act. Although somewhat embarrassed by all the publicity, Irene was encouraged to fight the case through so that other women would not hesitate to engage in union activity. A meeting was arranged with Skinner attended not only by Stanley and Reuther but also by UAW's second vice-president, Ed Hall, and stewards from several Ternstedt departments. Skinner opened the meeting with what he must have considered a surprise bombshell: "Before we start this meeting," he said, "let's get one thing straight, once and for all. Mr. Reuther has never worked at Ternstedt and therefore could never legitimately be a member of a union in our establishment." Reuther had been elected president of West Side Local on the basis of his supposed employment at Ternstedt's, and he was a delegate to the 1936 convention of the UAW in South Bend on the same grounds.

Reuther ignored Skinner's charge, and the meeting proceeded. Skinner's obvious ploy to disrupt the proceedings failed to achieve his purpose. Irene was reinstated and returned to her job. She was quickly surrounded by the jubilant workers she had signed into the union. When Skinner retaliated by transferring Irene to Fleetwood Plant he probably hoped to end her influence by placing her in a new department where she was a stranger. If so, he failed to reckon with Irene's capabilities. She soon organized all the workers in her new place.

Since Ternstedt was a division of GM, the successful ending of the Flint sit-down on 11 February gave a tremendous boost to the Ternstedt organizing drive. The master contract between GM and the UAW covered all GM plants, thus entitling Ternstedt workers to union recognition.

Before Stanley could get the first bargaining committee together and arrange a meeting with Skinner, he got that call from Addes on 17 February and became embroiled in the strikes of the cigar workers, breaking his foot on 20 February (for this story, see chapter 1). After that, Ternstedt stewards and committee members, as well as the cigar women, came to our apartment to consult with him and carried on negotiations in his absence. They frequently phoned for advice. He certainly had no chance to feel loneliness or isolation, even though confined to bed most of the time with his foot in a cast.

The Ternstedt workers were getting nowhere with Skinner, and about the last week in March the demand for Stanley's return to the Ternstedt drive became insistent. Dr. Shafarman gave permission, warning Stanley he must not bear his weight on the injured foot or drive a car. Local No. 174 got around these difficulties with the help of Tony Marinovich, Irene Young's husband. One morning before seven o'clock, Tony appeared at our door. "Hi, Stanley!" he grinned. "I'm your new chauffeur. Reuther sent me to bring you to the local."

Tony came from a Yugoslav family of miners in Illinois. One of the very first to join the UAW at Ford's, Tony hid union literature on his person and set a small stack of leaflets on the conveyor belt to travel down the line each day. He was eventually discovered and fired.

Organizing in the Ford plants was under the jurisdiction of the West Side Local No. 174, since Ford Local had not yet been established. No sooner was Tony fired than he volunteered his services to Local No. 174, and Reuther hired him to take Stanley about to resume his Ternstedt organizing duties.

Tony was tall, lean, and muscular, dark of hair and eyes, and bursting with nervous energy. When I saw how slender he was, I wondered how he would manage with Stanley, who was no lightweight. Our apartment was on the second floor, with no elevator. Without a moment's hesitation, Tony lifted Stanley to his shoulder, while Stanley held his crutches in one arm and placed the other around Tony's opposite shoulder. Tony held to the bannister with his free hand and carried Stanley down to the main floor. There Stanley could use his crutches to reach the car, and Tony helped him into it.

For weeks, Tony took Stanley daily to the West Side Local and from there to the Slovene Hall, which still served as headquarters for the Ternstedt drive. He took Stanley to all his meetings and saw him safely home at night. It could well be said that Tony Marinovich was responsible, as much as Stanley, for the organizing of Ternstedt's from that time until Stanley was able to get about without assistance.

On his return to the Ternstedt drive, Stanley contacted Mr. Skinner for some serious bargaining in view of the UAW victory at Flint GM. Reluctantly, Skinner set a date. By this time fully one-third of the work force had joined the UAW, and the bargaining committee consisted of representatives from all four Ternstedt plants.

The workers had begun to publish a paper, the *Ternstedt Flash*. When it announced the coming meeting between Skinner and the Bargaining committee, a wave of enthusiasm swept the plants, resulting in hundreds of new members. This meeting was regarded as the first step toward victory. However, the workers soon discovered the truth of the old adage, "You can lead a horse to water, but you can't make him drink." Skinner complied with that part of the agreement calling for meeting with the bargaining committee, but granted no concessions. This went on for weeks, creating a serious crisis.

Workers had joined the union for its benefits, yet Skinner refused to agree to any of the demands presented. The new GM contract specifically ruled out strikes. Moreover, there was tremendous antistrike agitation in the press. What could be done to compel Skinner to bargain, short of a strike? For several nights Stanley turned and tossed, sleepless, over the problem. Since Ternstedt's was a division of West Side Local No. 174, he consulted Reuther.

"Stanley," he warned, "you know you can't call a strike. We don't dare violate our new agreement."

"But what can you suggest to break the impasse?"

"You're an old, experienced hand, Stanley. I'm sure you can come up with something. You'll just have to work it out."

Shop stewards were now functioning in every department at Ternstedt's, numbering almost two hundred, all impatiently demanding action. Unless something was done quickly, further organizing would be stymied, and membership would drop. Stanley anxiously turned the matter over in his mind. Then he recalled reading about a strike in Vienna before World War I, where workers stood at their machines and went through the motions of working, yet produced very little. An old Polish worker in Chicago, who had participated in that strike, had told him about it years before and had given him a book in Polish describing it. He located the book in our library and spent most of the night reading it long after I was asleep. The next morning he seemed relieved.

Smiling, he said over breakfast, "Since the union contract cannot compel Skinner to grant concessions at the bargaining table, neither can it compel workers to produce while at their machines. If Skinner can make a farce of bargaining, I don't see why we can't use this tactic in return." Stanley first took the idea to Reuther.

"Sounds like a good idea, Stanley. Just see that the workers don't go overboard and lay us open to charges of violating the GM contract. To make sure, you had better check with Martin on this."

The first reaction of UAW president Homer Martin was, "Stanley, if you call a strike, I'll fire you!"

However, as Stanley outlined the method of the slowdown in detail, Martin became enthusiastic.

"You've got it, Stanley! Why hasn't someone thought of this before? Go ahead! You have my full approval and support!"

And so was born the first slowdown in UAW history. The problem now was to organize the new tactic. Of the twelve thousand Ternstedt workers, only a handful had any union experience. They had never heard of a slowdown but were ready for any kind of action.

The new technique was first carefully explained to the bargaining committee, then to the two hundred or more stewards, who then had to explain and demonstrate the idea to trusted workers in each department—all this while maintaining absolute secrecy. Fortunately, there were no company agents in the union leadership in the plants. Finally, the plan was ready to be put into operation. Production was not to be cut all at once in all plants but rather in each department at a different time. On the appointed day and hour, the cue was to be given successively in each department. A meeting of the bargaining committee with Mr. Skinner had been scheduled for the very morning when all this was to take place, and there was some apprehension among the group as they headed for Mr. Skinner's office.

"Good morning, Stanley," greeted Skinner as Stanley came in with his committee that morning in early April 1937.

"Good morning to you, Mr. Skinner," returned Stanley.

The committee members filed into the office and took their places around the big table in the center. Mr. Skinner looked every inch the business executive in his smart suit with his sleek, graying hair and trim build. He sat at his desk a few feet away, greeting each one with a great display of amiability, waving his long cigarette holder and moving papers around as he made conversation. At the bargaining table, small talk and laughter masked an undertone of uneasiness and tension. Skinner's unusual affability and exaggerated courtesy made the committee members wonder, "Does he know?" A surreptitious wink or shrug in reply to questioning glances expressed their hopes and uncertainty.

Irene Young came in and seated herself next to Stanley. "Goddamned bastard!" she swore under her breath as she watched Skinner's show of geniality. "That son of a bitch thinks he's got us over a barrel!" Then she grinned impishly. "If it works, he won't think it's so funny, I hope."

When all committee members had arrived, Mr. Skinner came to sit at the head of the table. As Stanley recalls, those present, besides Irene, were Al Warner, Richard Eager, John Bartosiewicz, Becky Lang, Joe Bedi, Rudi Kraft, and Joe Urban. Nowak put his crutches aside and drew from his briefcase a sheaf of papers. As each demand was presented, Skinner appeared to weigh it carefully, discussed it with the group, then turned it down for one reason or another. This had been the pattern of the meetings for weeks.

As the farce proceeded, a telephone call interrupted Mr. Skinner. The committee members looked at each other hopefully, and listened eagerly. Skinner was somewhat less genial when he returned to the table, but he continued with negotiations. In a few moments another call came. Skinner looked searchingly around the table as he resumed his seat. His good humor had vanished. Two more calls came. With each one he grew more disturbed. As he hung up the receiver from the last one, his face contorted with anger and he pointed an accusing finger at Stanley.

"You son of a bitch, *you* did this to me!"

"I did what?" Stanley asked innocently.

"*You* know what I'm talking about. How dare you have the gall to come here and go through the motions of bargaining when there's a strike in the plant?"

"A strike?" Nowak repeated. "Aren't the workers on the job? We don't know of any strike."

"Oh yes you do!" insisted Skinner.

"I don't believe it, Mr. Skinner. Take me through the shop and show me where there is a strike."

"Like hell, I will! Get out of here! All of you! You have a hell of a nerve to negotiate with a strike going on."

"All right," said Stanley, putting his papers back in his briefcase and reaching for his crutches. "Come on, everybody, Mr. Skinner is in no mood to negotiate today."

They left Skinner fuming and frantically calling the different departments in the factory. When scarcely out of earshot, the irrepressible Irene threw her hands in the air with a delighted, "Damn! We did it! It worked!" The others gleefully hugged and congratulated each other and Stanley on the success of their strategy.

"Don't be so sure!" cautioned Stanley. "We're not out of the woods yet. Wait until the day-shift workers report tonight at our meeting to find out exactly what is happening."

That night, the day-shift workers joyfully reported what had taken place in their departments. It hadn't taken long for department heads to notice the lag in production and reprimand the workers.

I'm doing the best I can," workers maintained. "Maybe it's the machine."

Machines checked out okay, but production was still slow. At first, workers were somewhat clumsy at appearing to work while producing little; however, they soon caught on, and then it became a wonderful game, each worker trying to outdo the others in making as many motions as possible and doing the least work. Production slowly dropped. Management had been taken completely by surprise. A new wave of enthusiasm brought hundreds of new union applications, until more than 80 percent of the work force had joined.

Within a few days, Martin, Reuther, and some members of the UAW executive board grew a little uneasy. Martin, who had given Stanley such unqualified approval at the start, now asked him to call a mass meeting of Ternstedt workers so that Ed Hall, UAW's second vice president could try to talk them into abandoning the slowdown.

"Do you think they will listen to me?" Hall asked Stanley before the meeting.

"I don't know, Ed. You can try, but I doubt you'll have much luck. They're very enthusiastic, and since I initiated the whole thing, they'd have my scalp if I tried to stop them."

Stanley introduced Ed Hall with the words, "He is here to discuss the slowdown with you."

"You know what a difficult fight it was to get the GM master contract," Hall began. "This is the first such agreement we have been able to obtain. That contract may now be in danger, because GM may charge that the slowdown here violates that agreement and might invalidate the contract."

Such an uproar of boos, shouts, and catcalls interrupted Hall that he could not continue for several moments. Usually at no loss for words, he stood helpless in the midst of the pandemonium. He pulled out his handkerchief, mopped his brow, ran a hand nervously through his hair, and looked at Stanley. Finally, Stanley signaled for silence and Ed Hall tried again: "In all honesty, I must say I was delegated by our president, Homer Martin, to say what I just did. And there *is* that danger. But now that I have done my duty, I'm sure this Polish brain [pointing to Stanley] will come up with something. Just follow his lead, and you'll be all right."

Cheers greeted these comments, and Hall sat down with relief. The slowdown continued. Production dipped to about 40 percent or 50 percent of the norm. In some departments it dropped to as low as 5 percent or 10 percent on some days. Skinner still refused to budge.

UAW vice president Wyndham Mortimer later told Stanley that William F. Knudsen, GM's president, had approached him and asked if he couldn't pressure Ternstedt workers to end their slowdown.

"They wouldn't even listen to such an idea," Mortimer declared, "unless Skinner begins to bargain in good faith."

Skinner must have been advised to abandon his hard-nosed attitude, for when Stanley phoned him soon after, he said, "Well, Stanley, I guess it's about time we got together again. Bring your bargaining committee and we'll get down to business."

In one three-hour session more was accomplished than in all previous meetings combined. Apparently Skinner realized that he was the one "over the barrel" this time. Union recognition was granted at once, and piecework was abolished, with hourly rates to be negotiated in place of piecework. *Glos ludowy* announced the end of the slowdown on 13 April.

There were so many who worked with Stanley to bring the union to Ternstedt's. One of the very earliest was Micky Moxham of the tool and die department, who served at different times on the grievance committee, the shop committee, and as vice president and later recording secretary of the Ternstedt unit. He often boasted that his department was the first to be 100-percent organized. Another was Ed Cote, chairman of the plant committee, who replaced Richard Eager when the latter was exposed as a Martin follower and disrupter. Cote was also vice president of Local No. 174 and later its president. Still later, he was a UAW regional director. Joe Bedi, another very early union member, was financial secretary of the Ternstedt unit for years. Bill Kiddon was another of the first rank-and-filers. Jack White served the Ternstedt unit as steward and member of the grievance committee. He was also a member of West Side Local's joint council and of its executive board, also recording secretary. As early as 1929, Jack had been an employee advocate and was involved in a work stoppage and fired. He had been working under the name "John White" and was later able to get back into Ternstedt's as "Jack White." When the

UAW organizing campaign began at Ternstedt's in 1936, Jack was ready and waiting. George Moran served as steward and committeeman. Steve Nagy was a very early supporter and rank-and-filer. Rudi Kraft was the first financial secretary of the Ternstedt unit. Art Reimal was a shop chairman. All these and many more whose names Stanley cannot remember helped establish the union and served at every step of the way and at every level.

Ternstedt unit celebrated the union victory at West Side Local, and Walter Reuther spoke at length about the hard work that had gone into it but never once mentioned Stanley. George Edwards, a fellow organizer who would one day be Detroit's police commissioner and later a judge in the appeals court in Cincinnati, showed concern over Reuther's omission of Stanley and the long fight he had waged to organize Ternstedt's, even on crutches. "Walter," he said, "you never once said a word about Stanley and his role in this. We all know he did it with very little help from us." Reuther just looked at George and Stanley, turned on his heel, and walked away. Stanley wondered about this. It was so unlike Walter, who had frequently consulted with him about problems in the local, even asking Stanley occasionally to substitute for him when he had to be away.

Stanley dismissed the incident from his mind and began the tedious process of negotiating hourly rates in place of piecework in the Ternstedt plants. Then on 26 May 1937 the infamous Battle of the Overpass occurred, where Walter Reuther, Dick Frankensteen, Bob Kanter, and many others, both men and women, were badly beaten by Harry Bennett's goons near gate 4 at the Rouge plant.

Stanley, still on crutches, was not allowed to participate in the giant leafletting planned for that day at Ford's. Instead, he was stationed at West Side Local No. 174 where medical facilities were set up to handle any injuries that might occur. Stanley recalls that Drs. Eugene Shafarman and Morris Raskin were there, and members of the Women's Auxiliary.

Ford Local was still part of the amalgamated Local No. 174, and there the wounded were brought, to be cared for or to be sent to a hospital. Frankensteen, Reuther, and others who had participated in the leafletting attempt were bleeding and horribly beaten. Among them was Irene Young's husband, Tony Marinovich, unconscious from a skull fracture and severe concussion after being thrown down the stairs and kicked and beaten. He would suffer the rest of his life from his injuries. Reuther, Frankensteen and most of the others would recover, though some had also been thrown and kicked down the stairs and kicked and slugged on the ground, their clothes torn and bloodied from their wounds.

As the excitement died down following this incident, Stanley again turned to the establishing of hourly wage rates instead of piecework at Ternstedt's. This culminated in a plantwide strike with traditional picket lines on 9 June, lasting until 17 June.

In the meantime, strange things were happening in the West Side Local office. Each day, Stanley carefully informed May Reuther where he would be negotiating and where to reach him. Yet people kept asking him, "Where the hell were you today? I called the office and they said they had no idea where you were or what you were doing. What is this?"

When this happened repeatedly, Stanley went to Reuther about it. Together they went to May in the office, who would say, "Well, I guess I forgot," or some such excuse. Walter flushed uneasily and cautioned her to be more careful. However, the "forgetting" went on.

Further, reports of comments by Walter about Stanley kept coming from many sources, all to the same effect: "Stanley has too much power. He holds Ternstedt in the palm of his hand." In conversations with Walter, Stanley had heard him make the same criticism against Bob Travis, namely, that he held "Flint in the palm of his hand." Obviously, something was amiss not only in West Side Local No. 174 but also in the International. Stanley had been so occupied with affairs at Ternstedt that he had not closely followed the ideological struggle that was developing in the UAW.

The story of the factional fight in the UAW has been written by numerous writers. It is a matter of record that UAW president Homer Martin was utterly incompetent to handle union negotiations or affairs because of his inexperience. He had been a Baptist minister and was ousted from his church for "conduct unbecoming a minister" (whatever that might be). His only asset was his gift of oratory. Recognizing his inadequacy, he gathered about him people who would support him, and from this developed his "Progressive Caucus." He also set about trying to get rid of anyone posing a threat to his power.

Early in 1937 the "Unity Caucus" was formed in opposition to Martin, consisting of many experienced and very capable union organizers and officials—Wyndham Mortimer, the three Reuther brothers, Bob Travis, Ed Hall, George Addes, Emil Mazey, to name a few, and of course, Stanley. Shortly after that, Stanley had broken his foot in the cigar strikes; had undertaken, while yet on crutches, the organizing of Ternstedt's and the slowdown there, with the long, tedious negotiations on hourly rates to replace piecework. Still later, he would organize other shops and campaign for election to the Michigan Legislature where he would sandwich organizing in between legislative work.

It must also be noted that along with all this Stanley continued his work in the Polish community—the radio broadcasts, speaking at Polish meetings and affairs, and helping organizers in various locals where there was a problem involving Poles and Blacks. He was on the go constantly and had little time or energy to take part in the factional struggle, although wherever he encountered those who were involved they informed him of most of the developments.

On 13 September a *Detroit Free Press* article headed, "Purge Demanded by UAW," told of a Flint meeting with Robert Travis and some board members. Travis was quoted as saying that Martin was "charging communism to anyone disagreeing with him."

On the twenty-eighth, when Stanley phoned Skinner to arrange a bargaining meeting, the latter said, "Not this time, Nowak, I don't have to deal with you any more. I have a wire from Homer Martin stating you were dropped from the international UAW organizing staff." On returning to his office, Stanley found a similar wire from Martin. The next day's *Detroit Free Press* (29 September) carried an article headlined, "Martin Ousting Three Aides," and mentioned Bob Travis, Stanley, and Robert Kanter of West Side Local No. 174. A *Free Press* article of 30 September was headed, "Nine in UAW Ousted" with a subheading, "Martin Rumored Ridding Ranks of His Enemies." The article mentioned the firing of Victor Reuther, Melvin Bishop, John Anderson of Local No. 155, and UAW publicity director Frank Winn, who had been writing the UAW's column for the Polish paper, *Glos ludowy.* That paper and the three regular dailies carried the above news.

The *Glos ludowy* article was more informative than those in the regular dailies and pointed out that all those fired had belonged to the Unity Caucus. The article mentioned that Martin had appointed a Ford organizing committee headed by Richard Frankensteen and Zygmund Dobrzynski – the same Dobrzynski whom Stanley had helped to establish Local No. 205 at Automotive Fibers in December 1936.

It was clear, Martin was ridding the UAW of anyone posing a threat to his power. Although he had fired Roy and Victor Reuther, Walter was beyond his reach, deriving his income and power from West Side Local No. 174 as its president. While Stanley was not actively engaged in the factional fight, he was a member of Unity Caucus, as were all those fired.

The *Free Press* of 30 September reported a meeting of fifteen hundred Ternstedt workers in the Finnish Hall (later purchased by UAW Local No. 155 for their headquarters). Angry Ternstedt workers had read of Stanley's firing and turned out to learn the details. Stanley read to them Martin's telegram, and a worker demanded the floor: "Who does Martin think he is? Nowak has been with us from the beginning, even on crutches. He came up with the idea of the slowdown to make Skinner negotiate in earnest. Martin has never once shown his face around here. The only thing he ever did was to send Ed Hall to try and stop our slowdown, and now the bastard wants to get rid of Nowak."

"To hell with Martin!" another voice exploded in anger. "Let's put Nowak on the West Side Local payroll and send a delegation to protest Martin's action." This was seconded by a dozen voices and a delegation was chosen from many volunteers, among them Irene Young.

At Martin's hotel the next day, 1 October, the delegation found about forty such protestors, as reported by the press. They waited for hours, and finally a committee of five, including Irene, went to Martin's suite. Failing to get a response to repeated knocking, someone kicked at the door, which Martin opened with a gun in his hand. There was a rash of photos and publicity in the press about this incident.

Nowak remained on the Local No. 174 payroll through 1937 and into 1938, continuing the time-consuming process of establishing hourly rates in place of piecework at Ternstedt's. One day Walter Reuther came to him with a proposal.

"You know, Stanley, that Martin fired both Roy and Victor. This is a big operation at Ternstedt's. Would you mind if we hire Victor to sit in with you at these negotiations and plant meetings, and maybe he can be of help."

Stanley readily agreed. Victor was a very likable person and pleasant to work with. He accompanied Stanley to the negotiations and frequently phoned our house to consult Stanley on questions. He always talked to me and was very proud of his wife Sophie, who was of Polish origin.

It wasn't long before people in the plants began coming to Stanley, somewhat disturbed over continuing comments made to them by Walter that Stanley should step aside and let Victor take over. Irene Young, Jack White, Martha Strong, and especially Frank Manfred of Kelsey Wheel, who was secretary-treasurer of Local No. 174, all related such comments by Walter. All of this seemed to indicate to everyone that since Ternstedt was now organized and functioning and had become the largest unit of Local No. 174, Walter wanted to control it through Victor.

At first Stanley was hurt and angry, for he had believed implicitly in Walter's honesty and decency and found it hard to believe he would go to such lengths to extend his power. Nevertheless, workers continued to report that when they tried to reach Stanley at the local's office they were told that no one knew where he was, even though he continued to inform the office daily where he would be.

The final break with Reuther occurred right after the founding convention of the Michigan CIO Council in April 1938. Stanley had been unable to attend that convention because of the press of his work, but he was told by Communist party people and others that a strategy had been developed by Unity Caucus to split away from Homer Martin the best elements of his Progressive Caucus. The plan was, reportedly, to adopt a slate that would include Richard Frankensteen and Richard Leonard, two able people from Martin's caucus. It seems that Walter wanted Victor to run for election to the office of secretary-treasurer, but that Leonard was elected instead. Walter was considerably angry and upset about this and related the whole matter to Stanley one day at West Side Local No. 174.

"But don't you think, Walter," said Stanley, "that it was a good idea to separate Martin from some of his able people in this way and split the Progressive Caucus by putting Frankensteen and Leonard on our Unity Caucus slate?"

"No, I don't," replied Walter, "and I think I'm through with Unity Caucus from here on." With that the conversation ended, and Walter hardly ever spoke to Stanley after that, carefully avoiding further personal contact.

When continued reports of Walter's comments came, that Stanley should step aside and let Victor take over Ternstedt, Stanley decided to step out of the picture. Many urged him to stay and fight, as I did, but Stanley feared such a fight might jeopardize the union he had worked so hard to establish in Ternstedt's.

"After all," he reasoned, "I can always find other shops to organize, and there are lots of them waiting out there. I've never had to fight for a union job in my life and don't intend to begin now."

Friends shook their heads over what they felt was his naïveté. He began organizing small shops on Detroit's west side, continuing on Local No. 174's payroll until the summer of 1938, when all the local's organizers, including Stanley, went off the payroll and applied for unemployment compensation. The union's funds were sharply reduced because of increasing unemployment of union members. Among the many small shops he organized during this period, Federal Screw Works was the scene, in early 1938, of the bloodiest and most violent struggle of all, a story all by itself.

10 A Neighborhood Battles Police

The municipal election in the summer of 1937 brought a complete change of atmosphere in the city of Detroit. For the first time, the CIO had entered a slate of its own candidates for the city council: Maurice Sugar, prominent labor attorney and later the legal counsel for the UAW; Tracey Doll, president of UAW Hudson Local No. 154; R. J. Thomas, then president of Chrysler Local UAW; Walter Reuther, president of West Side Local No. 174; and Dick Frankensteen, president of UAW Dodge Local No. 3. The CIO also supported Patrick H. O'Brien, a liberal Roosevelt Democrat, for the office of mayor. From this bitterly fought election the city emerged with a new mayor, Richard Reading, elected on an openly antilabor program, and a city council made up of conservative, antilabor leaders.

Very early in 1938, West Side Local No. 174 was presented with what appeared to be a routine organizing job in a small shop on Detroit's west side, when several men from the Federal Screw Works came for help and were referred to Stanley.

"Where is your shop located?" he asked.

"On Martin at Otis Street, about two blocks south of Michigan Avenue," one answered. Nowak recognized this predominantly Polish neighborhood. "How many are employed?" he asked.

"Normally about 300, but right now they're laying off until only about 150 of us are left."

"Yes, and they want to cut wages 20 percent across the board," someone volunteered.

"Our wages are already too low," another interjected. "The minimum wage for men is only seventy-five cents an hour, and they want to cut that to sixty cents; and they want to cut the minimum for women from sixty-five cents to fifty cents."

"Have you any union organization at all?" Nowak asked.

"No, but everyone is sore as hell and ready to join. We've heard a lot about the UAW, and the auto industry buys our products, so we thought you might help us."

"Would you like us to put someone in front of the plant with leaflets?" Stanley asked.

"Oh, no! Anyone seen taking leaflets or reading them would be fired immediately."

"Well, suppose we give each of you some application cards and literature. You could quietly sign up people in your department and give them the material. When you think you have enough members we can arrange a meeting here to make plans."

"Okay," all agreed. "We'll do it."

Soon they had half the work force signed up and called a meeting at Local No. 174, to which about 150 men and women came. Workers reported they had not only signed up workers in the shop but had also visited those laid off and signed them up, too. At this first meeting, they voted to reject the 20-percent wage cut and ask for union recognition and overtime pay. They elected a negotiating committee.

Within a few days the first bargaining session took place. Attorney Oscar Marcus, representing management, rejected all demands and insisted not only on the 20-percent wage cut for production but also a 10-percent cut for tool and die and other skilled workers.

"Things have changed in the City of Detroit," proclaimed Marcus. "Labor is going to be put in its place, and any strikes, sit-down or otherwise, will no longer be tolerated."

To justify its position, the company agreed to make public a financial statement by 18 February and schedule further bargaining. The financial statement showed a large margin of profit over the previous year, and on the twenty-third the Federal Screw division of Local No. 174 voted to strike if management persisted in cutting wages. At the next negotiation meeting, management practically dared the workers to strike by stating that unless the wage cuts were accepted, the company would close down on 10 March.

News came that Diamond Screw, a small unionized shop on Detroit's west side, had persuaded some workers to accept a 10-percent wage cut and to sign a statement that they did not want the UAW to represent them. Diamond Screw immediately laid off older workers and retained younger men who had agreed to the wage cut. Management fired the union steward on some pretext and announced that it considered the union contract void. The UAW informed the company that under the Wagner Act, a company could not break a union contract even if only 1 percent retained membership. Management then reinstated the union steward, promising to prepare a seniority list and put it into effect. This incident at Diamond Screw highlighted the significance of the struggle at Federal Screw Works. A growing number of employers, citywide, were exhibiting a tough attitude toward labor under the new city administration. If this continued, the UAW would lose ground in organizing or even in maintaining current membership.

The UAW declared that if Federal Screw carried out its threat to close down on 10 March because of the rejected wage cuts, it would be considered a "lockout," and the UAW would file a complaint with the National Labor Relations Board (NLRB). Management then lowered its wage cut demand to 10 percent, which was rejected by the workers with a threat to strike if management persisted.

The strike was scheduled for Monday the twenty-eighth, and the UAW sent out calls for mass pickets for 7:00 A.M. and 4:00 P.M., when it was rumored that Police Commissioner Heinrich Pickert was to provide protection for scabs going to and from work. Weekend reports came that foremen of the company had visited the homes of workers to organize a back-to-work movement. The union countered with home visits by strikers.

Several hundred pickets appeared on the morning of the 28th, mostly Federal Screw workers augmented by people from other shops responding to the union's call for pickets to support the strike. A temporary strike headquarters was opened that morning in an empty store on Martin Street one block north of the plant to provide coffee and food for the pickets and to serve as a first-aid station.

Stanley watched as a group of foremen with about thirty people, mostly strangers but including a few Federal Screw workers, assembled about a block away. Police officers appeared, obviously to march the scabs through the picket line. The pickets quickly changed to mass formation, joined by neighborhood residents standing on the sidelines, and assembled at the plant where the strikebreakers would try to enter.

The small group of scabs, surrounded by a large number of police in wedge formation, headed for the shop. All down the street, as the group passed, angry women shouted from porches and sidewalks, hurling insults at scabs and police and shaking their fists. Federal Screw strikers, recognizing fellow employees among the strikebreakers, called out to them to join the picket line but without results. Anger boiled over as the police returned from depositing the scabs safely inside the plant gate, and even children joined the enraged women in their shouts and irate gestures at this time.

The whole performance was repeated at 4:00 P.M. More people had come to swell the picket line, but not in sufficient numbers to prevent the police from achieving their purpose. They used their clubs on anyone coming too near, and one injury was reported in the press.

The next morning (29 March), as Nowak stood on the sidewalk to supervise the union forces, things went much the same as the day before. That afternoon, an estimated five hundred police were placed around two blocks to guard the scabs coming from the plant. Again the community showed its anger as the police ushered their charges out of the plant at 4:00 P.M.

Some scuffles occurred, and the whole community became aroused when elderly Mrs. Frances Bigos, visiting friends at 3434 Martin St. near the plant, was clubbed on the front porch of her hosts. Witnesses reported that a policeman drew a gun on a group of ten- and twelve-year-olds coming to the aid of Mrs. Bigos. The violence unleashed here was fully reported in the daily newspapers.

Those Federal Screw employees who had served as strikebreakers now became so incensed over the outrageous acts of police against neighbors and friends and the flagrant disregard for residents' property rights that they flocked to join the strikers on the picket line. The UAW wired Mayor Reading, Police Commissioner Pickert, and Governor Murphy, protesting the violation of the law by police and the unwarranted brutality shown to residents on their own property. An urgent campaign of wires and phone calls got under way to bring people from every union local in the city to help the Federal Screw strikers.

The next morning, 30 March, found more pickets present from various shops. The wedge of police and scabs again reached the plant successfully. There were some tussles and some wielding of police clubs, and one officer was injured; but the real test would be that afternoon when the scabs were to leave the shop and more pickets would be on hand. Federal Screw strikers on morning duty observed that all the scabs that day were strangers, obviously paid strikebreakers under police protection. Stanley had watched them assemble earlier on Michigan Avenue at Martin, under the direction of police officers.

The medical research clinic of the UAW brought equipment for a first-aid station near the plant. Doctors Eugene Shafarman, Frederick Lendrum, and Morris Raskin came to stay all day, and a number of the UAW auxiliary members and other women volunteers came to assist the doctors. Among them was Clara Van Auken, national committeewoman of the Democratic party.

By afternoon the plant was surrounded by thousands of workers. Estimates in the press ranged from five to ten thousand. A group came from Kelsey Hayes, headed by Chester Mullins; another from Cadillac Motor, including Dave Miller and Percey Keyes; another from Yale-Towne Lock and other small shops of West Side Local, headed by organizer George Edwards, who would become a member of Detroit's city council, then Detroit's police commissioner, then a member of Michigan's supreme court, and finally a judge in the federal court of appeals in Cincinnati. Still another group of pickets came from Ternstedt's, including Irene Young, Martha Strong, Joe Bedi, and Micky Moxham. People came from many other shops all over town, also from Pontiac, Flint, and other nearby communities.

When the time came for the scabs to leave the shop that afternoon 30 March, Nowak watched as nearly six hundred mounted and foot police formed a cordon around one block to the north and another block to the east of the plant and placed another force in front of the plant on Martin Avenue facing Otis, and a third on Martin and Edward. A tear gas squad was placed near the plant, and about thirty-five mounted police massed opposite the plant and nearby alleys. As this ominous deployment of police forces took place, thousands of pickets and aroused residents lined the streets for blocks around. Irene Young, who had been picketing for hours, had observed women and children accumulating piles of rocks, tin cans, and bottles on porches and rooftops in readiness.

When the factory gates opened, about ten mounted officers provided the advance guard with one in the lead, while several score more plus plainclothes detectives and foot officers surrounded the scabs on both sides and the rear to form a huge wedge. At this, an angry roar broke from the thousands of pickets and spectators.

Previously, police had herded their charges from Martin to Michigan Avenue and put them on streetcars or escorted them to their own cars. This time, because of the crowd and the furor greeting them as they took charge of the scabs at the factory gates, the police took them down Otis Street to Livernois. They were bombarded with sticks, stones, milk and pop bottles, tin cans, eggs, and tomatoes hurled by women and children from porches and rooftops. Some even threw pails of hot water. Strikers and spectators took their cue from the women, and the fight was on. Mounted police flailed their clubs wildly, and their horses trampled pickets and spectators, who were immediately set upon with clubs by the foot police. Pickets bearing signs tore them from the sticks to which they were tacked, and clubbed the police in return. One officer was knocked from his horse by Ken Young from Pontiac, the seventeen-year-old brother of Irene Young. Pickets immediately closed around the youth, easing him out of the area and down a back alley to safety while the fight went on. The police tried to continue the three blocks to Livernois, but under the hail of missiles and clubs, they broke ranks after only a block or so, and it was "every man for himself" for both pickets and scabs.

The officers then reformed their ranks and clubbed and arrested anyone booing or shouting at them. Spectators and pickets ran down alleys and streets with police at their heels and pursuing them up on their own porches, in between houses, and even into their own back yards.

Still limping and walking with a cane, Stanley tried to protect his injured foot and yet keep an eye on happenings as he stood on the sidewalk. As fists and clubs flew and sticks and stones came hurtling into the crowd, a big, stout woman dashed out of her house, grabbed Stanley's arm and half dragged, half carried him into the safety of her home, locking the door behind her. She had spotted a mounted policeman headed for her porch, and she immediately ran for a pail of water boiling on her stove, rushed upstairs with it and threw its contents down upon the officer just as he and his horse reached the steps. He raced away, howling. The woman locked Stanley in one of the upstairs rooms for his protection, scolding him roundly all the while: "You have no business out there in that fight. You already have a broken foot. Do you want a cracked head in the bargain? You should know better than to get mixed up in this!"

Stanley protested that he was all right and had to keep track of what was happening. "Never you mind! You stay right here!" she commanded. "There are others to do that."

As she towered over him, scolding, Stanley grinned and said, "Well, I'm certainly glad you're on my side."

She stood guard to make sure no harm would come to him, and she would not hear of his going out again into the fracas. She was bigger than he, and there was no arguing with her. She listened and watched for the return of the officer who had tried to reach her porch, and she was prepared to do battle with him if he did. Fortunately for both, he did not.

Stanley had never before met this woman, but she knew all about him. She said her sister worked in the cigar shop where he had broken his foot. We later learned, in talking to some of the cigarworkers, that she was Martha Drapinski.

The fighting continued around the house and the plant, with people being chased up alleys, onto porches, and into back yards by mounted or foot officers. Percy Keyes, the only Black man in the fray, was spotted by five policemen, witnesses told the press, and cornered in a backyard on Clippert near Otis. Several witnesses reported seeing him clubbed and stomped into unconsciousness, then dragged to a corner and slugged again. Dr. Morris Raskin, wearing an identifying arm band, pushed through the crowd to reach Keyes and was slugged on the head as he knelt to administer first aid. Witnesses also reported a ten-year-old girl struck down by a policeman on Otis Street and beaten, suffering three broken ribs. An elderly woman who saw this was reported to have thrown scalding water on the brutal cop from an upper window.

When scabs and police had been routed, Stanley's protector allowed him to leave. He rounded up some strikers to look for casualties, who were then directed or taken to the first-aid station, where the women washed the blood from wounds so that doctors could examine and care for them or send the victims to hospitals.

Stanley and his search party found Percy Keyes bleeding on the ground where he had been so mercilessly beaten. They rushed him to a hospital where it was found he had a broken spine and leg, and a fractured skull. Stanley was overwhelmed by remorse over the injuries to Keyes, for it was he who had brought Keyes to the union to organize the foundry workers at Cadillac Motor Company. Keyes had come to aid his union brothers and sisters. It was many months before he could be up and about, and he would always bear physical and mental scars from this day. Four other pickets were reported hospitalized with serious injuries, and some eight others were seriously hurt but not hospitalized. All were treated at the union's first-aid station. Physicians in charge stated they had treated twenty-four others for minor injuries. Several policemen were also reported hurt.

Ten men were arrested and held at the Fort Street station, to be arraigned the next day for "disturbing the peace," among them twenty-five-year old Jimmy Hoffa, who worked in a warehouse nearby and a was a business agent for the AFL Teamsters Union. Recorders court judge Christopher E. Stein later released Hoffa.

Walter Reuther offered to end the strike if the company would call off police and strikebreakers and begin negotiations. Company officials denied receiving that offer and announced the plant would close at least for the rest of the week, not to reopen before 4 April.

UAW president Homer Martin requested Governor Frank Murphy to investigate police lawlessness in Detroit and the systematic wage cuts in auto plants. He also stated he would make a protest at city council the next morning, 31 March.

For almost an hour that morning, about three hundred people demonstrated before the council meeting, carrying signs and booing the mayor, the police commissioner, and the police. Thousands of spectators gathered and joined in. Police came but nothing happened.

When council members assembled, pickets filled every seat in the council chamber and even the corridors outside. Representing the UAW were President Homer Martin; West Side Local president Walter Reuther;

CIO regional director Adolph Germer; Briggs Local president Emil Mazey; attorney Larry Davidow; and UAW publicity director John Tate. Representing the police were Commissioner Heinrich Pickert and Police Superintendent Fred Frahm, both of whom had led the police attacks at the Federal Screw strike.

Attorney Davidow introduced a resolution to prohibit the use of police as strikebreakers and the clubbing of pickets and spectators. In his presentation, Homer Martin condemned the use of police as strikebreakers and branded the company's wage cuts as "part of a general assault on the wage level of the city." He cited statistics showing that Federal Screw Works had tripled its profits in 1937 over those of 1936. *Glos ludowy* of 1 April 1938 quoted Martin: "The company made this wage-cut with apparent assurance that there would be no trouble. . . . We wonder what guarantees they had that they could cut wages. We think we know. The Police Dept. stepped in to act as strikebreakers, violating every principle of humanity. . . . One worker with a broken back was beaten with his hands in the air, defenseless. Another's skull was fractured when he tried to pick up a 13-year-old girl who had been knocked down."

During this tumultuous council session, union speakers were cheered by spectators, and reactionary council members were booed and jeered. At one point, Police Superintendent Fred Frahm rose in defense of the police to say, "Children and women were fighting police, who, thus attacked, had to defend themselves." Reuther retorted, "There was no violence until police provoked it," and pointed out that residents of the community were indignant at police brutality and trespassing on their property. "We expect police to be used to maintain peace and not to serve as a strikebreaking agency," he concluded. Following the session, about seventy-five people again marched briefly in front of city hall.

A week's truce between the UAW and Federal Screw management was arranged by the NLRB at a conference on 2 April. Stanley began negotiations, assisted by Walter Reuther and Adolph Germer. An agreement was reached on the seventh and overwhelmingly ratified on the ninth, rescinding wage cuts and granting union recognition, time-and-a-half pay for overtime, and seniority guarantees. The agreement was hailed by both Martin and Reuther as a "smashing victory," and Reuther added, "The settlement is an important victory because this was the national test case in the employers' drive to cut wages in the auto industry. We shall now make every effort to put the entire screw, nut, and bolt industry on the wage level required by the American standard of living."

On the night of the ninth, following the ratification of the contract, Walter Reuther was attacked in his home by two unknown men. Reuther was not seriously injured, and in his statement to the press, he said, "This was undoubtedly the work of paid gangsters, either of a certain large auto manufacturer or an association of manufacturers. . . . Our victory in the Federal Screw Strike evidently enraged the manufacturers who want to cut wages and bust the union. The labor movement is here to stay in spite of these gangster tactics." *Glos ludowy* of 16 April, reported that Reuther's assailants of the ninth had been apprehended and identified as having connections with the notorious Ford service department.

To create uniformity in wages and working conditions in the screw, nut, and bolt industry, the Detroit Screw Council was formed at West Side Local No. 174 on the twenty-second with twenty-five delegates from seven shops, representing about twenty-five hundred workers. Temporary officers were Stanley as chairman and James Staubaum as secretary.

On 10 May the press reported that charges against picketers arraigned in connection with police attacks at Federal Screw Works on 29 and 30 March were dismissed.

So one more battle was won, but the war would go on in the struggle for labor's rights. Stanley would continue in this field but would also be drawn into another where he would fight for labor and the people on a different level.

11 Citizen and Candidate

When we met in 1932, Stanley and I had lost faith in the political process. As we had studied U.S. history, both of us had been thrilled by the words of the Declaration of Independence. "Whenever any form of government becomes destructive [of the rights it was instituted by the people to secure]," says that document, "it is the right of the people to alter or abolish it." Tragically our government had become destructive of those rights, as evidenced in the economic and political world around us. We felt that some changes had to be made, but those holding political office lived in a world of corruption and self-interest, protecting the owning class against those who labored in their mills, mines, and factories, and we could see no hope for change there. Therefore, I had never registered to vote, nor had Stanley applied for citizenship.

It was Franklin Roosevelt's first term in office that renewed our hope in the potential of the political process to effect the radical changes we believed necessary. This is what motivated me to register as a voter and Stanley to apply for U.S. citizenship in 1936.

On a warm evening in early June 1938, Stanley and I were relaxing and reading the evening news. All evening he had been looking up from his newspaper with a speculative look and an amused twinkle in his eye, yet had said nothing. Finally I could stand it no longer. "What is it with you?" I asked.

His answer was unsettling, to say the least. "How would you like to be the wife of a state senator?"

"Are you serious?" I asked in reply.

"I was never more serious in my life," he said. "Many union people and some Democratic politicians think I should run for office and that I might even be elected."

My immediate reaction was shock and panic, and when I recovered my speech I exploded: "Stanley, you have made powerful enemies in your organizing work. If you enter politics, you know you will be a target. You might even be framed and sent to prison on some trumped-up charge. We both know many examples of such things happening to labor people. And besides," I continued, "what about the fact that you just recently obtained citizenship? Don't you think your enemies will make a big deal out of that? And another thing: Why haven't you told me about this before? And how did people get the idea of your running for office? Where would the money come from for the campaign?"

"Okay, okay. One question at a time," Stanley said after hearing me out patiently as usual while I got it all out of my system. He then reviewed with me the events leading up to the idea of his candidacy.

On 30 January Labor's Non-Partisan League (LNPL) of Michigan had been born at a conference in Lansing attended by 260 delegates from AFL and CIO unions and farm organizations and had been reported in the press. The purpose of LNPL was to establish a political organization in each Michigan district and precinct; to propose and support legislation to benefit labor and farmers; and to fight unemployment.

LNPL had studied Michigan's legislative districts to select candidates and come upon one of special interest—Senatorial District No. 21, comprising at that time wards 18 and 20 in Detroit and such municipalities as Dearborn, River Rouge, Ecorse, Inkster, Allen Park, and Wyandotte. Within this district was located the enormous Rouge Plant of the Ford Motor Company, and the majority of its workers also lived there.

The state senator from that district was Joseph Roosevelt, a Democrat who had changed his name from Cappola to facilitate his election yet who strongly opposed the liberal policies of both President Roosevelt and Governor Murphy.

Many workers from shops organized by Stanley had attended the growing number of conferences between labor people and Democratic officials, and they had begun to urge Stanley to become a candidate to oppose Joseph Roosevelt on the Democratic ticket. He had offered all kinds of excuses: he was too busy with organizing, he had no political experience, and so on. He thought of himself as a union organizer and was still involved in Ternstedt problems as well as negotiations at the Federal Screw works. He had also been assigned to organize smaller shops on Detroit's west side.

The idea of Stanley running for political office had intrigued many workers, and their enthusiasm had grown. Moreover, at one of the conferences between LNPL and Democrats, Governor Murphy had mentioned to Stanley that Joseph Roosevelt had blocked in committee Murphy's rural electrification program. Murphy had said he would like to see a liberal replace Roosevelt and had urged Stanley to become a candidate to oppose him. Officers of LNPL had concurred.

Soon the idea had begun to present possibilities in relation to organizing work. Chrysler and General Motors had union contracts, but the Ford empire remained impregnable. Its long campaign of intimidation had so terrorized Ford workers that they would not openly attend union meetings and feared even to be seen talking to known union members or to receive them in their homes. However, Stanley had noted, these same workers attended church affairs, club meetings, social affairs, and picnics where political candidates spoke. As a candidate he would be able to reach Ford workers and those from other industries within the Twenty-first Senatorial District with the union message.

This was considered the most highly industrialized legislative district in the nation, containing not only the giant Ford plants but also such industries as steel, ship building, salt mining, large chemical plants, and hundreds of small shops. The idea of bringing the union message to all these people by means of a political campaign had appealed to Stanley. He had consented to become a candidate provided I would agree, as this would change our lives considerably. Now I understood why he had not told me before. It had taken him some time to make up his own mind. With all the arguments in favor of his candidacy, how could I oppose it? I still had qualms, but as the campaign progressed these vanished and I became an ardent campaigner.

The first requirement was that he reside in the district in which he was running. This necessitated our moving from Detroit's east side to somewhere within the Twenty-first Senatorial District. It was already early June, and on such short notice we were unable to find a house and get moved in time for him to file with the city clerk by the 26 July deadline. Tony and Irene Marinovich came to our rescue: "We have a large upper flat with an extra bedroom. Come stay with us until you can find a place," they invited. So we stored our furniture, and my mother went to live with my sister a short distance from where Tony and Irene lived. Between my working every day and Stanley's organizing and campaigning, our stay with Tony and Irene became much longer than we had expected; for we had no time even to look for other living quarters.

Another legal requirement was to file with the county clerk petitions containing several thousand names or to pay a fifty-dollar filing fee. To explore the sentiments of people in our district, Stanley approached the Polish-American Ladies' New Deal Democratic Club and asked its endorsement and help in raising money for the filing fee. Club members had participated in every political conference of Democratic and union groups throughout the city, and some were members of the union in shops he had organized. The club not only endorsed his candidacy but also advanced the entire filing fee of fifty dollars. These women sparked the whole campaign. They rallied people from every nationality group in the district to distribute our campaign literature, raise funds, hand out cards and slates on election day, set up a kitchen in the headquarters, and prepare food and coffee for the election workers. They were full of energy and fun, singing their national songs as they worked. Such women as these came also from the Ukrainian, Russian, and Hungarian groups and their influence was widespread.

Stanley had expected his basic support to come from organized labor. He found, however, that it was impossible to get endorsement or help from the international UAW, riven as it was by factionalism at that time. The newspapers were full of the internal struggles between its president, Homer Martin, and the international officers and executive board members. Stanley turned to the rank and file at local union meetings, where he found a ready response. This was a big factor in this and subsequent campaigns. Shop workers fought on the floor of their local union meetings for endorsement and support for Stanley, and as delegates to the Wayne County CIO Council they sought and obtained that body's endorsement.

The Twenty-first Senatorial District had sent Democrats to Congress and the state legislature since 1932. Thus his main battle would be to win the Democratic nomination in the primary, which would be synonymous with election. The foreign-born in the district were overwhelmingly Democrats. The largest and most politically active group among the foreign-born was the Poles, followed by Hungarians, Ukrainians, Russians, Romanians, and Yugoslavs. Our districtwide campaign committee was made up or representatives from all these groups, as well as native-born citizens, both Black and white, active in local unions or in cultural and political organizations.

On 6 August the *Detroit News* reported that the state executive board of LNPL had endorsed eight legislative candidates, among them Stanley and Charles Diggs (of the Third district).

Our campaign workers rang doorbells and talked to people. They found additional nationality groups—Armenians, Greeks, Syrians—and got them to send representatives to participate in our campaign. Most language groups had a club, and often a meeting hall, where Stanley was invited to speak. Such groups were the backbone of his support throughout his ten years in the Michigan Senate.

Invitations poured in from business and professional groups, clubs, fraternal benefit societies, and churches; and Stanley found himself reaching with the union message people he would not have had access to apart from his campaign. Each evening he covered three or four meetings, and on Sundays five to seven picnics.

He observed other candidates, how they frequently repeated their names and promised to do all kinds of things if elected. Stanley refused to follow this pattern and developed one of his own. He showed how the problems of workers were related to state government and how important it was to elect candidates pledged to the interests of the people. His name was mentioned only when he was introduced by the chairman. This was in such sharp contrast to other candidates that many thought he must be a little "touched" or unbelievably naive, and some took him aside to offer friendly advice. Stanley thanked them for their concern. But their advice was unnecessary. Among the audience there were always employees of the many shops he had organized. By the time Stanley got around to urge his listeners to send people to the legislature who would fight for them, the audience was so enthused and eager for everyone to know who this man was and what he was running for that someone always shouted, "What about *you*? You're the kind of man we want. Tell them what office you're running for!" Someone usually rushed to the microphone as Nowak finished his speech to mention the many shops organized by him and to urge everyone to vote for him. I saw this happen repeatedly as I made the rounds with Stanley.

The UAW Polish Trade Union Committee extended its activities into the political arena. On 22 July at Dom Polski on Forest and Chene Streets, a conference of Polish unionists and Democrats took place to outline the overall political campaign in the city. Among members of the UAW Polish Trade Union Committee participating were Stanley as chairman; Vincent Klein as treasurer; John Zaremba, secretary; and Joseph Zylowski of Teamsters Local AFL. Prominent Democrats there were Lieutenant Governor Leo Nowicki; congressmen John Dingell, George Sadowski, and John Lesinski; federal marshal John Barc; and Joseph Kosky, secretary to Sadowski and himself a candidate to the Michigan State Senate. The conference unanimously voted to support the candidacies of John Zaremba and Vincent Klein to the Michigan House of Representatives, and Stanley for the Michigan senate.

Late in July Homer Martin announced he had appointed Zygmund Dobrzynski to head up a new UAW Polish Trade Union Committee—the same Dobrzynski whom Stanley had helped to organize and establish Local No. 205 of Automotive Fibers in December 1936. Dobrzynski had long since aligned himself with Martin in the factional fight and had been appointed late in 1937 or early 1938 as regional director for the Ford organizing drive. Now he was launching a rival UAW Polish Trade Union Committee to compete with the one that the UAW executive board had authorized Stanley to form in June 1936.

Stanley soon found that there was little to worry about. The record of the two-year-old UAW Polish Trade Union Committee was unassailable. It had aided every strike in the city involving large numbers of Poles, explained issues, rallied assistance from the Polish community, and gave the strikers moral and physical support. Its members were prominent unionists, many of them officials of locals; and the entire committee was much respected. Dobrzynski was unsuccessful in attracting Polish workers to his committee, and little more was heard of it.

Congressman John Lesinski's Sixteenth Congressional District was identical to the Twenty-first Senatorial District. Proof of Nowak's growing stature was the offer from Lesinski to share his campaign headquarters at 8000 Michigan Avenue, which was also headquarters for the Sixteenth Congressional District.

Democratic politicians, noting the new and dynamic forces entering the political arena through Stanley's campaign, were amazed at the energy, enthusiasm, and hard work of our campaigners. People old and young volunteered. There were dozens of young people who had never before worked in a political campaign, many not even old enough to vote. They were sons and daughters of workers in shops that Stanley had organized or of people who had participated with him in the general Polish work. These spirited and exuberant young people established and staffed five other centers for our campaign in various parts of our district.

Not to be outdone, their parents and other older people—many of whom had not participated in an election campaign for years, if ever—came out in large numbers. Often they proposed novel ideas for fundraising. They distributed leaflets from house to house, competing enthusiastically with young people. Their feet might hurt, and sometimes they huffed and puffed, but they were game. They stood on streetcorners near the voting booths on election day to hand out slates; challenged in the booths at night; and participated in all facets of the campaign. All this was done with boundless enthusiasm and the hope of electing a man from their own ranks who had helped organize their shops and had walked picket lines with them.

As we neared the end of the primary campaign, someone suggested at a campaign meeting that an effective finale would be a "Picnic of All

Nations," where each nationality would have a booth to sell its particular national dishes and exhibit its arts and crafts. The idea was enthusiastically accepted. In searching for a speaker who could be a real attraction, various names were mentioned.

"How about Governor Murphy?" someone offered.

"Are you crazy?" everyone laughed. You know that a governor comes into a legislative district only to support an incumbent, and in this case Murphy is displeased with Joseph Roosevelt."

"Let's ask him, anyway," several insisted, and a delegation was chosen. Surprisingly, he accepted. When it was announced, hardly anyone believed it. Many Democratic officials regarded the announcement as a mere publicity stunt to attract a crowd to the picnic. Even some of our own committee doubted Murphy would come.

Sunday, 11 September, was a beautiful day and people came in large numbers. About 1:30 P.M. a limousine drove into the grounds, escorted by state police, and everyone cheered as they recognized Murphy. He spoke to more than three thousand people from a platform in an open field, and the picnic was the talk of the district for weeks.

On election day (the thirteenth) our workers reported early in the morning. Women from the nationality groups prepared coffee and food for delivery to precinct workers throughout the day and evening. After 4:00 P.M., day-shift workers came for assignments, and at about the same time the midnight-shift workers reported to help for a few hours before going to work. The headquarters was a bustling, noisy, happy place. Democratic politicians visiting our headquarters marveled openly: "Where do you find such workers, Nowak? We couldn't get people to work like that even if we paid them shop wages." Still more amazing was the fact that besides their time and energy, these workers contributed money to the campaign.

When the voting booths closed, precinct workers came to report the sentiments they had heard. For the first time we began to feel that Stanley might win. Many were jubilantly certain that he would.

When all the reports were in from those who had worked outside the booths and as many booths as possible were supplied with challengers, everyone was wilting with fatigue. Experienced campaigners said it would take until morning for the final outcome to be known, and often results were uncertain until late in the day. We made sure each challenger had a way to get home, then everyone called it a day and went home.

Stanley and I alternately slept and listened to radio reports. At midnight, the first returns from our district showed Joseph Roosevelt and Stanley running neck and neck. This continued until about 4 A.M., when Roosevelt suddenly spurted ahead by two thousand votes. Only half conscious from exhaustion, we consoled each other that the real aim of the campaign had been achieved and that it had been a worthwhile experience, even if we had lost. Then we slept.

In a few hours, I left for work and Stanley went to a bargaining meeting at the Federal Screw Works. As he walked on Tarnow St. toward Michigan Avenue, neighborhood women all down the line ran out of their homes with tears streaming down their cheeks to say, "Oh, Stanley, too bad, too bad! We worked so hard and were so sure you would win. How could it happen?"

To comfort them as much as himself, he said, "We didn't do so badly for the first time. With your help we put on a tremendous campaign that was the talk of the whole state. The margin is very close. Maybe next time we'll win."

The women refused to be consoled. We had worked to win and were disappointed, but we did feel that Stanley had accomplished his goal of reaching large numbers of workers, especially Ford workers, with the union message through the medium of the campaign. We believed that the huge vote he received was actually a vote for the union. However, this did not satisfy those who had given so much to assure Stanley's victory.

He spent most of the day in negotiations, and late in the afternoon he went to the County Building for the final tabulation. As he approached, Mort Furay of LNPL came out.

"Congratulations, Senator!" he greeted.

"But I didn't win!" was Stanley's startled reply.

"What do you mean? Didn't you know you won?"

"No!" exclaimed Stanley in disbelief.

"Okay! Go in and see for yourself," said Mort.

Members of the election commission congratulated Stanley as he came in, informing him that his margin was 225 votes. They said an error had been made during the tabulation that had since been corrected. Mort Furay had spent the entire night in the County Building watching and checking returns. When the sudden drop occurred in Nowak's vote, Furay felt something was amiss and went to demand a recheck. It was then the error was discovered.

Stanley telephoned me the news at my office, telling about the women who had greeted him with tears on his way to work and about the error in computing the votes. I walked on air the rest of the day. Phone calls came that evening from people all around town who hardly dared believe and wanted to make sure. The women who had wept in the morning were dancing and singing in union and ethnic halls where Stanley's victory was celebrated.

When Joseph Roosevelt demanded a recount, Stanley consulted Lieutenant Governor Leo Nowicki. "What can Roosevelt accomplish by a recount?" asked Stanley.

"Well, since your margin is only 225 and there are 213 precincts, all he has to do is disqualify one or two votes in each precinct on a technicality, and your margin will be destroyed."

"So what do I do?" asked Nowak.

"Roosevelt has requested a recount of precincts where you have a margin," Nowicki explained. "You should demand a recount of those precincts that give him a margin. You can also disqualify votes, and both of you will probably wind up with about the same ratio as when you started."

We had heard rumors of votes being stolen during recounts, and Stanley asked Nowicki how to handle that. "I would suggest," said Nowicki, "that you select a crew of big, husky fellows and station one beside each recount worker with instructions to watch carefully, particularly the hands, where a tiny piece of lead from a pencil can be hidden under the nail to spoil a ballot and disqualify it. Tell your men that if they see anyone make a false move, they should not hesitate to hit that person's hand with a fist to dislodge the lead."

"Would we dare do that?" asked Stanley.

"Absolutely! If anyone tries to mark a ballot illegally, your man has the right to stop him."

"Thanks, Leo! This is more complicated than I realized."

"Good luck, Stanley!" said Leo as they parted.

From shops he had organized, Stanley soon had more volunteers than needed, among them Dave Miller, president of Cadillac Local; Chester Mullins from Kelsey Wheel; Jack White and Danny Gallagher from Local No. 174; Barney Majewski; and John Hell. Within twenty-four hours of the deadline, the same workers who had raised money for the campaign came up with three hundred dollars for the recount fee.

As the initiator of the recount, Roosevelt began first. One of our men stood behind each of Roosevelt's. Observing one of them doing exactly what Nowicki had warned of, Dave Miller brought his fist down sharply on the worker's hand, and sure enough, a small piece of lead hidden under a fingernail rolled out on the table. Our crew threw the man out of the room, and the recount continued.

After finishing thirty precincts, Roosevelt had reduced Stanley's lead from 225 to 190, approximately one vote per precinct. Realizing that Stanley could do about the same to him, Roosevelt abandoned the recount. Stanley then withdrew his demand for a recount and his money was refunded. His margin was now only 190 votes, but he was the official Democratic nominee. His problem now would be to defeat the Republican nominee in November. This would be Orville Hubbard, age thirty-six, ex-marine, attorney, and for five years a member of the Detroit bureau of the *Wall Street Journal.*

In the Sixteenth Congressional District, paralleling our Twenty-first Senatorial District, John Lesinski was the Democratic nominee. He had already served three terms and was a member of the Committee on Immigration and Naturalization, a little detail to which we paid no attention at the time, but which may have been of some significance to us in later developments.

Once again the campaign rolled and the Nowak forces merged with those of the Democratic party. On 1 October *Glos ludowy* announced the formation of the Senator Nowak Club, and the people who had helped so enormously in the primary campaign now enrolled in the club.

At the state convention of the Democratic party in Grand Rapids in early October, Stanley got his first inkling of things to come, when U.S. Marshal John Barc invited him to dinner. He described this event to me on his return to Detroit. Over dinner, the two had discussed events of the primary.

"You certainly staged a brilliant campaign," said Barc. "Some of us in the leadership of the Democratic party, including myself, had not the slightest notion that you could defeat the incumbent. We completely underestimated you. We realize now how mistaken we were and want to welcome you into the 'family,' so to speak."

"That's very kind of you," replied Stanley, somewhat embarrassed and wondering what all this was leading up to.

"It was very clever of you," Barc continued, "to play for the labor vote. That is what elected you. But such ties can be a chain around your neck if you are interested in a political career. You can have a real future in politics if you free yourself from your link to organized labor."

Stanley made no comment, and the conversation turned to other things. On returning to his hotel, he thought over this conversation. It was clear that many Democratic politicians needed and wanted labor's vote but at the same time feared its power. Stanley had not "played" for labor's vote, as Barc had put it. Organized labor had been his life since the age of seventeen. If he abandoned labor and its concerns, he would be just another professional politician, interested only in being elected, wooing business for financial support and kidding labor and the people for their votes.

He thought of the hundreds of people who had worked long hours in the rain and cold to hand out slates on election day, who had rung doorbells and passed out leaflets, raised money to finance his campaign, and even reached into their own pockets to contribute. He thought of all the hopes and dreams that his campaign had engendered among these people. He remembered the women in tears the morning after the primary and their boundless joy that night when they learned he had won.

These were the people responsible for his victory. How could anyone even think he would turn his back on them? He was part of their struggles, hopes, and dreams. Whatever was in their interests he would work for in the legislative field just as he had as a union organizer.

Barc was the self-appointed spokesman for some of the leading Democratic politicians, even though they varied in their political orientation, some being liberal, others conservative and even reactionary. He also assumed the role of spokesman for powerful reactionary circles closely tied to the federal government, the FBI, and certain ultraconservative and reactionary elements in the Catholic community. There was an ominous undertone to the conversation with Barc that evening, even though it was, on the surface, friendly. Stanley believes that most of the troubles he later encountered stemmed from his steadfast refusal to act on that "friendly" warning.

Once again he campaigned by speaking before every possible meeting or affair. All was disturbingly quiet on the eve of the election. Our campaign committee, anticipating a last-minute attack over the weekend before the election, made preparations accordingly. Radio time was purchased for Monday night. A printer stood ready on Saturday afternoon for any leaflets desired. A crew of men with cars volunteered for Sunday morning distribution of leaflets if needed.

About 2:00 P.M. Saturday afternoon, 5 November, a worker rushed to campaign headquarters with a leaflet printed in red ink, denouncing Stanley as a "red" alien agitator and carrying a photograph of him doctored to resemble Joseph Stalin. Since the leaflet was libelous in character, it bore no address; and the names of the sponsoring committees were completely fictitious. Henry Kraus, former editor of the UAW paper, the *Auto Worker,* immediately drew up an answering leaflet. The printer spent the better part of the night producing fifty thousand copies. Early Sunday morning, a crew of about a hundred men and forty cars took the leaflets to every church and almost every home in the district.

As they went from house to house, our opponent's leaflets were found on porches. Our men picked them up and substituted our own. In front of churches they found children distributing our opponent's leaflet. Since it was so libelous, adults dared not openly circulate it. In exchange for a quarter, the youngsters happily surrendered their bundle of leaflets and our workers proceeded to hand out our own.

A message later came from the chairman of the district Democratic organization that Stanley was not to attend any of the scheduled meetings for Democratic candidates that afternoon and evening. This success of the leaflet attack was disturbing news; but after some consideration, Stanley decided to ignore the message.

The first meeting, at Fordson High School in Dearborn in the early afternoon, would be the crucial one, indicating people's reaction to the leaflet attack. When Stanley arrived, the meeting was already under way and some candidates seated on the platform. As he strode down the center aisle, the audience broke into spontaneous applause and stood to cheer him. This heart-warming demonstration brought tears to his eyes. In response to the ovation given Stanley, the chairman who had sent the message to stay away was compelled to extend a welcoming hand as Stanley reached the platform. It was some time before the cheering could be quieted and the meeting allowed to continue.

Governor Frank Murphy arrived soon after, and again the meeting was interrupted by cheers and applause. Murphy deliberately seated himself next to Stanley on the platform and shook hands warmly. He advised Stanley to ignore the leaflet attack. The two arranged to follow each other to the remainder of the scheduled meetings so that one would always follow directly after the other to the speakers' platform. Stanley was cheered at each meeting; and whether he or Murphy arrived first, Murphy always made a show of cordiality. In speaking, Murphy always mentioned Stanley and said, "You can elect this man with confidence. He will serve you well."

The last-minute leaflet attack aroused the fighting spirit of friends and supporters and won new forces to our side. No further mention of it was made by Democratic officials except to comment on how smoothly our crew got our answering leaflet into the hands of the people.

As usual, the Democratic ticket won in our district, and Stanley became the first CIO Senator in the Michigan legislature. The morning after the election, Orville Hubbard, the defeated Republican candidate, stopped briefly at Tony and Irene's residence, where we were living, to offer congratulations on Stanley's victory. This was the same Orville Hubbard who served later as Dearborn's mayor for so many years.

While the Democratic party had won overwhelmingly in Wayne County, our joy was tempered by the fact that Michigan went heavily Republican outstate and Murphy was defeated by the openly antilabor Republican, Frank Fitzgerald. Stanley would be going into a Michigan Senate of twenty-three Republicans and nine Democrats, a crushing blow to our high hopes. It made our personal victory seem a very small one. Although the Democrats would be in a hopeless minority, Stanley felt that they could be a vocal one and even do much to protect the interests of the people.

One of our primary concerns was education. We had met Frances

Comfort, president of the AFL Teachers Union, in the early days of the UAW. She and John Elder, an associate in the leadership of their union, got a number of teachers to meet with us for an evening to give us ideas and suggestions. This marked the beginning of a working arrangement that held throughout Stanley's legislative years. When all others refused, educators knew they could always rely upon him to introduce or support any school legislation.

There was not sufficient time to meet separately with the many interest groups in our district. Stanley proposed to Congressman Lesinski that they jointly call a legislative conference and invite groups in the district to bring their concerns and suggestions. Such a conference was held on the afternoon of 17 December at Miller High School in Dearborn, and seventy-nine organizations sent 191 delegates. Attorney Vincent Fordell served as chairman. Delegates represented labor; veterans; educators; fraternal organizations; business and professional groups; and political, church, and social groups. Besides Stanley and Lesinski, the CIO state chairman Adolph Germer spoke. A permanent legislative committee was elected, and each organization was to send a delegate to a monthly meeting to present problems, suggestions, and support for the work of the legislators.

During the holidays, Stanley and I prepared for the new life ahead in Lansing, to which we looked forward with some apprehension, for this would be a new arena about which we knew very little. Moreover, Zygmund Dobrzynski had been busy testifying before the Dies Committee in Detroit and Washington. This was a congressional committee headed by Congressman Martin Dies, to investigate subversives in unions and other organizations and was the forerunner of the notorious House Committee on Un-American Activities, known as HUAC. In his testimony, Dobrzynski labeled almost every official of the CIO, the UAW, the Teachers Union, and others (including Stanley) as Communist. Because of all this we could not but wonder how we would be received in the legislative world of Lansing.

12 Stanley's First Senate Term

Both Stanley and I were on hand for the formal opening of the legislature on 4 January 1939. The stationery on his desk told us what his committee assignments were: Apportionment, Education, Michigan State College, Public Health, and Taxation. The powers that be apparently feared to put him on the Labor Committee, as he had requested.

We were aware of the guarded scrutiny of many people as the veteran senators moved about, greeting newcomers and renewing acquaintance with others who had survived the election. In the entire nation, Stanley was the only one elected by labor to any legislative body, and certainly the first in Michigan. There was much curiosity about this man, whose campaign was the talk of political circles and who was regarded by some as a dangerous radical.

Many senators had brought their spouses and family members for the opening ceremonies. We knew the Democrats from Wayne County. Some from outstate, as well as some Republicans, came to introduce themselves and their families to us.

Promptly at noon, the sergeant at arms closed the heavy doors to the Senate Chamber; and the senators went to their desks, where additional chairs had been placed for family members. Following the invocation, the first order of business was the administration of the oath of office to the senators. This was the moment we were awaiting with some trepidation, as it had been rumored that Stanley might not be allowed to assume his elective office. He seemed nonchalant and relaxed, but I knew he was watching, as I was, for any move against him.

The Senate secretary called the front-row senators to stand before the rostrum, and Stanley walked up with the others. They raised their right hands and repeated the oath in unison; then a Senate page handed each a printed copy of the oath to sign. This took only a few moments but seemed an eternity. Suddenly, Stanley was walking back to his seat before I realized it was all over. I let out a breath of relief; and a load must have lifted from his shoulders, too, for his steps seemed lighter.

Governor Fitzgerald's Message to the Legislature was scheduled for the next day, 5 January. All the pomp and ceremony surrounding this event was to take place in the House. Some of the senators' wives took me under their wing, and we went to gallery seats in the balcony to watch the House of Representatives convene. The House Speaker appointed a committee to escort the senators to the House. Another was designated to bring the senate officials; another to bring the members of the Michigan Supreme Court in their judicial robes; and finally, a committee to fetch the governor.

Fitzgerald's message promised a labor act "with teeth in it." He interpreted his defeat of Frank Murphy as a mandate to launch a sharply antilabor program. To solve the plight of Michigan's troubled farmers, he proposed a twenty-five-thousand-dollar advertising program for Michigan farm products.

Governor Murphy's parting message to the legislature was shelved by a motion "to consider it read." It was clear, they wanted no more of him. I watched and heard all this with a sinking feeling, which was fully shared by Stanley as we talked about it later. If what we had just witnessed indicated the tone of the entire legislature, we wondered how he would be able to work effectively in a Senate body of twenty-three Republicans and nine Democrats, and he the lone labor man among them. It did not look hopeful. We would have to take one day at a time and see what would happen.

Neither of us had realized what Stanley's new status would do to our personal lives. On 6 January we returned to Detroit, parked our luggage in the room we still rented from Tony and Irene Marinovich, and picked up what we needed for the weekend. Then Stanley took me to my sister's home and flew to Washington for a conference. I enjoyed a carefree Friday evening with my mother, my sister, and her family. Saturday morning my pleasant relaxation ended abruptly when Tony Marinovich appeared. "I think you had better come home with me, Margaret," he said with a rueful grin. "Some people are there to see Stanley, and there isn't anyone to take care of them."

"Can't they wait until Monday?" I asked hopefully.

"You don't seem to realize you're a senator's wife," Tony scolded affectionately. "You just can't run around like an individual. Our phone has been ringing all morning and people are waiting in our living room. Since Stanley is away, you will have to see what you can do."

Seeing my dismay, he laughed and ran his fingers through his hair in amused annoyance: "Yes, I know, this is all new to you. But you must get used to being a senator's wife, and you might as well begin now."

My dismay came from the sudden awareness of how rudely Tony and Irene's home life must have been disrupted. We had continued to rent a room in their home, since we were required by law to retain a Detroit residence even during the legislative sessions in Lansing. Tony and Irene's home was the only place where our constituents could reach us.

I hastily collected my things and went home with Tony where several people waited, most of whom I knew from campaigns or the Polish work. I typed letters that I could sign for Stanley, filled out forms, and made appointments for them with Stanley for the following weekend, if they had problems I could not handle. I was busy the whole day, returning to my sister's for the night and Sunday; and returned Monday to take care of calls and more visitors. Stanley arrived home in time to drive to Lansing for the evening Senate session.

Life soon fell into a pattern. The daily deliberations usually began at 1:00 or 2:00 P.M. to permit senators to attend morning committee meetings or take care of correspondence and visitors. Friday's session convened in the morning so the senators could leave around noon for the weekend. We lunched when the session adjourned and left for Detroit.

People usually awaited us at Tony and Irene's, and there was the weekly accumulation of mail. The phone rang constantly. Friday evenings there were usually meetings. Saturday brought people to our door, and there was often an afternoon meeting at some local union or with some language group and always an evening meeting or social event requiring our presence. Sundays, besides the phone and visitors, there were usually meetings throughout the day. Monday morning was reserved for people with language problems, whom Stanley had to take to the department of welfare or the Old-Age Assistance Bureau. By midafternoon we usually headed for Lansing to arrive for dinner before the 7:00 P.M. session that began the legislative week.

We stayed at the Hotel Roosevelt when we first came to Lansing, and within a very short time we wakened to some serious financial problems: a hotel bill we couldn't pay and no money for food or transportation for the coming weeks. We had been told—but had refused to believe—that a legislator's salary was only $3 a day. We had assumed that additional pay was given for committee work. Our wants and needs were simple, and we had anticipated no difficulty. We soon learned that the salary actually was only $3 a day, a yearly total of $1,095, with no compensation for committee work. Moreover, reimbursement for travel between the capitol and the legislator's home was covered for only one round-trip each term.

On 12 January, the Senate passed a resolution allowing each Senator to draw $50 a week against his annual salary during the legislative session, after which a return would be made to the usual monthly check at the rate of $3 a day until the $1,095 was used up. This resolution eased our immediate situation. Friends loaned us enough to pay off our obligations, and we found less expensive living quarters.

During these first weeks of the session, Stanley took little part in Senate proceedings except to vote or ask a question. He listened, observed, and tried to master the complicated Senate rules and regulations. He also studied his colleagues for clues that might indicate how he could work with them.

The press representatives were curious and sometimes skeptical about Stanley, watching him and listening intently to his rare comments. We remember especially James M. Haswell and Hub M. George of the *Detroit Free Press;* Don Gardner of the *Detroit Times;* and Guy E. Jenkins of the Booth newspapers, the senior member of the group. Occasionally, the young, fair-haired Scotsman, Billy Allan, of the Communist paper, the *Daily Worker,* came to Lansing to sit in the press section to record some special debate. His biting humor and sharp observations had livened many a picket line as he had followed Stanley and other organizers in the 1937 and 1938 strikes and reported on them.

Also during this initial period when Stanley and his colleagues were taking each others' measure, I began doing Stanley's secretarial work. A corps of stenographers was provided, but there was only one for every three or four Senators. Stanley's correspondence was heavier than most, for labor people throughout the state regarded him as their emissary. Moreover, the stenographers had trouble with Stanley's diction. Stanley had used the Polish language as he grew up in a Polish home; in his work on the staff of a Polish paper as a youth; in the Polish community wherever he lived and worked; and in the Polish segment of the labor movement in Chicago and Detroit.

Because of his constant use of the language, he had difficulty in articulating the final consonants of English words. For example, when he wanted to say *asked* or *wished,* the words came out *ask* or *wish; girl* came out as *gir; most* or *best* came out as *mos* and *bes.* The drafts of his dictated material contained singulars in place of plurals and present, instead of past, tenses. I was familiar with his speech patterns and corrected his material or asked his meaning if I were not sure. The stenographers hesitated to do this. It must have been a relief to them when I took over his work, and it was a welcome chore for me. I was not paid for this, but it gave me a sense of sharing Stanley's work.

When he had no committee meetings, we went over his mail and he indicated replies to be made. Sometimes he dictated a press statement or radio speech for delivery in Detroit on the Polish program. The original weekly program, financed by the UAW, had been canceled by the station on the eve of the Flint GM sit-down of 1936, and in 1939 the UAW Polish Trade Union Committee bought time from the "Polish Hour" on station WMBC for an occasional speech by Stanley on legislation or labor issues. During the afternoon sessions, I found an available typewriter in the stenographic office or went to the office of the Workers Alliance, an organization of the unemployed with headquarters nearby, to transcribe my notes.

Another matter came to Stanley's attention in those early weeks, when Mort Furay of LNPL came to see him: "Stanley I want you to read something I picked up at Hudson's Department Store in Detroit."

He handed Stanley a booklet, "Know Your Sales Tax," by Daniel Wells of the Michigan Sales Tax Department.

"I think you will find it interesting," said Furay, "particularly the item on page 32, which I have marked."

The booklet gave a history of sales and use taxes and proved informative. On page 32 he found the author had used a Jewish druggist as an example of a tax chiseler, thus implying that Jews are tax cheats. Stanley immediately wrote to the Michigan Tax Commission calling attention to the anti-Semitic example and objecting to it. He received a prompt reply that the pamphlet was being withdrawn. It soon disappeared from bookstores.

Twenty-five January brought the event we had been anticipating with some apprehension. Governor Fitzgerald submitted simultaneously to the House and the Senate his dreaded labor bill "with teeth in it," and a transmittal letter. Senator Hittle, chairman of the Labor Committee of the Senate, introduced the bill in the Senate that same day; but as it would make its way through the legislative mill it would always be referred to as the "Fitzgerald labor bill."

Stanley sought ways to link his legislative work with his activities outside the Senate chamber. In his radio broadcasts and his meetings with labor, liberal, and language groups each week, he continually reported events in Lansing. Most labor people were so busy fighting battles on picket lines and in negotiations that they did not fully realize how victories won in the field can be lost in the legislature.

Stanley found that one effective way to show the relationship between the legislature and daily life was to ask groups to draft resolutions or laws in their field, which he introduced in the Senate. Then the groups organized mailing campaigns and visits to the legislators to request hearings before the proper committees. In this way people learned the procedures involved in creating laws and the role that people outside the legislature can play in that process.

On 9 February a closed or "executive" session was called to confirm some appointees of Governor Fitzgerald to the Department of Labor and Industry. Stanley described the events of that session to me later. One of the appointees was the notoriously antilabor Daniel A. Knaggs, former mayor of Monroe, Michigan. Stanley could not allow this to pass unchallenged even though he knew it would be a lost cause. A number of Republicans spoke favorably on the confirmation. Not a single Democrat raised his voice until Stanley signaled for the floor: "The Department of Labor and Industry is supposed to be an impartial body," he began, "but the governor is appointing to it a blatantly antilabor person who flouted labor's rights in Monroe, Michigan during the steel strike by brutally attacking pickets. How can such a man act impartially or objectively in the Department of Labor and Industry?"

Senator Joseph Baldwin, a conservative from Baldwin, Michigan, rose to direct some questions to Stanley: "Do you not believe in law and order, which Mayor Knaggs was trying to restore during the strike?"

"Of course," retorted Stanley. "But picketing is legal, a guaranteed right of labor. When Mayor Knaggs attacked picketers, he was not defending the law, he was breaking it by violating labor's legal rights."

Baldwin hurled one question after another, unaware that he was dealing with a seasoned veteran of many streetcorner meetings that had subjected him to sharp heckling and opposition. The freshman senator, rumored to be uneducated, crude, perhaps even violent, had given a quietly expert account of himself by the time Baldwin gave up.

Encouraged by Stanley's successful clash with Baldwin, the Democrats voted solidly against Knaggs's appointment, but their votes were buried under the Republican avalanche. Many senators, both Republican and Democrat, who had been routed in tilts with Baldwin, were delighted that someone had stood up to him. It didn't matter much what Stanley had said; it was enough that Baldwin had met his match. A number of senators from both parties shook Stanley's hand and congratulated him. Since the press had been excluded from the closed session, Stanley dictated a press statement expressing his disapproval of the appointment and his reasons. To Senator Baldwin's credit, he held no enmity for this incident. If anything, it seemed to win his respect, for whenever Stanley went to him on any issue he found a ready listener and a fair one.

That same evening (9 February) a fiery hearing was held in the House on the governor's bill, which had just been released by the House Labor Committee. Representatives of both the CIO and AFL, as well as church and community groups, spoke against the bill. Following this, on the fifteenth, the Association of Catholic Trade Unionists issued a statement that the bill should be scrapped.

Stanley continued his low-key role in the open sessions of the Senate, merely voting on measures and continuing to study his colleagues. He found certain liberal Republicans could be reached on the basis of justice and fair play. When they sounded off with democratic and liberal views, he simply took them at their word and approached them on that basis. The Democrats were mostly small business people who had started out as workers. Some, of ethnic background, responded well to minority problems and usually reacted favorably to liberal measures.

The Democratic senator, Charles C. Diggs, the lone Black member, responded well to matters touching his race and other minorities; but was largely the businessman, tending to make deals to push desired legislation through the Senate. As Stanley worked with him on issues, Diggs reacted wholeheartedly as a human being. In him Stanley found a staunch ally on civil liberties, the rights of minorities, and organized labor. A friendship developed, and Diggs often rode with us to Detroit on Friday afternoons, sometimes having us to dinner when we took him home. There we met his wife, Mamie Diggs, and their son Charles Junior, who would one day become the U.S. congressman from the Thirteenth District. Sometimes Senator Diggs rode to Lansing with us on Mondays.

Most legislators stayed in hotels or apartments near the capitol, but Senator Diggs could not obtain such accommodations. He stayed with a private family in the Black community. Stanley spoke to the lieutenant governor, to the president of the Senate, and some senators in an effort to get them to pressure hotels or apartments to change their policy, pointing out how ridiculous it was that a member of Michigan's highest lawmaking body could not obtain convenient housing because of race. All reacted to Stanley's comments sympathetically but did nothing.

One of the most colorful personalities in the Senate was Republican Earl Munshaw of Grand Rapids. A slim, dapper figure moving with quick, nervous energy, he radiated a warm personal charm and humor. He was a successful lawyer, making no pretensions as to his purpose in the legislature. Admittedly there to make money, he scorned the pious and patriotic phrases used by some of his colleagues to hide their real motives and practices. At first Munshaw made no friendly overtures, even turning Stanley down a few times when approached on legislation. "Your bill has merit," he would say, "and I would like to vote for it, but I can't. My vote is committed."

Stanley entered the Olds Hotel one day, looking for someone, and encountered Munshaw.

"Come have coffee with me, Stanley," he insisted, drawing him to a table and ordering something.

"You know, when I was in college," he said, "I was strongly attracted to the socialist movement and did considerable reading and thinking along those lines."

"You surprise me," commented Stanley.

"Yes, but as I left college and tried to establish a law practice in a small town, I found I could not succeed as a socialist. When I married and began acquiring a family, it became important to make money, so I withdrew from socialist and labor circles and concentrated on my career until I achieved some measure of success.

"I've been watching you," he continued. "You are much like I was years ago. But you can't make money working for labor, and what you earn here is really just pocket money. You should work for the interests that have the real money."

"You don't understand," Stanley protested. "I've been part of the labor movement from an early age. It was always the little people who pushed and prodded me to learn and grow and who helped me along the way. They are the ones who waged my campaign and paid for it, trying through me to realize their dream of a people's legislator to represent them. How could I turn away from them and betray their hopes?"

"You're very foolish, Stanley!" declared Munshaw, shaking his head. "But I must say, I admire your integrity."

From that time, Munshaw took Stanley under his wing, advising him on steering bills through the maze of rules and regulations. He could anticipate, almost to a word, what the windbags and flag-wavers would say on issues; and took the keenest pleasure in telling Stanley how to punch holes in their arguments. His desk was next to Stanley's; and he frequently leaned over with dancing eyes to say, "Watch this jerk wrap himself in the flag!" or "Listen to this hypocrite hold forth on patriotism and high motives." I often saw Munshaw do this, and Stanley told me later of the comments exchanged.

Senator Baldwin had introduced a bill on 20 January to establish a state committee to investigate seditious activities. It made Baldwin unhappy when Stanley immediately dubbed the measure the "little Dies bill" because it approximated the intent of the congressional committee headed by Martin Dies, later known as the House Un-American Activities Committee (HUAC). Letters had flooded the Senate, pro and con, and Stanley invited Baldwin to debate the bill at a public meeting in Detroit.

"I'd be skinned alive!" Baldwin protested.

"Not at all," Stanley assured him. "People want to know your reasons for introducing the bill and your arguments for it. They may disagree sharply with you, but no harm will come to you. That I can guarantee."

Baldwin reluctantly agreed, and the Civil Rights Federation arranged a meeting in the Detroit Leland Hotel on 21 February, which was reported in the *Detroit Times* of the 22nd. A. E. MacDonald of the Federal Veterans Administration supported Baldwin's position. The two main opposing speakers were Stanley and Rev. Owen Knox, pastor of the Bethlehem Methodist Episcopal Church and leader in the Civil Rights Federation. Vigorous discussion came from the floor. Baldwin declared his bill was designed to fight fascism yet was unwilling to limit it enough to prevent its use for a witch-hunt. Opponents of the bill argued that sufficient federal legislation existed to make a state investigative body unnecessary. Letters pro and con flooded the Senate as Baldwin's bill proceeded through the legislative process; many letters demanded public hearings.

In the meantime I developed some unusual physical symptoms, and Dr. Shafarman informed Stanley and me that we would be parents in October!

For weeks, Stanley's desk had been swamped with letters and petitions from individuals and organizations, asking for his promised investigation of the job selling racket in the Ford plants. He showed the letters to some colleagues and asked their advice on procedure. As he opened his mail one morning, one of the Detroit newsmen stopped at his desk and noticed letters and petitions on the matter and a Senate resolution ready for introduction.

"Do you really intend to introduce this?" the newsman asked.

"I certainly do," replied Stanley. "I promised during my campaign, and you can see the volume of mail I receive on the question."

"Would you wait a day or so, Senator, until I contact the Ford Motor Company and perhaps get a statement from them?"

"Okay," Stanley agreed.

The next morning a young man of tall, athletic build was sitting beside Stanley's desk when he came in. He was built like a football player, and Stanley was not surprised when he introduced himself as Harry Newman, representing the Ford Motor Company. Newman was a former All-American quarterback at Ann Arbor.

"I hear you are introducing a resolution asking an investigation of job selling at Ford's," said Newman.

"Yes, I am."

"Senator Nowak, I think you are making a mistake. All this talk about job selling is just rumor."

"Is that so?" Stanley replied. "Then what about all the affidavits and letters that come to me? And what about the people offering, at risk to themselves, to testify under oath as to the existence of this practice and how it is done?"

"This is all a misunderstanding, Senator. I am sure we can clear it up. Mr. Bennett would like to see you and discuss it."

"I would be happy to talk to Mr. Bennett here and to receive any information he has on the matter," replied Stanley. "I will study it and consider it carefully."

"But Mr. Bennett is too busy to come here," protested Newman. "He would like to see you at his office."

"I'm sorry, Mr. Newman, but I see my constituents here in the Senate, not in their homes or private offices, particularly when they represent large firms such as the Ford Motor Company. Mr. Bennett can talk with me here in the Senate Chamber or in one of the Senate offices."

Newman was persistent. Morning after morning, he was at Stanley's desk until Stanley's patience was exhausted: "Mr. Newman, the only persons allowed at my desk are family members or invited guests. You are neither. If I find you here again I will have the sergeant at arms throw you out bodily. Now go!" Mr. Newman left and did not come back.

Stanley introduced the resolution on 8 March and it was referred to the Committee on Rules and Regulations. In his weekend radio broadcast and at meetings Stanley reported his introduction of the resolution. More letters flooded the Senate, demanding that the committee release the resolution for discussion. The introducer of a measure is entitled to appear before the committee to which it has been referred, and Stanley did this. The senators listened politely, but their attitude indicated they had no intention of reporting out the resolution. There the matter would rest until the Senate term of 1941–42, when Stanley would again take action. Wide press publicity had greeted the introduction of the resolution, and Stanley's sources reported a sudden cessation of job selling in the Ford plants. Eventually the organizing and recognition of the union would eliminate the practice, in any case.

Governor Fitzgerald died of a heart attack on the sixteenth, and the next day Lieutenant Governor Luren D. Dickinson was sworn in as the new governor. His policies were every bit as conservative as Fitzgerald's had been.

On the sixteenth the Fitzgerald labor bill had been up for its second or third reading in the House. Several amendments were adopted that made the bill more vicious than it had been originally, in spite of heated opposition by all the Democrats and some Republicans. After four hours of furious debate and controversy, the bill was passed fifty-seven to thirty-eight, given immediate effect. It would now go to the Senate. The bill proposed a labor relations board of five members to be appointed by the governor for two-year terms; to try to head off strikes, curbs were placed on mass picketing, and provisions made for elections to determine employee representation. More than a dozen Republicans joined the Democrats in voting against the bill.

Welfare and old-age assistance problems had become acute. On our return to Detroit every weekend, we found increasing numbers of people pleading for Stanley's intercession with the welfare department or the Old-Age Assistance Bureau. Each time he approached the agencies, the problem was tossed right back to him. "Senator Nowak," the harried social worker would say, "you know very well that the legislature makes the appropriations we have to work with. You also know those appropriations are never adequate. Why don't you do something about this in Lansing?"

On 20 March Nowak introduced an emergency resolution asking for two million dollars for relief in Detroit, and made his maiden speech in open session on the inadequacy of relief and the need for money to relieve the desperate situation.

Harrumphing loudly, Senator George P. McCallum rose in pompous indignation to label Stanley's remarks as "campaign rhetoric." He was unalterably opposed to welfare. The resolution was referred to committee and stayed there for weeks in spite of letters and delegations from Detroit.

Stanley's status as a state senator had brought additional demands for his presence at conferences and affairs in other cities both during the week and on weekends. His legislative work had been interrupted for a trip to Chicago the weekend of 4 March for a conference of the national body of Labor's Non-Partisan League; for the UAW convention in Cleveland on 28 March; and for the Polish-American Trade Union Council in Cleveland and meetings of the striking McCormick and International Harvester employees in Chicago, both in mid-April.

In the Chicago strike there had been some attacks on pickets and union members by company goons, and here Stanley was able to help in a way that no one, least of all himself, had imagined. The strike leaders had thought that Stanley's status as a state official might lend weight to the strikers' cause. When he finished speaking at one of the meetings, he sat down at the front table while the meeting continued; and a stranger approached to whisper in his ear, "Senator Nowak, could I see you alone for a few moments?"

Obligingly, Stanley went into a small adjoining room with the stranger, who turned to him and said, "Don't you remember me, Stas?" Stanley looked him over intently, then said regretfully, "Sorry, I can't place you."

"You don't remember Alex?"

Stanley again studied the man, and suddenly the years fled as he recalled his childhood friend and protector from his parochial school days in Chicago. "Alex! Of course!" said Stanley, and they hugged each other in remembrance and talked about their respective families and some of the old days. Alex had been a big, bumbling fellow who had difficulties with his studies. Stanley had helped him and in return Alex had protected him from the roughhousing of the boys in some of their games.

Suddenly serious, Alex said, "Stas, what kind of an outfit is this CIO union these men belong to? Is it a good organization? And what does it do?"

Stanley explained the whole question of unionism and why one was needed to protect the interests of workers. Finally, Alex shook hands warmly and took his departure, moving swiftly without a word through the group of anxious men clustered around the door as he went out.

"What went on in there, Stanley? Are you okay?" they all asked.

"Of course! Why not?"

"Well, he's one of the guys we told you about who have been slugging our pickets and union members."

They were quite surprised at Stanley's explanation about the boyhood friendship and his conversation with Alex. It must have had a lasting influence on Alex, for he never appeared again.

Whenever Stanley was away on one of these trips, I went to the Senate Chamber each morning, opened his mail, answered what I could and put aside the rest for his return. The senators talked to me as I went about my duties, and I soon came to know a number of them. I also became acquainted with the stenographers as I worked in their office and lunched with some of them.

The Senate Labor Committee met the evening of 13 April to see what they could do with the version of the Fitzgerald Labor Bill that the House had passed to them. The next day, the fourteenth, Harry Hittle, chairman of the Senate Labor Committee, reported out a substitute version of the labor bill in the Senate. The new bill was modeled after the New York labor law.

A measure passed on 3 May, after bitter Senate debate, took the heart out of the Civil Service Law. His valiant fight on the matter won friends for Stanley in all walks of life and brought approval of the Detroit Citizens League on the only occasion during his ten years in the Senate. The secretary of the league publicly congratulated him for his battle to retain civil service as it had been. Throughout the state, the press lauded Stanley. While civil service was not completely destroyed, much of its effectiveness was lost. Stanley would battle on this issue in every Senate term.

On the eighth, as we entered the capitol grounds, we noticed a group of pickets carrying a long, wooden box, like a casket, and some signs. Both of us laughed in relief as we saw the words painted on the side, "Here lies John Doe, who died of starvation." Inside was a dummy. It was a Workers Alliance picket line, and the marchers' signs bore statistics on the number of unemployed and the meagre welfare allowance. Some people stopped to talk to the marchers. Others carefully avoided them. Later that morning, Stanley spoke in the Workers Alliance hall, and at 5:00 P.M. at a mass meeting on the capitol steps with state representative Raymond E. Garvey of Ironwood, an area heavily hit with unemployment. That weekend in Detroit, Stanley discussed the relief crisis with local unions and Unemployed Councils, describing the Workers Alliance picket line and demonstration. Detroit groups wanted to follow suit.

"Wait until I go before the committee next Monday," Stanley suggested. "If I get no results we can organize a march on Lansing later."

On his return to Lansing, Stanley encountered the same callous indifference from the committee. The senators were flip, making jokes at the expense of the unemployed who, they contended, were lazy loafers who would not accept a job if offered one.

"Gentlemen," said Stanley, "unless funds are immediately forthcoming, I will return to Detroit this afternoon and bring thousands of unemployed to camp on the capitol grounds until the appropriation is made."

"You can't really mean that!" scoffed the committee chairman.

"I assure you, gentlemen, I was never more serious in my life."

Uneasy glances were exchanged and the senators' flip manner vanished. They were still unhappy over the previous week's rally of people from upper Michigan. If so many could come that far, how many more might come from Detroit?

"Senator Nowak," said the committee chairman, "would you step out for a few minutes so we can discuss the matter?"

Within an hour, the chairman approached Stanley in the Senate Chamber, smiling ingratiatingly. "The committee recommends an appropriation of a million dollars for relief in Detroit," he said hopefully. Nowak had set two million as a bargaining figure, but realized that one million would handle the present emergency. If needed, further action could be taken later.

Since Senator Baldwin's debate in Detroit in late February, his "little

Dies bill" had been making its way through the legislative maze. There had been a fiery hearing on it on 29 April in the Senate Chamber, with supporting arguments from the American Legion, the Veterans of Foreign Wars (VFW), the chamber of commerce, and the Lansing Junior Chamber of Commerce. Opposing arguments came from the Detroit chapter of the National Lawyers Guild; Detroit attorney and war veteran Charles Lockwood, active in consumer affairs; Adolf Germer of the CIO; the Michigan Council of Churches; the Socialist and Communist parties; the Workers Alliance; and Rev. Owen Knox of the Civil Rights Federation.

Now, on 19 May, the bill was to be reported out of committee; and when it came to the Senate floor for a vote, I was on hand but with little hope. Stanley knew that Republican Senator D. Hale Brake, chairman of the State Affairs Committee, had serious reservations about the proposed legislation but was unwilling to admit it publicly. When the bill came to the floor, Stanley rose to say, "I believe Senator Brake has some opinions on this matter that would be worth hearing. Would the senator mind making a statement?"

With obvious reluctance, Brake slowly rose to his feet, skirting the subject for a moment or two before launching into it. His approximate comments were, "I am not opposed to the idea of the bill but am strongly of the opinion that such investigations should be made by experts. I do not believe any of us here are qualified to do this. On that basis, I will vote against the bill."

Baldwin spoke for his bill, then Stanley signaled for the floor. Aware of the accusations of the Dies Committee during Stanley's campaign and knowing his labor record, all senators and newsmen paid full attention as he rose to say, "This bill would permit a select few to decide what is American or un-American, and there is a wide divergence of opinion on this. This could easily be used for a witch-hunt. Further, there are in existence sufficient federal agencies to do the job that Senator Baldwin's bill proposes, and we don't need any more. The Dies Committee has been used as a political weapon against liberals and labor leaders in the last election, and we have every reason to believe that Senator Baldwin's bill would serve a similar purpose, regardless of the senator's intent." When the vote was taken, I couldn't believe it. Some of the most conservative Republicans voted with the Democrats to kill the bill by a margin of sixteen to ten.

The last two weeks of the Senate session were hectic to say the least, with the afternoon sessions extending into the evenings and even the wee hours of the morning sometimes. Yet there were pressing bills still undecided and not released from committees. Probably the most controversy surrounded the Fitzgerald labor bill.

The *Detroit Free Press* announced on 7 May that the House and the Senate were worlds apart on their versions of the bill. Even as late as the twenty-third, the *Free Press* stated there was a possibility that there would be no labor legislation this session, since the House had refused the proposed modifications of the Senate version and tabled the committee report and observed that "the proposal fostered by the late Governor Fitzgerald appears doomed for the present."

The legislature was to adjourn on the twenty-fifth. Finally the House called a Republican caucus on the twenty-third to decide the fate of the labor bill. On the twenty-fourth the *Detroit Free Press* reported that the House caucus had voted sixty-eight to twenty-two to approve the compromised report, and sent it to the Senate at once. There, in spite of strong opposition from the Democrats and a number of Republicans, the measure was adopted, given immediate effect, and sent to the governor for his signature. The bill set up a mediation board of three and a five-day cooling-off period with no cessation of operations; outlawed sit-downs; and prohibited mass picketing.

One little personal item that had given Stanley and me some uneasy moments was a bill introduced early in the session by Senator Baldwin, validating marriages of Michigan residents solemnized in another state. Stanley and I had gone to Indiana to be married in 1935, and as Baldwin's bill had made its way through the Senate with some discussion, we had often wondered, "Are we married or aren't we? And with a baby on the way!" The matter was settled when Governor Dickinson signed the bill on the twenty-fourth. We were saved from sin. On our return to Detroit at the end of the session, Stanley spent weeks job hunting. We were anxious to establish our own residence, as our way of life was a constant invasion of Tony and Irene's privacy. Further, our impending parenthood made it imperative to find a place and get settled.

Stanley participated in the organizing work of Local No. 174 on a volunteer basis, picketing with strikers at Cadillac Motor and other GM plants and providing help and leadership wherever he could.

A new role began for Stanley that summer and continued through the years. Many foreign-born workers came from countries where the collaboration of church and state, in many instances, had oppressed and kept the people in ignorance and poverty. As a result they were alienated from the church and religion, even while rearing their families in the church.

When their last illness came upon them, many such people requested that no priest or minister should officiate at their funerals but that Stanley should speak instead. He was a worker, a foreign-born U.S. citizen like themselves, knowing their problems and dreams. They were proud of him as "their" senator. They knew he would put into words what was in their hearts as he had done so many times. Stanley had walked picket lines with them, battled for them in negotiations, worked with them for social and economic improvements. He obtained from families or intimate friends the personal details of the individual's life and combined these with his own knowledge of the person, so that often a new image of the deceased emerged for the family as Stanley spoke. He pointed out how in many cases parents had been branded as radicals because of their struggles to provide a better life for their families and make this a better world for them to grow up in and how such parents were sometimes ridiculed or rejected by the very children for whom they had sacrificed so much.

When Stanley concluded, family members often realized for the first time the contribution made by the parent or spouse to the quality of U.S. life. Sometimes family members had doubted whether to respect the deceased's last wishes and violate tradition, and often a priest was asked to say a prayer or a few words following Stanley's remarks; yet they were always deeply touched by Stanley's presentation and came to thank him with tearful eyes.

Tom Mooney, the AFL leader who had been the victim of one of the most notorious frame-ups in U.S. labor history in 1916, had been released from prison in January 1939 by California's Governor Culbert Olson. Labor and liberal Democrats arranged a national tour for Mooney, with Detroit and Hamtramck on his schedule for 10 June.

As Michigan's labor senator, Stanley was asked to participate in the reception committee at the airport and in the parade escorting Mooney about the city. We attended the evening banquet for him. He was stooped and gray, but his glowing eyes showed that his inner fire still burned. Stanley introduced me to him after the banquet; and as I looked up into the craggy face and Mooney took my hand, I was deeply grateful that we had been privileged to be among those who had fought over the years to vindicate and free him.

A few days after the close of the Senate session, we received an unexpected and heart-warming letter from Senator McCallum dated 1 July, as follows:

> I cannot lay aside my legislative activities until I have written you a letter expressing my appreciation of the opportunity to make your acquaintance and to work with you in the Senate. Your attitude in the committee was always a very helpful one, and I felt at all times that if I had a meritorious measure to lay before the committee I would have your earnest consideration, also your sympathetic consideration, because you impressed me at all times as desirous of trying to understand what we were all about and your wish always was to do the wholesome thing and particularly what-

> ever would grant relief to those who were in tax distress. . . . I want you to know how much I appreciate your attitude.

Stanley had been quite surprised to find himself on the Senate Committee on Taxation, about which he knew very little. He made it his business to learn all he could about it, since taxation provides the revenues from which appropriations come for the people's needs. Taxation was the domain of Senator McCallum, an expert in the field, and it was a real trial to him that some of his committee members did not regard the subject seriously, sometimes falling asleep during committee meetings or skipping them altogether. Stanley's serious approach and faithful attendance pleased him, and he went out of his way to teach Stanley all that he could. The two were on opposite sides of the fence on almost every issue except taxation; but conservative though he was, and bitterly as he opposed Stanley on the Senate floor, the old gray veteran of many Senate battles would exhibit real regard and appreciation for Stanley's earnestness and sincerity in the future.

Although 1939 was not a campaign year, our home life continued at a frenzied, campaignlike pace. There were increasing demands for Stanley's presence at labor and social gatherings. He helped organizing drives wherever he could. A brief comment in a letter of 17 July from Earle Fisch, secretary of Lodge No. 1297 of the Steel Workers Organizing Committee CIO, illustrates the kinds of activity Stanley undertook: "We wish to thank you from the bottom of our hearts for the fine consideration you showed . . . during our strike at Palmer-Bee. Your presence on our picket line and at our strike meetings did a great deal, we believe, to keep 90 percent of the membership on the picket line during the entire strike."

Stanley was also volunteering his time and services in the Ford drive, as the majority of Ford workers lived in our senatorial district and came to him for advice and help in leafleting and speaking.

In July Stanley went temporarily on the payroll of Local No. 174 as a full-time organizer. We immediately found a three-bedroom upper flat on Daniels Street near McGraw, which we furnished on credit through some friends who owned a furniture store. The move to our own residence on 1 August must have been as great a relief to Tony and Irene Marinovich as it was to us. My mother again came to live with us, and life returned to normal, or as normal as it would ever be as long as Stanley was in the legislature. Friends rented a hall near us for a baby shower, which gave us the money for the doctor and hospital. I turned our extra bedroom into a nursery. The shower had provided a crib, Bathinette, scale, and a chest of drawers. I made a cover and cushions for an old rocker, with matching curtains.

On 23 August 1939 the Hitler-Stalin pact was signed, causing a furor around the world. We were naturally surprised and shocked by this event but soon recognized it as an attempt by the Soviet Union to buy time to prepare for what they knew would inevitably happen, an attack on the Soviet Union by Nazi Germany. The Polish community, representing, as it did, every ideological viewpoint from left to right, was split wide open; and at meetings throughout the Polish community the arguments raged. However, as international developments occurred, the controversy died down. Poland had been offered a mutual assistance pact by the Soviet Union earlier but rejected it out of hand and made such a pact instead with England and France. We saw Poland attacked by Nazi Germany on 1 September and a very tardy response from England and France.

We would later see the Soviet Union attacked by Hitler's forces and his ruthless subjection of the Balkan nations, which would bring together not only the Poles but all Slavic nationalities in the United States in a unified attempt to help their Slavic brothers and sisters in Europe. However, that story belongs in a later part of our lives (see pp. 000–00).

In September 1939 Stanley's organizing post with Local No. 174 was made permanent; and on 10 October our daughter, Elissa Gail, put in an appearance, bringing added responsibilities and problems as well as great joy. When she became fretful at times, a previously undiscovered facet of Stanley's personality surfaced as he took her in his arms and walked the floor, singing Polish lullabies remembered from his childhood. The cries would cease as she appeared to listen intently. It was a wonderful time in our lives in spite of the world's turmoil.

The developing war in Europe had created a war atmosphere in the United States, especially in Detroit, which would be the center for the hardware of war. The fear of fascism was growing, and debates raged in the press and in Congress on legislation to compel noncitizens to register. Factories producing armaments began to discriminate against aliens because of the fear of sabotage. Foreign-born workers had to offer proof of citizenship, or at least first papers. Even native-born citizens had to produce birth records. These developments brought a new rush of people to our home for letters or forms to be filled out. People waited in our living room office every evening before I could clear the dinner table and put Elissa to bed.

We had a nursing infant on a three-hour feeding schedule. Then there were the meals, grocery shopping, laundry, and the interminable list of household duties. Where, I wondered, could I find additional time and energy to handle the phone, the doorbell, Stanley's correspondence and speeches, and the clerical work needed by the many people coming to us in the evening? Half of our living room had been converted into an office with typewriter, desks, and other equipment inherited from our 1938 campaign. We placed chairs around the other half of the room for a reception area. Our large dining room became our living room. Seeing the tremendous demands made upon our time and energy, friends often brought their daughters and their typewriters to help with the work.

Nineteen hundred thirty-nine had brought us enormous adjustments to the many new and varied demands of political life, combined with organizing, picketing, and work in the Polish community and language groups, in addition to becoming parents. This hectic pace would continue through 1940.

13 The Ford Organizing Committee

The year 1940 saw the rapidly developing war in Europe, increasing attacks on the rights of the foreign-born and noncitizens in the United States, and growing unemployment.

On 3 January the Senator Nowak Club mailed letters to key people in the Twenty-first Senatorial District, calling for the establishment of a Nowak Federation of Clubs and setting a conference date. The club initiated monthly meetings to prepare for the 1940 elections, and the sons and daughters of many who had participated in our 1938 campaign came to help with typing, mimeographing, and stuffing envelopes. This was all done in our home under my supervision until a headquarters could be obtained.

On the 7th, Stanley inaugurated a new half-hour Polish radio program, "Promien prawdy" (Ray of Truth) on station WMBC, paid for by the UAW Polish Trade Union Committee. It was later extended to an hour.

Early in March Stanley participated in a national conference on the rights of the foreign-born in Washington. The call had been issued by a hundred prominent citizens, among them Mary McCleod Bethune; Dr. Franz Boas, noted anthropologist; Sidney Hillman of the Amalgamated Clothing Workers; Heywood Broun, famous newspaper columnist and later president of the Newspaper Guild; novelist Fannie Hurst; California's governor Culbert Olson; famous explorer Viljalmur Steffanson; and Nobel prize–winning scientist Harold Urey. The conference chairman was President Emeritus William Allan Nielsen of Smith College, and the co-chairman was Ernest Hemingway.

Over six hundred delegates participated. Stanley spoke in the panel on legislation, chaired by Detroit probate judge Patrick H. O'Brien, and Detroit attorney Ernest Goodman reported resolutions against antialien bills, against discrimination in employment, and for the right of asylum for political and religious refugees.

Early March press reports indicated twelve million people unemployed in the United States. Throughout the month, demonstrations took place all around the country under the banner of the Workers Alliance. In Detroit a huge meeting of the unemployed was held on 23 March in Jefferson School, where Stanley and prominent Democratic politicians, Democratic officials, and union officials spoke.

On 28 June President Roosevelt signed into law the alien Registration Act, requiring every noncitizen to be fingerprinted and registered within four months. The number of people waiting nightly in our office–living room increased sharply. Some of the work had to be shifted to our campaign headquarters, where volunteers helped fill out applications for citizenship.

The primary campaign that summer brought a new language group to the Nowak forces when a young Ford worker invited Stanley to speak at a picnic arranged by an Italian fraternal society at one of the parks in August. Stanley arrived alone at dusk, parked his car, and started for the dance pavilion where speaking programs took place. He noticed several young men wearing T-shirts bearing the name of Bob Ford, a Republican candidate for Congress in our district and somehow related to the Ford family. Stanley wondered if he had misunderstood the invitation or had come to the wrong park. Thinking that some of Harry Bennett's Ford service department sluggers might be around, he felt a little uneasy and was considering trying to slip out of the park unnoticed, when a young fellow spotted him and waved. "Hi, Stanley," he shouted. "Glad you came!" Short, slight, and dark of hair and complexion, he grinned and shook Stanley's hand in hearty welcome, introducing himself as Johnny Gallo, a Ford worker. The young men in the Ford T-shirts quickly surrounded Stanley, and Gallo introduced them as fellow workers at Ford's. Seeing Stanley eye their T-shirts, they all laughed.

"Don't believe everything you see," they reassured him. "Our foreman gave us the shirts with instructions to wear them everywhere over the weekend. We never know when some of Bennett's stooges may be around, so we wear the shirts to keep our jobs."

They escorted Stanley around the park, introducing him to everyone and winding up at the bar. Stanley recalls Paul Boatin, Mark Cinzori, and a very young lad, Angelo Dei Tos.

"Stanley, we've been warned there are some Ford servicemen in the crowd who have threatened to rough you up," said Gallo. "Look behind you occasionally so that no stranger gets too close. And don't worry! We'll keep an eye on you and stay close by."

When Stanley was called to the speaking platform, he looked out over the audience and noted uneasily that his "guardians" had disappeared. He continued speaking and was immensely relieved when the soon reappeared, each bearing a heavy glass mug of beer. They ringed the speakers' platform, standing and sipping their beers nonchalantly but watching the crowd intently. Any troublemaker would have had a heavy mug dropped neatly on his head and strong arms would have seized him. After the program, Stanley's young friends carried their beer mugs to conduct him to his car and out of the park. They told him later they had watched to make sure no one followed him. These young workers would be active in all of Stanley's future campaigns and would work with him in the Ford organizing drive.

The same forces that had conducted our 1938 campaign rallied in greater numbers than before, for Stanley's legislative record had won new friends. Campaign picnics took place throughout the summer.

Joseph C. Roosevelt once again opposed Stanley in the primary, contending that Stanley was a Stalin agent taking orders from Moscow. Thirteen other Polish candidates registered in the Democratic primary, obviously to split the Polish vote. Six of these were persuaded by friends or family to withdraw from the campaign. The primary vote in September gave Stanley 9,483 compared to Roosevelt's 7,343, with the other candidates trailing far behind.

Ford workers grew more insistent in their demand for help in organizing. Ford Local No. 600 had been established by charter from the CIO in August 1938 but was still under the jurisdiction of West Side Local No. 174. In September 1940 the UAW announced an intensified organizing drive among the ninety thousand Ford workers. Michael F. Widman, Jr., national CIO assistant organizing director, was appointed by John L. Lewis to head the drive, with an organizing fund of $100 thousand contributed largely by the United Mine Workers Union. Two headquarters were opened on Michigan Avenue, one near Wyoming and the other near Addison, both located near where we lived. *Glos ludowy* carried an appeal by Widman in both Polish and English for support and help in the Ford drive.

On 8 October the U.S. Circuit Court of Appeals upheld the decision of the NLRB in the Rouge case, filed in 1937 as a result of the brutal beatings of union people at Gate 4 on 26 May 1937. The court decision placed the sole responsibility for the battle at Gate 4 on the Ford Motor Company and its service department and ordered the company to cease anti-union activities and rehire, with full back pay, the twenty-three men discharged for union activity. This decision helped Tony Marinovich, which pleased Stanley and me very much.

Following the court decision, the UAW decided to challenge the constitutionality of a Dearborn ordinance banning the distribution of leaflets on Dearborn streets. On 1 November Stanley and twenty-four other organizers appeared at the Ford gates with leaflets. With them were Maurice Sugar, the UAW's legal counsel; Richard Frankensteen; Bob Kanter; and Walter Reuther. They were aided by volunteer organizers, both men and women, from all language groups.

When Dearborn police arrested the crowd and took them to jail, the "victims" joked and sang labor songs all the way there. They were brought before Dearborn Judge Lila M. Neuenfelt, who immediately recognized Stanley. "What are *you* doing here?" she asked in surprise.

"Your Honor," he replied, "your Dearborn police arrested me along with these people while we were passing out leaflets at the Ford factory gates."

"You don't belong here, Nowak!" declared Neuenfelt. "Go on, get out of here! All of you!" she added, turning to the others, and smilingly waved them out.

Judge Neuenfelt announced to the press that she was taking the matter of the constitutionality of the Dearborn ordinance under advisement and would make a decision shortly.

Michael Widman appointed Stanley to the Ford organizing committee on 3 November. Nowak's overwhelming primary vote and the vast forces drawn into the Ford drive as a result of his organizing and political work in the district no doubt contributed to this decision. His campaign speeches still sounded more like union appeals than election bids.

Glos ludowy immediately announced Stanley's appointment with an appeal to all Poles and Slavic organizations in the city to help in the Ford drive. A similar appeal was also issued by the Italian paper, *Il corior del Michigan* (Michigan courier). Also active in the Ford drive was an Italian committee headed by Monsignor Joseph Ciarrochi of Santa Maria Rectory on Cardoni Street. Some committee members were Felix Bernardia, Dominic Cecarelli, Peter Recchia, John Gallo, Paul Boatin, and Angelo Pagott, almost all of them active in our election campaign. In the Ford drive Stanley would also work with many Blacks who had participated in, and even initiated, organizing attempts at Ford from the very beginning before Stanley was appointed to the drive. Among these were Shelton Tappes, Chris Alston, John Conyers, Sr. (father of Congressman John Conyers), Marcellus Ivory, Douglas Lee, James Simmons, Harold Robertson, and many others whose names we cannot remember. Many of these were also active in Stanley's legislative campaigns.

The Ford organizing committee gave Stanley two specific assignments. The first was to canvass from house to house on behalf of the union in the downriver community of Allen Park. Besides Allen Park, the downriver area included the communities of Del Ray, Lincoln Park, Ecorse, River Rouge, and Wyandotte, all within his legislative district. Stanley's second assignment was to organize the Poles and Slavic workers in the Ford plants.

Since Poles constituted a large segment of the Ford workers, Stanley felt it would help if a number of prominent Detroit Poles would form a broad sponsoring committee for the organizing drive, and direct its appeals to Polish workers in all plants and in the Polish community at large. Stanley made this proposal to the UAW Polish Trade Union Committee, and its members went with him to visit leaders in Detroit Polish circles. Such a broad sponsoring committee emerged and included attorney Arthur Koscinski (later a federal judge); Nicholas Gronkowski, Hamtramck justice of the peace who had held the fact-finding hearings in the 1937 Hamtramck cigar strikes; Frank Danowski of Plymouth Local; and Edward Danielewski and John Zaremba of Dodge Local No. 3. Committee members frequently spoke on the Polish radio program. Nowak's weekly broadcasts dealt with various aspects of the Ford drive, and sometimes Arthur Koscinski, Michael Widman, or Maurice Sugar spoke.

On 16 November Judge Lila Neuenfelt courageously declared the Dearborn ordinance on leafleting unconstitutional.

On 1 December 425 delegates and friends attended a conference called by the Ford organizing committee and the Nowak Federation of Clubs at Chadsey High School. Stanley chaired the conference and many prominent Polish and Democratic officials were present. The conference issued a call to a broader one of all Polish organizations in Wayne County to develop countywide support for the Ford drive. Stanley was authorized to draft the call for the Wayne County conference to be held sometime in January.

On the seventh, Judge James E. Chenot of the Wayne County Circuit Court upheld Judge Neuenfelt's decision regarding the Dearborn leafleting ordinance, declaring it "unreasonable, arbitrary, and discriminatory" and stating that it had made a mockery of free speech and free press. He granted an injunction forbidding the enforcement of the ordinance in Dearborn. Overnight, Ford workers sprouted union buttons. Within forty-eight hours of Judge Chenot's decision, Stanley and other organizers and volunteers were at the Ford gates with handbills. From that time on, members of the Ford organizing committee and Ford Local No. 600 appeared at the plant every two weeks with fifty thousand copies of "Ford Facts," the official publication of the local.

Even while getting the wheels moving in the Polish community and conducting his reelection campaign, Stanley had begun the other part of his assignment, to visit the homes of Ford workers in Allen Park. Accompanied by Local No. 600 members and some from the UAW Polish Trade Union Committee, Stanley had begun in early November to knock on doors. Many a Ford worker in Allen Park was surprised to find his state senator on his doorstep. In the privacy of their homes, Ford workers described the prisonlike regulations in the factory, the nerve-racking speedup, the unhealthy, often dangerous working conditions, and the constant intimidation by the ever-present Ford servicemen.

The house-to-house canvass brought increasing numbers to the union, and small home meetings began. All Ford workers in one block met in one of the homes with Stanley and others from the Ford organizing committee and Local No. 600. Workers took courage from each other, and the meetings grew to include workers from a two- or three-block area. The sons of the workers served as lookouts to report any strangers lurking about, in which case decks of cards, food, and drinks quickly appeared to convert the gathering into a social event. It was at such a neighborhood meeting that Walter Dorosh, later president of Ford Local No. 600, met Stanley. John Gallo, the young Ford worker whom Stanley had met earlier at the Italian picnic, came to these meetings. Carl Stellato, one-time president of local No. 600, often told how he had first met Stanley at one of these home meetings.

The struggle to organize Ford's was carried on in many places by many people. Stanley's part in it was only one sector of a huge battlefront. Along with his campaign for reelection, the Ford drive occupied the major portion of his time and energy until he left for the legislative session in January 1941. The November 1940 election gave Stanley a vote of 75,255 compared to 47,644 for his Republican opponent, Elbert Hawkins.

In the midst of the Polish work and the Ford drive, another matter came to Stanley's attention toward the end of the year. The State, County and Municipal Workers Union CIO had established a local among the employees of the Detroit department of Public Welfare. Some members had discovered abuses in the department and brought them to Stanley's attention, asking that he do something about it as a legislator.

He conferred with State Senator Charles C. Diggs, and they prepared a joint press statement. Ray Pearson of the *Detroit Free Press* came to our home on 1 December and made notes for a news article. Stanley wanted Diggs to come and be photographed with him, inasmuch as it was a joint statement being issued, but Pearson said it was against the policy of the three daily papers at that time to show photos of Black and white persons together. Stanley refused to allow his picture to be used without one of

Diggs, so no photos accompanied Pearson's article in the *Detroit Free Press* on the fourth.

In an appearance on the third before the Detroit Welfare Commission Diggs and Stanley had requested an investigation and audit of Detroit welfare records because of the hundreds of complaints from persons who were callously treated and denied relief. Diggs and Stanley requested that an investigating committee be set up, to which they could present evidence. They also asked to have a representative on the committee, which was established immediately.

Stanley revealed that two state auditors and a field representative had already been given some of the evidence collected and were making a preliminary survey. He stated he and Diggs were forwarding to the State Social Welfare Commission and to the attorney general's office a resolution signed by the entire Wayne County delegation of the state legislature, asking an investigation and action by the attorney general if charges of misuse of funds were substantiated.

Still another matter was brought to Stanley's attention in late December by the State, County, and Municipal Workers Union, concerning housing of welfare recipients. Ray Pearson reported in the *Detroit Free Press* on 22 December on a letter from Nowak and Diggs to the Detroit common council charging that hundreds of welfare clients were housed in "rat-infested, firetrap shacks whicih the Dept. of Buildings & Safety Engineering had termed unfit for human occupancy" and asking for public hearings where the two senators could present evidence. The letter asked that the housing investigation be separate from that of the welfare department. Pearson's article of the twenty-third said Stanley had announced that several civic and labor organizations would join the demand for a public hearing on the housing question.

And so ended the full and hectic year of 1940. The Ford drive would continue into 1941, as would the welfare and housing investigations.

14 The Second Senate Term

The elections of November 1940 gave Michigan a Democratic governor, Murray D. Van Wagoner of Pontiac, and ten Democratic senators instead of nine as before, with new faces among both parties.

This would be the most active and aggressive session of Stanley's ten legislative years, both in the Senate Chamber and outside. He would introduce many petitions of a routine nature for constituents—common councils and schoolboards of downriver communities in his district, union locals, school employees, citizens, and civic groups. He would introduce a total of twenty-seven Senate bills, four Senate resolutions, and four concurrent resolutions, in addition to spearheading vigorous battles against antilabor legislation introduced by others. He would work with Senator Harry F. Hittle, Republican, of East Lansing and chairman of the Senate Labor Committee, to improve and liberalize workmen's compensation and measures of a similar kind. Hittle represented the AFL as an attorney; and, while generally conservative, he responded well to issues concerning workers and farmers and sometimes voted with the Democrats.

The United States was heading rapidly into war, and the unrest and turmoil among workers was matched by an upsurge in repressive elements. Stanley would be involved simultaneously in struggles in several areas. For the duration of the 1941 session of the legislature we sublet our Detroit flat, retaining one room for Stanley's use when in Detroit. In Lansing, we rented a furnished flat where I stayed with Elissa when Stanley returned alone to Detroit over weekends. Sometimes I was joined in Lansing by my mother for a week or two.

For a long time, constituents had been coming to Stanley with injuries due to negligence by operators of public or private conveyances. When he referred such cases to attorneys, he was usually told there was no legal remedy. Walter Nelson, prominent Detroit criminal attorney, often talked with Stanley about the need for reforms in negligence and insurance laws.

"Why don't you and your colleagues draft such legislation and have someone introduce it in the legislature?" asked Stanley.

"We did, but no one has been willing to sponsor our bills, since many legislators are retained as attorneys by corporations opposing such reforms."

"You write the bills, and I'll be happy to introduce them," Stanley offered.

Nelson involved some of the finest brains in the legal profession, some from the office of UAW legal counsel Maurice Sugar, some from the National Lawyers Guild, and some prestigious attorneys who realized the need for such laws and were willing to draft them but did not wish to be publicly associated with Stanley because of his controversial reputation. On 17 January Stanley began introducing these insurance bills as fast as Nelson could get them to him, and correspondence came immediately from attorneys all over the state, commending Stanley and offering help in any way possible. Copies of the bills were requested by bar associations and individual attorneys, some of whom wrote that the bills were discussed in their local bar association meetings.

In the meantime, Stanley continued his efforts in the Ford organizing drive, particularly among the Polish community. On the twenty-sixth, a historic countywide conference on the Ford drive took place in Dom Polski on Forest and Chene Streets in Detroit. Over a thousand delegates, representing every Polish organization in Wayne County, were present, with political ideologies ranging from the extreme Left to the extreme Right. Stanley opened the conference and John Zaremba was chairman. Prominent speakers were Arthur Koscinski, chairman of Lodge No. 150 of the Polish National Alliance and later a federal judge; Judge Nicholas Gronkowski of Hamtramck; Leo Krzycki of the Amalgamated Clothing Workers; Michael Widman, Jr., Director of the Ford organizing committee; and UAW legal counsel Maurice Sugar. A series of resolutions emerged in support of the Ford drive, and the resulting publicity brought wide support from forces throughout Wayne County.

The investigations initiated by Diggs and Stanley in December 1940 into the misuse of welfare funds in Detroit and the deplorable housing of welfare clients, continued through January 1941, with hearings before the Detroit City Council.

Letters once again were coming to Lansing, urging action on the job-selling racket at Ford's. The practice had stopped after Stanley's introduction of a resolution in the matter in 1939 but was apparently revived. On 29 January 1941, Stanley introduced Senate resolution no. 27, asking for an investigation. It was referred to committee and "killed" before he could present any evidence. However, there was so much publicity and so many letters and wires asking for a public hearing, that the committee chairman notified Stanley during an afternoon session that he could appear before the committee that afternoon immediately following the Senate session. This short notice gave Stanley no time to bring witnesses, affidavits, or other material to substantiate his arguments; but he met with the committee. Its members did not question the accuracy of Stanley's charges but expressed the opinion that legislation, not investigation, was needed. "All right, suppose I introduce such legislation. Would the committee members support it?" asked Stanley. All agreed they would, and Republican senator D. Hale Brake even offered to help draft it.

Accordingly, Brake met with Stanley a few days later. They found on the Michigan Statutes an act prohibiting the sale of jobs without a license but providing no penalties. Brake had assumed that petty foremen or supervisors accepted money or gifts for jobs, in which case the party receiving payment would be a company employee and easily traced and prosecuted. Stanley explained that the sale of jobs was done quite differently, making it difficult, if not impossible, to trace. In various communities, an individual went to a Ford dealership, beer garden, real estate office, hotel, or boarding house and left his name and address with fifty to ninety dollars. Within a few days he would receive a postal card to report to work. Brake and Stanley added a clause to the existing law to the effect that any party aiding the sale of jobs without a license would be considered a company employee and conspirator in the transaction and subject to a penalty of six months in prison or a five-hundred-dollar fine, or both. Senator Brake agreed to serve as co-sponsor of the amendment.

In the meantime, the U.S. Supreme Court, on 10 February, ordered the Ford Motor Company to comply with the NLRB order to reinstate without further delay the workers discharged four years earlier, all with full back pay. UAW president R. J. Thomas then appealed to the federal government to deny defense contracts to Ford in view of the court decision. Ford workers reported that compliance notices were posted in Rouge Plant on the eighteenth. Bennett continued to harrass the union, issuing wholesale transfers to place union committeemen in strange departments among workers who did not know or have confidence in them and would therefore refuse to sign union applications.

The regional office of the NLRB was flooded with affidavits concerning Bennett's continued defiance of the court order. This was bringing retaliatory action by Ford workers, and matters were rapidly approaching boiling point. Very early in March, three thousand rolling-mill workers sat down until their demand for reinstatement of several shop stewards was met. Other departments followed suit throughout March, bringing the total of sit-downers at one time or another to fifteen thousand according to reports in all the daily papers.

While this went on, bitter and impassioned debate was taking place on a Senate bill introduced by Senator Brake, proposing penalties for sabotage in defense industries. On 16 February Stanley stated in a radio address over station WJBK,

> Apparently the authors of this bill assume that the owners of factories, mills, and mines will not impede national defense or carry on any kind of sabotage. Yet we know, how manufacturers in various wars . . . have sold the government guns that were defective and airplanes that failed to work.
>
> While severe penalties are provided for workers and farmers for possible negligence and oversight during work on material for national defense, there is no provision made to punish manufacturers and owners of industry for selling defective material.

Stanley also quoted a statement issued by the labor advisory board of the National Defense Advisory Commission after careful study of this bill:

> Under the act, a strike, slow-down, temporary stoppage, loafing, quitting work in midshift, and picketing would be treated equally with violent sabotage. . . .
>
> A union member who joins his brothers in obeying a strike order and peaceably walks out of a plant producing airplanes under contract with the U.S. Army can be arrested, convicted, fined $10,000, and imprisoned for ten years. This is so unless the right to strike is specifically exempted from and protected by the terms of this act.
>
> The union leader who calls a strike in the above case is likewise criminally liable either as a conspirator or as a principal since the terms of the act do not specifically exclude striking.

In the debate on the bill in the Senate, Stanley quoted these same arguments with their source. Hundreds of labor leaders, professional people, members of the clergy, and concerned citizens came to Lansing at various stages of the debate on this bill. The original was withdrawn and a different version introduced; but it, too, was protested by large numbers of people. A watered-down version was finally passed and signed into law despite public clamor and outrage.

In early March, the senators debated Stanley's bill on job selling. Quivering with indignation at the aspersions cast upon his folk hero, Senator McCallum rose to protest the passage of this bill: "I am sure that Mr. Ford does not know about this practice, and I am not at all certain that Senator Nowak has the evidence he claims to have. If he does, and if Henry Ford were informed of these facts, he would certainly put an end to the practice a once." Laughter from some quarters greeted these remarks, and Stanley signaled for the floor: "Senator McCallum, you may find it disturbing and difficult to believe, but Mr. Ford has been informed of this practice by many people. There is no question as to its existence, as evidenced by the many sworn affidavits in my possession and the many individuals ready to come before this body at the risk of their safety to testify. With all the publicity in the press, I don't know how Mr. Ford could avoid knowing about it. The intent of this bill is to provide penalties for this practice not only in the Ford plants but elsewhere." The bill was passed, sent to the House, and buried in committee. Stanley was not deeply concerned, as the growing storm in the Ford plants indicated the inevitability of a strike. The establishment of the union would eliminate the job-selling practice without need for legal action.

Correspondence continued to stream into the Senate on the negligence and insurance bills Stanley was introducing. On 5 March, when he went to Senate secretary Fred I. Chase to introduce two more, Chase called to his attention the fact that one of the bills would be numbered 200.

"Is that of some significance?" asked Stanley.

"Yes, Senator, when a bill carries the number of an even hundred, its sponsor is expected to throw a party for his colleagues. Do you wish to do that?"

"Wait a minute," Stanley requested, as an idea occurred to him.

"Can you hold that number for me until tomorrow so I can make some phone calls and get back to you?"

Chase obliged, and that evening Stanley phoned Walter Nelson, the Detroit attorney under whose auspices the bill had been drafted.

"This could provide some publicity for the National Lawyers Guild, Walter. Do you think they might foot the bill?"

"Sounds like a great idea, Stanley. Let me talk with the fellows here, and I'll call you back."

The next day, Nelson phoned his okay, and Stanley immediately introduced Senate bill no. 200. When Chase announced Stanley's invitation in the Senate Chamber, it caused a sensation. The news traveled, and among the many letters on the merits of the insurance bills was one from attorney Thurman B. Doyle of Menominee, Michigan, a Democrat who was for ten years Menominee's city attorney, for three years assistant U.S. attorney, a member of the American Legion, the VFW, and Knights of Columbus. Doyle's letter stated, in part, "The enclosed correspondence between myself and attorney Leigh Caswell of Crystal Falls might be of interest to you. If there is anything I can do to assist you in the passage of . . . the legislation which you have pending and which were endorsed by our Bar Association, I will be only too glad to lend my assistance." Enclosed with Mr. Doyle's letter to Stanley was a copy of a letter Doyle had received from attorney Caswell, dated 25 March, stating, "The majority of the lawyers in this county are not in favor of the large portion of the proposed legislation . . . and discarded the first communication from this self-styled 'Lawyers Emergency Committee,' thinking no responsible person was back of it. . . . The bills are introduced by Senator Nowak, who was elected from a district infested with communists—and now the senator is giving a dinner Thursday of this week at $2.50 a plate. Rather expensive eating for the poor lawyers."

With the copy of Caswell's letter, Doyle enclosed a copy of his own reply, dated the twenty-seventh, in which he said,

> I presented your letter to most of our attorneys and they, as I, got a hearty laugh out of it. The boys here all feel now that every night . . . we should look under the bed to make sure there aren't any ghosts, witches, communists, or members of the "Lawyers Emergency Committee" lurking there to gobble us up.
>
> After receiving the communication at Menominee from the committee, we called a meeting of our Bar Association and spent several hours seriously considering the proposed legislation. Mr. F. J. Trudell presided. As you know, Mr. Trudell is Dean of the Upper Peninsula attorneys, . . . a "corporation lawyer," . . . represents the Chicago, Milwaukee, & St. Paul Road, . . . the local branch of Wisconsin Public Service Corp., . . . a conservative Republican.

Mr. Doyle's letter to Caswell also named several other equally prominent attorneys at that meeting and stated that all had endorsed the "Lawyers Emergency Committee" that had drafted Stanley's bills. Doyle's letter continues,

> I do not know Senator Nowak nor his constituents. . . . I do know that the legislation he proposes is almost identical to what has been on the Statutes of Wisconsin for many years.
>
> Are you aware that the imputed negligence rule . . . has been repudiated either by law or court decision in, I believe, forty-seven states, leaving Michigan alone on this subject?

> Do you know that the Wisconsin Supreme Court many years ago sustained the comparative negligence statute abolishing the contributory negligence doctrine, companion legislation sponsored by Senator Nowak?
>
> Do you know the Wisconsin Supreme Court has approved much of the legislation which Senator Nowak has introduced?
>
> You refer to the $2.50 dinner Senator Nowak is giving. . . . Did you attend the dinner given within the last year to the lawyers of Upper Michigan which didn't cost us lawyers a cent but was paid for by a prominent insurance company, . . . to which . . . our Circuit Judge was invited but [which he], like myself and most of our Bar, declined to attend?"

The party to celebrate Stanley's introduction of Senate bill no. 200 was held in the ballroom of the Olds Hotel on 27 March with a bar set up at one end of the room before dinner. Among the guests were Simeon P. Martin, president of the Farmers Union; Redmund Burr of the Railroad Brotherhoods; Darrel Smith, CIO state legislative representative; and Walter Nelson. Stanley introduced each senator to the guests for brief comments and then introduced the guests to the senators.

The insurance lobby had already done its work, and none of Stanley's insurance bills became law. Nevertheless, their introduction spotlighted the need for reforms and helped lay the basis for later improvement in this field. Stanley had discussed the proposed legislation at labor and political gatherings and in his radio speeches, thus providing widespread education on insurance matters among people who knew little about the subject.

Throughout March, outbreaks of short-term sit-downs in various departments at Ford's continued, and on the twenty-fifth, the NLRB opened hearings in Detroit on the situation with a fanfare of press publicity. Continued harrassment by Bennett evoked retaliation by rank-and-file workers, finally forcing the UAW to file formal notice of intention to strike without setting a date. Wires to President Roosevelt and Governor Van Wagoner asked intervention to compel the company to bargain.

Things were at this impasse when Stanley left Detroit for Lansing on 2 April, after a morning meeting with the Ford organizing committee. During that afternoon session of the Senate, the governor sent for Stanley.

"What's the situation at Ford's?" he asked.

"Well, when I met with the steering committee of the organizing staff this morning, we found the workers enraged over the continued harrassment by Bennett, and they want to strike right now."

"Do you think they will?"

"It was a stormy meeting this morning," Stanley replied, "but the steering committee prevailed and the decision was made to prepare more adequately for a strike and wait to see what you and President Roosevelt can do to compel management to bargain."

The governor seemed satisfied with this, and Stanley returned to the Senate Chamber. That evening, Van Wagoner threw a dinner for all Democratic legislators and the press, during which Stanley noticed the governor's secretary hurrying to the governor to deliver what appeared to be an urgent message. Van Wagoner at once became agitated and sent the secretary to summon Stanley.

"What are you trying to do to me, Nowak?" he demanded.

"What do you mean?" asked Stanley in surprise.

"You surely must know that the Ford workers struck this afternoon. Remember what happened to Governor Murphy? What do you think this will do to me?"

"I think that will depend upon you, Governor. You could emerge a hero, depending upon what action you take."

"But why didn't you tell me about the strike when we talked this afternoon?" persisted Van Wagoner.

"I did *not* know anything about it," replied Stanley. "The situation was exactly as I described it when I left Detroit this morning. Something must have triggered the strike after I left."

"What would you suggest I do, Nowak?"

"You might go immediately to Dearborn, contact union leaders, and make whatever arrangements you feel necessary to ensure the peaceful conduct of the strike."

The governor excused himself and left for Detroit at once. Stanley also headed for Detroit, excusing himself from further Senate sessions for the week. At strike headquarters he found the strike had been set off by Bennett's discharge of all eight members of Ford Local's bargaining committee and his refusal to bargain further or deal with the union. Unplanned, the strike had proceeded haphazardly from department to department and building to building, but the speed of its momentum attested to the strength and unanimity of the strike sentiment.

At the scene, Stanley found the union in control, dominating the area through sheer numbers. Thousands of strikers and sympathizers surrounded the plants. Massive numbers of pickets guarded the three main gates. Other groups were stationed at tunnel ways and railroad tracks and patrolled surrounding roads. At the local a thousand men were in reserve for day or night emergencies. John Gallo was picket captain.

Outnumbered and outmaneuvered, Bennett gambled on a deception designed to bring outside intervention to crush the strike. Charging that a sit-down was in progress and that the Rouge plant had been seized from the inside by "Communist terrorists," he appealed for federal and state troops. He also charged that the sit-downers were saboteurs, deliberately wrecking tools and dies of vital importance to the manufacture of aircraft parts. Federal Conciliator Thomas J. Dewey investigated and found that the alleged sit-downers (numbering over a thousand) were Ford servicemen pretending to be sit-downers. They were commanded by Bennett's Black aide, Don Marshall. Most of the men were new to Detroit, largely Black, brought from the South by Bennett. Dewey appealed to the men to leave, promising safe-conduct. The union even cleared the way for them by removing pickets from certain gates; however, when the servicemen "sit-downers" tried to leave, Ford servicemen outside shoved them back inside. From the rootfop and an open gate, Bennett's gang peppered the pickets outside with small lengths of pipe and other missiles. Pickets responded by hurling the objects back upon their assailants.

Since the majority of the men inside were Black, it was feared a race riot might develop. To prevent this, a number of prominent Black community leaders volunteered their services, among them Senator Charles C. Diggs, Sr., and Rev. Charles A. Hill of Hartford Avenue Baptist Church. Together they spoke from loudspeakers at strategic points along the picket line around the Rouge plant, appealing to the occupants to join their Black union brothers outside. Walter White, then secretary of the NAACP, also came to the scene and appealed to the men to come out.

This is where Stanley first met Rev. Charles Hill, who had long been sympathetic to the efforts of the union. He had been one of the first ministers to open his church to the infant Local No. 600 as a meeting place. Hill and Stanley developed a warm friendship that would take them through two joint campaigns for election to Detroit's common council and bring them together to work on community issues through the years.

Two or three hundred of Bennett's men came out in response to the appeals, but the rest remained to plague the strikers and continue their drunken, violent brawling. The situation was a time bomb waiting to explode. Fortunately, neither President Roosevelt nor Governor Van Wagoner yielded to Bennett's demand for intervention.

From the strike's inception *Glos ludowy* issued a daily four-page supplement in both Polish and English to hand out on the picket lines. The 5 April supplement reported that moving sound cars, on loan from other locals, were keeping pickets in step with lively music and that hundreds of automobiles patrolled the surrounding roads to prevent the entrance of scabs. That same supplement also reported that twenty thousand Ford workers and their families had jammed the State Fair Coliseum the previous evening to hear Ford organizing director Michael Widman, Jr.; UAW president R. J. Thomas; UAW secretary-treasurer George Addes; Richard

Frankensteen; and Walter Reuther. A tremendous standing ovation was reportedly given state senator Charles C. Diggs, Sr., as he assured strikers that former UAW president Homer Martin was not going to tell the Black Ford workers what to do and that they would remain solidly with the strike.

The following evening (the fifth) Martin's AFL Ford Workers Union was able to muster only a couple hundred people at the State Fair Coliseum to call for a back-to-work movement. *Glos ludowy*'s strike supplement of the seventh revealed that news and also revealed that the AFL Teamsters, Bricklayers, and Streetcar unions were all honoring the Ford picket line.

The strike supplement of the eighth reported forty-five thousand meals and ten thousand sandwiches being served to picketers each day, and hundreds of thousands of cups of coffee. More than three hundred wives and relatives of Ford workers, along with UAW auxiliary women, worked in soup kitchens throughout the city preparing food, clearing tables, and washing dishes—at Local No. 155 Tool and Die West Side Local No. 174, Briggs Local No. 202 and Dodge Local No. 3, to mention a few. The main kitchen was at Bayside, an old school near the Ford plants. Within ten days, Governor Van Wagoner arranged an agreement whereby five of the eight committeemen were reinstated, unresolved disputes referred to a mediation board, and the current NLRB hearings temporarily suspended. Both sides agreed to speed the holding of a government-supervised election.

During all this upheaval, Stanley continued his work in the Polish community in support of the strike, speaking on the radio program and at Polish affairs. At the picket lines, he repeatedly spoke in Polish and English to encourage the strikers. He also joined Senator Diggs and Rev. Charles Hill on both the radio and the picket line, appealing for Black and white unity. Nowak permitted the Ford organizing committe to take over the radio program during the remainder of the strike.

On his return to Lansing the first Monday after the outbreak of the strike (8 April), Stanley was bombarded with questions. His colleagues were surprised by his eyewitness account, for Bennett's misleading press statements had given quite a different impression.

After the strike truce, the organizing drive was intensified. Stanley continued to meet with the Ford organizing committee and members of Local No. 600 on weekends and sometimes midweek. He continued to report and discuss strike issues on the Polish radio program to rally the Polish community behind the drive.

Other matters also claimed his attention, as he battled to get the Senate committees to release his bills on improvements in workmen's compensation and the investigation of the welfare mess in Detroit. One strange incident came out of these battles on 9 April, as he left the Senate Chamber after a stormy and unsuccessful debate with McCallum and others on the workmen's compensation amendments. As he entered the deserted hallway, he heard someone call his name and saw a shadowy figure emerge from the dark stairway, swaying unsteadily. It was one of the lobbyists who had avoided him until now. "Nowak," said the man, extending his hand, "I want to shake the hand of an honest man. I never believed it possible to find one in this place. In my experience, every man has his price. Since you have never played ball with us, I felt the only difference between you and the others was that your price was higher. But, by God, after today I believe you're one honest guy! That was some fight you put up in that Senate Chamber today, even when you knew it was a lost cause."

"Listen, friend," Nowak said caustically, "you did everything possible to defeat me on those measures, and you certainly succeeded. I should be congratulating you!"

"Well, that's my job, and I did the best I could," the other replied, "but you did a good job, too, a damned good one!"

He shook Stanley's hand and turned to go. Then he came back to shake a warning finger unsteadily under Stanley's nose. "Don't you ever turn crooked, you little son of a bitch, or I'll break every bone in your body!"

Ashamed of his outburst, the man smiled foolishly. "I know, I know, I've had too much to drink. Otherwise I'd never have the nerve to say what I did. But I meant every word, and don't you forget it!"

As his questionable admirer made his way uncertainly to the elevator, Stanley felt oddly warmed by the strange encounter.

On 22 April Stanley introduced Senate bill no. 336, proposing a complete reorganization of the state's welfare setup and procedures. Many professional social workers and attorneys, and even some senators on the Welfare Committee, complimented him on the merits of the bill.

"It should be a good bill," Stanley retorted. "It was prepared by professionals in the field." (He knew that the senators were merely making goodwill gestures to soften their refusal to allow the bill out of committee.)

In addition to the many letters, there were delegations of social workers, professional people, labor representatives, and concerned citizens coming from all over the state to appear before the committee on behalf of the welfare bill and to visit every legislator; but as Stanley had expected, the bill was not released from committee.

The union election at Ford's was scheduled for 21 May. Two days before, Diggs and Stanley issued a joint appeal to Black and white workers to vote CIO, and their leaflet was distributed throughout the plants. The election was a landslide victory with 70 percent of the votes for the CIO, slightly more than 25 percent for the AFL, and less than 3 percent for no union. Bennett found this bitter medicine and branded the election "a great victory for the Communist Party, Governor Van Wagoner, and the NLRB," according to the *Detroit Free Press* of the twenty-third.

It must have been disturbing to the Ford interests that the legislative district containing the Ford plants was represented in the Michigan Senate by a new dealer and union organizer, whose electioneering had been more of a union organizing drive than an election campaign, and that he had ousted from office a senator sympathetic to Ford interests. No doubt they had been even more disturbed when Stanley introduced legislation in 1939 and again in 1941 to investigate job selling in the Ford plants and later joined the Ford organizing committee.

Stanley's work with the Ford organizing committee ended with the union election in May 1941, and at the end of the legislative session in June he went job hunting again. At the time District 50 of the United Mine Workers was conducting a national drive to organize chemical workers and had established a regional office in Detroit. Most of the chemical industries lay in the downriver area within Stanley's senatorial district, and he was placed on the organizing staff.

Many chemical workers came from nationality groups with which Stanley had worked in his election campaigns and legislative work. Therefore, he channeled his organizing approach through them. In each of the chemical companies, a large segment of the workers belonged to some ethnic club—Hungarian or Polish—with an ethnic meeting hall. Club members called meetings at their hall, helped Stanley distribute leaflets and sign up fellow employees, and finally established a local. In this manner Stanley organized employees at Solvay Process Company, the Michigan Alkali Division of the Wyandotte Chemical Corporation, and the U.S. Gypsum Company. Stanley's work with District 50 would continue through 1941.

That summer of 1941, Labor's Non-Partisan League (LNPL) sought a candidate for election to the Detroit Common Council. Because of his successful campaigns in the past, LNPL approached Stanley. He agreed but pointed out that there had never been a Black member of the council and suggested Senator Charles Diggs, Sr. Stanley was delegated to approach him, and Diggs agreed to run, too. When the candidacy of Nowak and Diggs was endorsed by the Wayne County CIO Council, friends of Walter Reuther in that body suggested that George Edwards, a former coworker of Stanley's at West Side Local No. 174, be added to the slate of LNPL candidates. Both Stanley and Diggs agreed.

Stanley and Diggs established a joint campaign headquarters at Broadway and Gratiot Avenue and several other places. Among volunteers staffing the main office were Erma Henderson, who would later become president of Detroit's city council; and Esther Shapiro, who would later head the Consumer Affairs Department for Detroit. They would be aided by many others of both races in handling the office and leg work of the campaign. Diggs and Stanley arranged joint rallies and speaking engagements in both the Black and Polish communities and jointly held a huge campaign panic. In their appearances together in their respective districts, they stressed unity in both the election of candidates and the organizing of unions.

Besides appearing with our spouses, Mrs. Diggs and I campaigned in our own way with "chain" meetings. I invited to my initial meeting women from my neighborhood, from the language groups, and from unions. Mrs. Diggs came to my first meeting, and each woman there pledged to arrange a gathering of friends where Mrs. Diggs and I could appear. She then started her "chain," and I attended the initial meeting, composed largely of women from churches, clubs, and political groups.

Throughout 1941, during Stanley's work with the Ford organizing committee and in other phases of the Ford strike and even during his work with District 50 and his council campaign he had also engaged in local and national efforts to unify the Slavic nationalities behind President Roosevelt's policies. The slavic nations of Eastern Europe were under attack by Hitler, and there was a growing movement in the United States to unite all Slavs to send aid to their embattled brothers and sisters in Europe.

In early August the UAW Polish Trade Union Committee distributed in Polish communities throughout the city a leaflet in Polish and English appealing for unity in support of anti-Hitler forces in Europe. On 28 September, at the Belle Isle Shell, under the auspices of the Citizens Committee to Fight Hitlerism, several thousand people heard Stanley urge Slavic unity in the United States to support fellow Slavs in Europe. UAW secretary-treasurer George Addes and Senator Charles C. Diggs, Sr., spoke. Vincent Klein chaired; and two members of the Polish Army, Colonel Witold Urbanowicz and Colonel Wladyslaw Jakubowski, were introduced for comments. A resolution was passed supporting the anti-Hitler coalition of nations in Europe and urging full U.S. support. Such meetings as this took place in Seattle, Pittsburgh, Washington, Chicago, Toledo, Pawtucket, and Passaic to mention only a few. Sentiment was growing for a national Slav organization.

On 10 October, in a special session of the Michigan legislature, Senate concurrent resolution no. 66, introduced by Stanley and passed by both houses, urged the national leadership of both the Democratic and the Republican party to give full aid and assistance to those countries fighting Hitler, condemned anti-Semitic propaganda, and urged unity behind Roosevelt's efforts.

In the meantime, all three LNPL candidates were nominated in the October primary race for election to the Detroit City Council. At once, the press began featuring unfavorable articles and editorials designed to alienate Diggs's forces from Stanley's. At the same time, expensive billboards appeared in prominent places throughout the city, featuring Edwards, while the same newspapers lauding him attacked Stanley and Diggs. Apparently big business was alarmed by the large vote drawn by the three labor candidates. It appeared that at least one of them would be elected in November, and big business interests evidently decided it should be the one most palatable to them. Certainly, funds for large, well-situated billboards could not come from the labor movement at that time, and the conservative forces controlled the newspapers. Diggs and Stanley continued their joint campaign, and Stanley's election activities went hand in hand with his work to unify Michigan Slavs.

The first all-Slav meeting in Detroit took place 19 October at Dom Polski, sponsored by the UAW Polish Trade Union Committee and attended by representatives of thirty Slav nationalities. At this meeting the Michigan Slav Committee was formed, with Dr. W. T. Osowski – a dentist from Detroit's east side and a conservative Republican – as chairman; Dr. D. K. Yatich of the Serbian Radio Club and Stanley as vice chairmen; George Pirinsky, national secretary of the Macedonian-American People's League, as secretary; and Marie Tomasik from the Croatians as recording secretary. A plan emerged from this meeting for an all-Slav banquet at the Masonic Temple on 7 December, and committees were appointed to plan details and make all arrangements.

When the November election came, Stanley and I spent the whole night until the wee hours going with Charles and Mamie Diggs, Rev. John Miles and his wife Lennie, and members of the campaign staff, to visit one headquarters after another, trying to cheer each other and the workers as election returns showed Edwards steadily gaining and Diggs and Nowak trailing. Edwards climbed from sixteenth to seventh place to become a member of the city council. We were all disappointed, especially since victory had come so close, yet everyone was pleased that such a large number of people of both races had, for the first time, waged a harmonious election campaign and made such a good showing.

On the afternoon of 7 December twelve hundred people from all over Michigan assembled in the Fountain Room of the Masonic Temple for a banquet sponsored by the Slav-American Defense Savings Program of Michigan. The printed program listed the following distinguished guests:

Hon. Francis Biddle, U.S. Attorney General
Frank Isbey, Chairman, Michigan Defense Savings Program
Murray D. Van Wagoner, Governor of Michigan
Edward J. Jeffries, Jr., Mayor of Detroit
Hon. Joseph Belina, Czechoslovakian Minister of Labor
Gen. Bronislaw Duch, Brigadier General, Polish Armed Forces
John J. Barc, U.S. Marshal, Eastern District, Michigan
Stephen Sudek, State Commissioner, Polish National Alliance
Adolph Bazant, President, Czecho-Slovak National Alliance
Michael Kammer, President, Federation of Slovak Societies
Ray Travnik, National Vice President, Slovene NPJ Federation
Vasil Dicoff, President, Bulgarian-American Citizens Committee
George Pirinsky, National Secretary, Macedonian-American Peoples League
George Marksity, President, Serbian Vivovdan Congress
Thomas Besenic, Past National President, Croation Fraternal Union
Steve Pawloff, President, United Russian War Relief Committee
Stanley Nowak, Michigan State Senator
William Shewchuk, Ukrainian-American League
Rev. Fr. Kulinatycki, Carpatho-Russian

A booth was set up in the hall outside the Fountain Room for the sale of defense bonds.

At one of the banquet tables a number of people from the local U.S. Justice Department were seated along with U.S. marshal John Barc and some of his associates. Stanley approached their table to greet them, but instead of the usual friendly greetings from fellow Democrats, he was met with cool courtesy bordering on outright antagonism. This surprised and puzzled him, as their relations in Democratic circles had always been cordial. He dismissed it from his mind for the moment, but would recall this as future events unfolded.

Dr. D. K. Yatich chaired the affair, with Arthur Koscinski as toastmaster. The atmosphere was electric with excitement. Minor officials were introduced and musical numbers presented, when suddenly someone rushed to the speakers table with a message for Biddle. He hurriedly left after a quick consultation with the master of ceremonies. Tension hung in the air. Uneasy whispers sounded. The gaiety had vanished. Biddle soon returned and spoke briefly with the master of ceremonies, who rose to say that Biddle had a momentous announcement to make. In the stillness, Biddle said the Japanese Air Force had bombed Pearl Harbor and that we were now at war. A groan swept the crowd. A very hushed and sober audience heard the rest of the program. Biddle saluted the efforts to establish unity among American Slavs, which, he said, would be of great importance in the struggle ahead. He congratulated Stanley, Dr. Osowski, and the others for their work in this regard. Greetings were read from President Roosevelt and other national figures.

After the banquet, the booth in the hall outside became a busy place as people bought defense bonds. People lingered, seeming to feel the need to draw comfort from one another. Groups chatted everywhere. Finally, people began to leave and Stanley and I headed for home, weary and fearful of the future. What would it hold for us? For everyone?

The Michigan Slav Committee immediately began arranging a national tour for Stanley for early 1942 through industrial centers of the northeastern and central states to rally Slavic support for the war. The strain of the campaign and our manifold political activities had left me utterly exhausted and unhappy at the prospect of Stanley's being away for weeks at a time in the next few months and my having to cope all alone with all of our obligations. Both of us faced the Christmas season of 1941 and the New Year of 1942 with apprehension and uncertainty.

15 Slavic Unity and an Indictment

On New Year's Day 1942 Stanley left for a series of meetings in Massachusetts and Rhode Island. This was the beginning of a three-month tour during which he would visit large Slavic communities in twelve states. The importance of rallying the Slavs nationally behind the war effort was pointed up by government statistics indicating that 51 percent of all war workers were of Slavic origin. The committee arranging the tour realized that the only money coming in for our household expenses was the monthly check from the state of Michigan figured at three dollars a day, and that Stanley would have to put off any organizing assignments until after the tour. Therefore arrangements were made for a modest sum of money to come to me each week; and all of Stanley's expenses on the trip would be fully covered by the local Slav committees wherever he appeared to speak. Besides the general goals raised in all the Slav groups, the Poles aimed specifically to raise funds for the new Polish Army on the eastern front in the Soviet Union, in accordance with a treaty between the Polish government-in-exile in London and the government of the Soviet Union. As Nowak visited Slav communities they formed Slav committees on the spot that began communication with like committees in other cities and states.

Stanley came home from his first week of meetings for a special session of the Michigan legislature on the sixth, which he attended alone, returning to Detroit nightly. Further meetings took him to Massachusetts and Connecticut, then to Rochester and Buffalo, New York and home in time for another brief Senate session on the nineteenth. By the twenty-third, he was off again for Pennsylvania, New Jersey, Delaware, and Maryland, returning for another brief Senate session on 16 February. On the twenty-sixth, he left for meetings in Syracuse and surrounding towns in New Jersey, New York, and Pennsylvania, followed by meetings in Cleveland, Ohio; South Bend, Indiana; and Muskegon and Grand Rapids, Michigan.

Stanley returned for a conference of the Michigan Slav Committee on 15 March at the Book Cadillac Hotel, where three hundred delegates representing twelve Slav groups made preparations for a national Slav conference at the end of April in Detroit, the national center of the arms industry, and already called "the arsenal of democracy." On the twenty-second, Stanley was off again for Buffalo, New York; Kenosha and Milwaukee, Wisconsin; and Calumet City and Chicago, Illinois. He was home again by 1 April.

As a legislator and a leader in the Democratic party, he enjoyed extensive cooperation from government officials in every city and state on the tour. In Newark, New Jersey the mayor met him at the train and took him to dinner with a prominent manufacturer. Following the afternoon meeting, Stanley was the guest of a well-known Catholic priest, and the evening meeting was held in the parish hall. From every walk of life, Slavs flocked by the hundreds to these meetings. Stanley was almost always given radio time in addition to the scheduled meetings.

Members of Slav committees in other cities also made such tours. One was undertaken by B. K. Gebert, president of the Polonia Society of the International Workers Order, a sick-and-death benefit society. Leo Krzycki, vice president of the Amalgamated Clothing Workers, spoke to labor bodies around the country on the need for uniting the Slavs behind the war effort.

Growing out of all these tours was a strong desire for a national Slav organization. This was felt to be of special importance, since among the Slavs were some elements strongly anti-Soviet, carrying on disruptive activities against the war effort. It was believed that unifying the U.S. Slavs would help quell such activities.

On the morning of 25 April 2,458 delegates from many parts of the United States assembled in the Masonic Temple in Detroit for a weekend of deliberations. Nationalities represented were Polish, Russian, Czech, Serb, Slovak, Bulgarian, Croatian, Slovene, Macedonian, Ukrainian, Carpatho-Ruthenian, and Montenegrin. Philip Adler, reporting in the *Detroit News* of 27 April said, "'Unity, Production, Speed!' the battle cry of the congress, in a way sums up its achievements expressed in the numerous resolutions." A fight against fifth-column activities was one of the principal planks of the congress platform. A special committee was created to investigate such activities among Slav groups, and Stanley was named chairman. Leo Krzycki was elected national president of the Slav Congress; Professor J. J. Zmhral of Chicago, first vice president; Stephan Zeman, Jr. of Pittsburgh, second vice president; George Pirinsky of Detroit, secretary; Blair F. Gunther of Pittsburgh, chairman of the board of directors; and Vinko Vuk of Pittsburgh, treasurer. Representatives of each nationality were named vice presidents and members of the board of directors.

Following the final business session on the morning of April 26th, delegates and guests numbering nearly ten thousand gathered for a victory rally in the State Fair Coliseum in the afternoon to hear Paul V. McNutt, chief of the new War Manpower Commission. McNutt commented "The Axis strategy of 'divide and conquer' did not envisage this meeting. Hitler did not dream of it when he boasted: 'America will be easy to conquer. It is not a nation. It is the raw material of a nation.' Today, by coming here, you gave Hitler the lie. Yes, in this Slav-American Congress you have shown the world the miracle of American unity." McNutt also pointed up the relation of the Slav congress to his own war task: "I have just received a mandate from the President to coordinate the mobilization of American man power. The fact that thousands of you have come here today . . . to offer your services to your chosen country strengthens me in my hope and belief that this great recruitment of labor skills can be kept on a voluntary basis." Other government officials present represented the U.S. Treasury, the War Production Board, the Department of Labor, and the Commission of Facts and Figures. Greetings came from President Roosevelt.

This is the only time in history that all twelve Slavic nationalities were united in a common effort; they had often been at each others' throats in Europe. But Hitler's onslaught against the Slavic nations had the effect of uniting U.S. Slavs, from the extreme Left to the extreme Right, both workers and professional people, to support their fellow Slavs under attack in Europe by Hitler. With the vanquishing of Hitler and his forces and the ending of the war, the Slav congress would disintegrate, but during the war it was a powerful force for victory.

Shortly before the conference took place, Stanley had begun to work for the Hotel and Restaurant Workers CIO. Paul Domeny, financial secretary, was formerly a waiter in the Book Cadillac hotel. He headed the organizing drive among workers employed by companies supplying box lunches to auto workers, cafeteria workers in factory lunchrooms, and those working in restaurants, bars, and small hotels near auto shops and patronized by auto workers.

Nowak was assigned to help organize employees of box lunch companies serving the River Rouge Plant of the Ford Motor Company. The majority of these workers were organized within a few weeks, but management delayed several weeks before consenting to negotiate.

When Nowak and Domeny arrived with the negotiating committee for the first session, they found that management's attorney was Larry Davidow, former general counsel for the UAW under Homer Martin. It was said that Davidow was doing legal work for Bennett and the Ford Motor Company after leaving the UAW, and this seemed to be borne out by his presence at this meeting, representing companies rumored to be controlled by Bennett. Davidow showed surprise and displeasure at seeing Stanley, with whom he had often worked, and he became almost hysterical when he realized he had to deal with Stanley as an official representative of the food workers. "This man is a Communist, a troublemaker," he shouted, pointing to Stanley. "We've never had trouble with you before," he said turning to the box-lunch company employees on the negotiating committee. "You've been satisfied with wages and conditions up to now, haven't you? This radical, Nowak, is pushing you into demanding more, now isn't he?"

Davidow ranted on during the whole meeting, permitting no one else to talk. With nothing accomplished, a second meeting had to be scheduled. At the next one, to prevent a repeat performance, Paul Domeny led off. "Gentlemen," he began, "we are here to negotiate. Our time is valuable. We have no time to listen to the ravings of management's attorney. Therefore, let us get down to business."

Management representatives sat in silence while Davidow again went into his act, wasting the whole time. As Stanley and Domney left the meeting, Domeny said, "It appears they are trying to provoke us to strike so they can charge us with obstructing the war effort."

"Obviously," returned Stanley. "But we're not going to let them. It isn't necessary. We'll go see Paul St. Marie."

St. Marie, then president of Ford Local No. 600, grasped the situation quickly and proposed a solution: "Ford workers don't care much for the food served by the lunch wagons, and I'm sure they would be only too glad to stop buying from them. Let me pass the word, and I'm sure you will soon see results."

Within a few days, most workers were bringing their own lunches. Day after day, huge quantities of food came into the factory only to be taken out again, unsold. After a week of this, the box lunch companies were desperate. Their employees had not struck, yet the companies were losing money. Finally, Harry Bennett offered to mediate between management and the food workers, but only on condition that neither Stanley nor Davidow were present. Recognizing this as a face-saving maneuver,

Stanley suggested the union accept Bennett's offer. Accordingly, Domeny headed the negotiation committee at the next session. A contract emerged, recognizing the union and granting a substantial pay raise.

That summer and fall Stanley spent every Thursday evening in the Sochachewski Department Store on Michigan near Central, selling war bonds. He announced this on the Polish radio program and in *Glos ludowy.* People came to see him at the store on various matters and bought several thousand dollars in bonds. Even on his speaking tours early in the year, he had specified that arrangements be made to sell war bonds at each meeting; and this was also done at Detroit meetings.

Stanley again campaigned for nomination to the Michigan Senate. In the primary he was once more opposed by Joseph C. Roosevelt, but Stanley emerged with a substantial margin to win the Democratic nomination. Congressman Lesinski was also renominated. At the Democratic state convention in Grand Rapids in September Governor Van Wagoner appointed Stanley to a study commission on education.

Stanley continued to discuss the progress of the war on the Polish radio program. Some conservative Poles disapproved of his position on the issues. A representative of the federal government came to see him. "Senator," he said, "there are people from another Polish program who strongly disagree with you and even suggest that you should be charged with treason. They have asked me to check your speeches."

"Well, English copies of all my speeches are on file at the radio station. There you can see what I've been saying."

In a few days the man returned and said, "Senator, I wish the speeches on the other radio program were like yours. They would certainly help win the war. I have talked to the people on the other Polish program and told them the same thing. I don't think they are very happy about it."

In the 3 November election, Stanley won reelection to the state senate with 42,097 votes, and Congressman Lesinski was reelected with 42,911. The close approach of Stanley's vote to the number of votes drawn by Lesinski was noted in many quarters.

On 7 December, the first anniversary of Pearl Harbor Day, Stanley led a group of two hundred people to the Red Cross to give blood. Then on the eleventh our lives were disrupted by a completely unexpected happening that struck like the proverbial bolt from the blue. The phone rang, and I picked up the receiver. "Margaret," said a man's voice, "this is a friend. The grand jury has issued an indictment for Stanley's arrest. Tell him to pack a bag and scram!"

The caller hung up without identifying himself, and I stood numbly by the phone for I don't know how long, with sinking heart and rising fear, before beginning hurriedly to assemble things Stanley might need and put them into a suitcase. My trembling hands and dragging feet did not seem to be my own, and my brain was in turmoil.

Suddenly a hand tugged at my skirt, and I became aware that three-year-old Elissa had been talking to me. "Mama! Why don't you answer me?" she demanded.

I hugged her to me in relief. She had brought me back sharply to reality and I knew at once I must unpack the bag. Why should Stanley run away? He had done nothing wrong. His life and work were a matter of public record and one in which he could take pride. He had never run away from a fight in all the years I had known him. Certainly, he would not begin now! Quickly I unpacked the suitcase and put it away. I was expecting Stanley momentarily, as he had phoned earlier that he would soon be home. Together we would decide what to do.

It was already late afternoon. The strange, warning call had interrupted my housecleaning chores in preparation for guests. Stanley and I had long before agreed never to delay dinner on his account, because of the unpredictable nature of his work. When our guests arrived, we proceeded with dinner and awaited developments. The meal was long over and Elissa asleep for the night, but still no word from Stanley! My anxiety grew with each hour. Where could he be? Why hadn't he phoned? My questions were answered when the evening edition of the *Detroit Free Press* was delivered to our door, announcing Stanley's arrest in banner headlines and carrying his photograph on the front page. He was charged with fraud in obtaining his citizenship.

By that time the phone calls were coming in. Jack Raskin of the Civil Rights Federation was the first. "Don't worry, Margaret," he reassured me. "We're on the job doing all we can. Attorneys Ernie Goodman and Mort Eden are trying to get Stanley released, and many people are calling to offer help."

All over town, people went into action as the *Detroit Free Press* hit the streets. At least a dozen people phoned to say that when someone had brought a newspaper into their meetings, further business was suspended to discuss what they could do to help Stanley. Others phoned to offer help in a personal way. Warmth and gratitude filled me with the realization that *when one does not work for self alone, one does not fight battles alone.* For months I had been ill from exhaustion and the never-ending pressures. My recovery was hampered by Elissa's frequent infections requiring round-the-clock medication. Friends feared I would crack under the added strain and shock of Stanley's indictment; but the warmth and assurance shown by numberless friends and the deep concern and support from broad masses of people all gave the needed courage and strength to sustain me.

At midnight Stanley phoned, eager to reassure me and learn how I was faring. He was vastly surprised and relieved when I reassured *him* and relayed messages describing activities in his behalf all over town. Soon our attorney, Ernest Goodman, called to tell me where to go in the morning and what to do.

The next morning, friends took me to the office of federal marshal John Barc. When Stanley was brought from jail, Barc greeted him with exaggerated courtesy tinged with mockery. "Now that you have been fingerprinted, we shall soon know all about you," he said with humor edged with malice. He seemed elated over the turn of events.

From Barc's office we went to the courtroom of Judge Edward J. Moinet, where attorney Goodman joined us. Stanley was arraigned and then released on bond. As we left the courtroom, photographers' flashbulbs greeted us all down the corridor. We then went with Goodman to his office, where we conferred with him and his partner, Morton A. Eden.

"Tell us what happened last night, Stanley," said Goodman. "You must have had quite a session, for Mort and I tried all evening to reach you. They kept putting us off with excuses."

Stanley related the events of the previous day, which he had spent in contract negotiations for the cafeteria workers at the navy arsenal on Mound Road near Eight Mile Road. On the way home his car had developed motor trouble on Michigan Avenue near Central. Finding that repairs would take an hour or two, he had crossed the street to the Russian Cooperative Restaurant to eat and telephone me. He had ordered his meal and gone to a phone only to find it out of order. "I'll find a phone elsewhere and call later," he had thought.

The clientele of this restaurant consisted largely of Slav workers from the community. All knew Stanley and kept stopping at his table for a word with him. He was just finishing his meal when two young, athletic-looking young men had caught everyone's attention as they entered and sat at a table. Stanley had gone to pay the cashier and become involved in conversation with friends standing there. They had all stepped outside and were about to enter the bar next door to find a telephone and have a drink, when a hand had been laid politely but firmly on Stanley's arm, and a voice had said, "Could I see you for a moment, alone, please?" Stanley had looked up into the face of the man, one of the two strangers who had entered the restaurant a few moments earlier. The other stood behind him. It was not unusual for him to be approached in this manner wherever he went. "Be with you in a minute," he told his friends, and walked a few steps way with the strangers. The one who had stopped him had held an FBI badge in the palm of his hand. "Mr. Nowak, a warrant has been issued for your arrest. Will you be good enough to come with us?"

"Who issued the warrant?" Stanley had asked.

"The U.S. grand jury. Please do not insist on our producing it at this moment or resist arrest, for it would only cause an unpleasant commotion."

Surprised and confused, Stanley had been uncertain what to do. He had not been sure these were really FBI agents. Threats received in the past and dismissed as of no importance now came to mind. To avoid trouble for his waiting friends, Stanley had gone to them and excused himself: "I'm sorry, something unexpected has come up and I'll have to take that drink with you another time."

He had entered the waiting car, noting with relief that it headed for town, for he had felt that gangsters would probably have made for the open country. Asked if he had a gun or weapon on his person, Stanley had assured the men he never carried one, and they had accepted his word.

In the federal building, Stanley had been left alone in a small room. A young man had entered; identified himself as Mr. Gordon, special agent in charge of the case; and showed Stanley the warrant for his arrest. The charges were so ridiculous Stanley had burst into spontaneous laughter. He was accused of being both a Communist and an anarchist, two different things; and with concealing this from the immigration authorities at the time of his naturalization, thus committing fraud. It was a criminal indictment, calling for revocation of citizenship and a fine of five thousand dollars and/or five years in prison. Surprised by Stanley's unexpected reaction, Mr. Gordon had studied him carefully but had said nothing except that a doctor would examine him shortly. The doctor had paid particular attention to Stanley's ears, nose, and the soles of his feet, making written notations. Stanley had asked why this kind of examination, but the doctor had refused to say. Stanley had been allowed to dress and told to stand by the door, which had soon opened to reveal a crowd of press photographers, whose flash bulbs had flared with each step as Stanley was escorted down the hall. Among the press representatives he had recognized some from Lansing, their faces serious and questioning.

In another room, Mr. Gordon had been waiting. He had asked Stanley to be seated, inquired what brand of cigarettes he smoked, and then sent for some even though Stanley had insisted he was well supplied.

"How about sandwiches and coffee?"

"Thank you, I had just finished my dinner when your boys picked me up."

After coffee and cigarettes, Gordon had taken some papers from the desk in front of him and proceeded to interrogate Stanley until almost midnight. After what seemed an eternity of sparring back and forth, Gordon had said, "You're an intelligent man, Mr. Nowak, and could render our government a valuable service. After all, this country has treated you kindly, and you should seriously consider cooperating in return; otherwise, things might not go so well with you."

"Mr. Gordon, I refuse to be intimidated. I value the advice and opinions of my able attorneys and friends far more than any you may have to offer."

"Do you mind if I transcribe my notes?" Gordon had asked.

"Do as you like," Stanley had said, knowing it would be done anyway. After a few moments at a nearby typewriter, Gordon had handed him a statement to sign, amounting to a confession and utterly unlike the interrogation.

"Give me a copy for my attorney and I will do whatever he advises," Stanley had said.

Gordon had repeatedly urged him to sign the statement, but Stanley had stubbornly refused and demanded to see his attorney. At that very moment attorneys Goodman and Eden, along with Jack Raskin of the Civil Rights Federation, were in another FBI office where they had tried vainly to reach him all evening, while Stanley's repeated requests for permission to call me or his attorneys had been put off with "Later, not just now." Finally, at midnight, Gordon had allowed Stanley to call me. His voice was the most welcome sound I had ever heard. After that call to me, a different physician had examined him and, like the first, paid special attention to his ears, nose, and the soles of his feet. Stanley had concluded that this must be the manner in which the government protected itself from charges of coercion or mistreatment. Stanley was, after all, a state official, and the examinations had immediately preceded and followed his interrogation.

Frustrated and angry over the negative results of his questions, Gordon's facade of courtesy had disappeared: "You will have to spend the night in the county jail, Mr. Nowak, since the federal government has no prison facilities here. Also, I must insist on applying handcuffs, a regulation over which I have no control."

Enroute to the jail, Stanley's escorts had bought the evening edition of the *Detroit Free Press* for him. The front page article was by Hub George, who had represented the paper in Lansing. It was a good story. The accompanying photograph, considered one of Stanley's best, was used in subsequent election campaigns. At the county jail he had been fingerprinted and registered by fellow Democrats who knew him personally and received him with warmth and kindness. They had made sure he had whatever he needed. The cot in his cell was hard and narrow, but he had fallen asleep immediately from exhaustion.

The next morning he had been escorted, without handcuffs, to the marshal's office. From there, we had gone together to Judge Moinet's courtroom for the arraignment, and from there to Goodman's office, where Stanley was now relating yesterday's events to Goodman, Eden, and me. Stanley and the attorneys discussed plans for the defense, then he and I left.

On our way home from Goodman's office, we discussed the strange behavior of Marshal Barc. Stanley recalled his confidential chat with Barc following the 1938 election, when he had been urged to break with labor in order to advance politically. Both Barc and Lesinski had aided Stanley in his early campaigns, particularly that first one, when he had unwittingly served their purposes by ousting from office Joseph Roosevelt, who had posed a possible threat to their private hopes and schemes. As Stanley had been twice reelected, each time with a growing margin of votes approaching the number received by Lesinski for Congress, both Barc and Lesinski must have noted that fact uneasily. Stanley recalled with me one other occasion when Barc had become confidential, revealing that it was agreed between the two that if anything should happen to Lesinski or if he should decide not to run for office, Barc would run for Lesinski's post. Stanley had recognized this revelation as a warning not to reach for the office of Congressman himself. Though he had no such intent or desire, neither Barc nor Lesinski could know that. Barc's conduct this morning now became understandable as Stanley and I reviewed these things.

A press statement by Stanley appeared in the *Detroit Free Press* of 14 December, from which I quote:

> This indictment against me is an attempt by reactionary forces to use the Dept. of Justice to disrupt the unity of the people in the war effort.
>
> I have been organizing workers into labor unions . . . in the campaign . . . to increase war production; I have sold thousands of dollars worth of War Bonds; I have agitated for blood donations.
>
> In the American Slav Congress I have been active in uniting Americans of Slav descent in support of the government and the war effort. Further, I am chairman of the committee to investigate and expose Fifth-Column activities among the different groups of American Slavs.
>
> In the Michigan Senate I was responsible for introducing and obtaining passage of a resolution in both houses . . . supporting the foreign policy of President Roosevelt. I have introduced . . . many progressive measures, including one . . . to protect men in the armed forces against mortgage foreclosures because of debts.
>
> I introduced and was successful in passing in the Senate a bill to prohibit racketeering in the sale of jobs. I fought successfully for an increase in the benefits of unemployment compensation, workmen's compensation, and old-age pensions. During both terms in the Michigan Senate I have fought bitterly all anti–New Deal, anti-labor, and anti-democratic bills. . . .

By all these activities I have brought down upon my head the anger of anti-labor employers, reactionaries, and anti-war forces. . . .

The charge that I am a disbeliever in organized government is ridiculous in the face of my many activities on behalf of and as part of organized government.

Among the many reassuring letters coming to us was one from the internationally famous artist, Rockwell Kent, of Ausable Forks, New York, dated 17 December, in which he said, "It is too bad that the highest honor our Department of Justice can bestow continues to be the arrest of the most active and fearless partisans of labor and democracy. I send you a copy of a letter that I have addressed to Attorney-General Biddle." The people of our Twenty-first Senatorial District were indignant at Stanley's indictment and immediately established the Nowak Defense Committee. Members of the committee called on Attorney General Biddle in Washington on the eighteenth, to urge dismissal of charges against Stanley, as reported in the *Detroit News* of the nineteenth:

Biddle told the delegation he would consider their request and give his answer within "a day or so."

Included in the delegation were State Senator Charles C. Diggs, Sr.; John Zaremba, an international representative of the UAW-CIO; Mort Furay, state director of the State, County, and Municipal Workers (CIO); James Lindahl, Secretary of Packard Local 190 (UAW-CIO); Ernest Goodman, an attorney; and Dr. D. K. Yatich, a member of the Executive Board of the Michigan State Council of American Slav Congress.

It was also announced in Detroit that three national organizations will assist Nowak . . . the American Committee for Protection of Foreign-Born, the International Labor Defense, and the National Federation for Constitutional Liberties.

"The charge against Senator Nowak can only be explained as persecution because of his pro-war, pro-labor activities and record," the organizations' joint statement said.

Outraged by the indictment, and recognizing it as a political move, many people spoke out publicly. In a joint statement to the press on the twenty-third, UAW president R. J. Thomas and UAW secretary-treasurer George F. Addes said

This seems to us an attempt to intimidate the foreign-born and is a coldly legalistic means of attempting to get rid of political enemies. As a matter of fact, the prosecution was instituted within five days of the time in which it would have been outlawed and we have a strong suspicion that it comes as an expression of the increasing boldness of the sources of reaction in the United States.

The UAW-CIO will support the cause of Senator Nowak in this

prosecution, not as an individual, but as an example of reactionary persecution.

Rumors appeared in the press that Stanley might not be permitted to assume the Senate seat to which he had just been reelected. One of the first to protest this was Republican senator Joseph Baldwin, Stanley's frequent opponent in the Senate. The *Detroit News* of 25 December quoted Baldwin: "Senator Nowak has been elected to the Senate by his constituents three times, and the charge that he was a Communist, which is the basis for this indictment, was voiced in Nowak's first campaign. The Senate did nothing about it then, so I see no reason why it should now. A man is innocent until he is convicted under our form of government." Baldwin had written to Stanley personally on the fifteenth: "I observed in one of the papers tonight a report to the effect that there might be an attempt to deny you your seat in the Senate when that body convenes on Jan. 6th. If anyone has such an idea, they have forgotten the basic doctrine of the presumption of innocence until proof of guilt. I want you to know that, as far as I am personally concerned, I shall resist any prejudgment of your case. And I say that as one who has consistently opposed the influence of the Communist Party."

The 25 December issue of the National Maritime Union (NMU) publication, the *Pilot*, reported that temporary headquarters for Stanley's defense had been set up in the NMU Hall and that attorney Ernest Goodman was to be the chief defense counsel. The paper also reported that resolutions condemning Stanley's indictment were coming in from many sources—labor, political organizations, and professional groups, some with sizable donations. The article further reported that NMU agent E. J. Cunningham blasted the charges against Stanley and declared the indictment "another Bridges case . . . an attempt to deprive a man of his citizenship because he is an outstanding labor leader."

On the afternoon of the twenth-seventh, over three hundred people attended a conference called by the Nowak Defense Committee in the Ukrainian Temple on Martin Street near Michigan Avenue. Speaking at the conference were Percy Llewellyn, vice president of Ford Local No. 600; James Lindahl of Packard Local; and Dave Miller, president of Cadillac Division of Local No. 174, which sent five hundred dollars for Stanley's defense. Plans were made for a larger conference on 3 January 1943 to rally citywide support. In reporting this 27 December conference, the English page of *Glos ludowy* of 2 January had this to say:

> The call was sponsored by a long list of men in public life and the labor movement, including Senators Charles S. Blondy and Charles C. Diggs, Sr. who is temporary chairman of the proposed Jan. 3rd conference; Pro-

bate Judge Patrick H. O'Brien; State Labor Commissioner Harold A. Bledsoe; Principal Walter Allmendinger of the Greenfield Park School; the Rev. Charles A. Hill of Hartford Ave. Baptist Church; Vice-President Arthur Bowman of the Young Republicans; attorneys Ernest Goodman, A. M. Lebedeff, and C. LeBron Simmons; Editor Louis F. Martin of the Michigan Chronicle; Secretary George Pirinsky of the Michigan Slav Congress; and Executive Secretary Jack Raskin of the Civil Rights Federation, who is temporary secretary of the conference.

Among labor sponsors are Regional Director Leo Lamotte of the UAW-CIO; President George W. Miller of the UAW Tool & Die Council; President Harry Campbell of the CIO Downriver Council; President Tom Curtin of United Steelworkers Local 1299; President John Hudson of Budd Wheel Local 306; President Ned D. Coleman of Fiber Local 205; most of the officers and building chairmen of Ford Local, including Recording Secretary Shelton Tappes, who is temporary vice-chairman of the conference, as well as many UAW international representatives and other local officers. Recording Secretary James Lindahl of Packard Local is chairman of the conference labor committee.

Senator Nowak's defense has also been indorsed by the UAW-CIO International Executive Board; Detroit and Wayne County CIO Council; the UAW Tool and Die Council; Ford Local 600, and many other local unions as well as by civil organizations.

The *Detroit News* of 28 December quoted from a letter written by Paul St. Marie, president of Ford Local No. 600, to Senator George P. McCallum, president pro tem of the Michigan Senate and to Lieutenant-Governor-Elect Eugene C. Keyes: "Many sincere persons believe Nowak is the victim of unfair persecution because of his political beliefs, or because of his connection with organized labor. It would be a destructive thing to the war effort and to the morale of Michigan workers, were they to become convinced that their government, in the midst of a war for freedom of speech and freedom of opinion, should persecute anyone for holding opinions, no matter how false or unpopular these opinions may be." St. Marie's letter also asked that Stanley be seated pending the outcome of his case in the courts.

We were heartened by the willingness of so many prominent people to speak out publicly in our behalf. This and the overwhelming turnout at the 27 December conference and the vigorous enthusiasm displayed in planning the 3 January conference to come made us aware that we were not alone in our battle. This gave us the courage and the needed strength to face the year 1943, with all its problems.

The 3 January conference drew over five hundred people to Hotel Statler in Stanley's behalf. Almost every CIO union was represented, also many nationality and Black organizations, ministers, professional people, and legislators. In addition to Republican senator Clarence Reid, the gathering heard council member George Edwards (later a member of the federal court of appeals in Cincinnati and still later a member of Michigan's supreme court) and probate judge Patrick H. O'Brien, who declared, "I recommended Senator Nowak for citizenship. I've never been prouder of anything I did in my life. . . . Senator Nowak is as good an American as there is in the United States today. . . . This indictment is an outrage not only against Senator Nowak but also against every liberty-loving American." UAW secretary-treasurer George F. Addes said, "If Nowak is allowed to be railroaded, many trade union leaders will be subjected to the same treatment."

Out of this conference came a citywide Nowak Defense Committee, which merged with the one already established in our senatorial district. Congressman George Sadowski was named honorary chairman, and George Addes chairman. Vice chairmen elected were state senator Charles C. Diggs, Sr.; UAW vice president Richard T. Frankensteen; Percy Llewellyn, then chairman of the Ford National Council UAW; Judge Patrick H. O'Brien; Wayne County CIO council president Pat Quinn; Professor John Shepard of the University of Michigan; and Dr. D. K. Yatich, vice president of the American Slav Congress.

Labor was the backbone of the defense. Resolutions and wires from various international and local unions poured into the office of the U.S. attorney general, Francis J. Biddle, branding the move against Stanley as a frame-up instigated by enemies of labor and of unity in the war against Hitlerism. Professional and business people, Black leaders and organizations, the foreign-born, and members of the clergy joined labor to demand that the proceedings against Stanley be dropped.

I accompanied Stanley to Lansing for the opening of the legislature in 1943. He presented himself for the swearing-in ceremony without incident. Every senator had received a letter from Gerald L. K. Smith, noted red-baiter and fascist demagogue, branding Stanley a Communist and naming me as the real "red" in the family. Smith had also addressed a petition to the Senate, protesting the seating of Stanley and demanding the right to speak before that body. The petition was referred to committee and appropriately "buried." As for the letters, these were also taken care of in a suitable manner. Many of the senators called either Stanley or me, sometimes both, to their desks. "Have you seen this?" they asked. "Well, this is what I think of it." The senators then very ceremoniously tore the letter to shreds and deposited them in the wastebasket.

In his column in the *Michigan Chronicle* of 9 January Rev. Horace A. White wrote,

> In order to keep the common people from really embracing a liberal movement after the war, the reactionaries start now to discredit the liberal leadership.
>
> Everybody knows that Stanley Nowak has been a liberal. He has fought for the common people always. He has believed in the idea of equality for all people. In his mind this meant the Negro, too, with no reservations. Stanley Nowak has sought to change the government of our country. If he had not he would not be worthy of its citizenship. . . . There is not one bit of evidence that he ever advocated any change in the Constitution. Nowak has been liberal and many times left wing. Good indeed. Progress for the people comes only when we have a clear cut clash of opinions.
>
> Labor has not had a stronger friend than Nowak. . . . Then Nowak becomes a symbol, around which people in the State of Michigan can rally for a peace that the people can believe in. Let us not miss the chance.

At a meeting of the Nowak Defense Committee on 16 January George Addes read a telegram that had been sent to President Roosevelt by thirty-two delegates from all provinces of Canada, meeting in Toronto the week before, condemning Nowak's indictment and asking that charges be dropped. Addes promised to ask for cooperation in Stanley's defense during a scheduled tour to midwestern cities to visit UAW-CIO leaders. He announced that petitions in Stanley's behalf were being circulated, with a goal of 125 thousand signatures by early February, when a mass rally would be held and a delegation elected to take the petitions to President Roosevelt.

At this 16 January meeting, many union members reported that their local's edition of the UAW paper was devoting considerable space to Stanley, and Packard Local members reported that their local had issued a special four-page supplement on the case, with twenty-five thousand additional copies printed for distribution by the Nowak Defense Committee. Contributions came from many UAW-CIO locals and from the State, County, and Municipal Workers Local No. 78.

Support came from other sources. A Polish banquet on the twentieth attracted three hundred fifty people and raised defense money. The Amalgamated Clothing Workers CIO named Jack Ellstein of its joint board to the executive committee of the Nowak Defense Committee.

Then, as suddenly as it had begun, the case came to an end. Out for a walk in Lansing the evening of 9 February, Stanley and I picked up the Lansing edition of the *Detroit Free Press* to find the banner headline, "U.S. Drops Fraud Indictment against Nowak." The accompanying article laid bare the chagrin of the antilabor elements who had hoped to end Stanley's political career. It revealed that John C. Lehr, U.S. district attorney, had refused the request of the Justice Department to quash the indictment.

Forced to go over Lehr's head, U.S. attorney-general Biddle sent a special representative, Henry A. Schweinhaut, to Detroit to handle the matter.

At the following morning's Senate session, 10 February, Stanley rose to a point of personal privilege, mounted the platform at the invitation of Senate secretary Fred I. Chase, and read a statement that he and I had sat up late to prepare the night before, from which I quote briefly:

> Since I have been vindicated of the charges made against me by Attorney-General Biddle's dismissal of the indictment, may I now take this opportunity to thank my colleagues . . . for the fine American attitude you have adopted toward me, namely, that a man is innocent until proven guilty. I appreciate your confidence in my integrity and loyalty to our Constitution and our government.
>
> May I further thank you for the stand you have taken in defense of democracy and justice by ignoring the slanderous charges made against Mrs. Nowak and myself by this infamous disrupter of national unity, this pro-fascist, Gerald L. K. Smith. You have shown that the Michigan Senate, like the rest of the people of our country, does not fall for tricks borrowed from Herr Goebbels.

The Senators broke a long-standing rule with their immediate and spontaneous applause. By unanimous vote, Stanley's statement was ordered printed in the *Senate Journal* for that day. After the session, his colleagues came to congratulate both of us. It was a beautiful moment.

On 16 February, at Local No. 157 in Detroit, a rally celebrated our victory. R. J. Thomas, Dick Frankensteen, and George Addes spoke, hailing our triumph over the forces of reaction. The main speaker was Leo Pressman, CIO general counsel. Many friends embraced and congratulated us. Stanley addressed the rally briefly in our behalf: "The thanks of the defense committee, myself, and Mrs. Nowak go out to all who assisted in bringing the facts of the case to the attention of President Roosevelt, Attorney General Biddle, and those in position to see that justice was done. We are grateful to the unions which took a stand, to the civic and nationality organizations, the clergy, the newspapers, and all individuals who gave money and effort. . . . The antiwar forces, . . . in singling me out for attack, apparently thought they could split labor by playing upon and exaggerating differences that arise at times within the labor movement as within any democratic movement. . . . This attack upon me served, instead, as a unifying force far greater than anything that has happened in the ranks of labor for a long time. Labor made answer in unmistakable terms. This applies not only to organized labor but also to . . . the leaders of the Democratic party and such Republicans as senators Reid and Baldwin, also to the leaders of nationality groups, churches, and professional people."

With all this now behind him, Nowak immediately plunged into greater activity toward unifying U.S. citizens behind the war effort. He was one of the signers of the call for a conference by the Polish panel of the Michigan Slav Congress for the afternoon of the twenty-first at Dom Polski. Almost every prominent Polish leader in Detroit and Hamtramck signed the call, with two notable exceptions—Federal Marshal John Barc and Congressman John Lesinski.

The 21 February conference drew 97 delegates from labor, political, and professional groups, who planned a larger conference in March. On 14 March at the Book-Cadillac Hotel, 224 delegates and 405 registered guests attended. Also present were Frank N. Isbey and Colonel G. E. Strong. A collection of $1,028 was taken for the Polish Army, and greetings sent by shortwave radio after the meeting to the Yugoslav, Czech, and Polish partisans. This was done through the U.S. State Department in cooperation with the Slav congress.

I went with Stanley to New York, where he was honored with forty-two other foreign-born citizens by a United Nations in America dinner, sponsored by the American Committee for Protection of Foreign-born, at Hotel Biltmore on 17 April. Leo Krzycki was one of the honorees. Famous guests included film actor Edward G. Robinson and authors Maurice Hindus and Stefan Heym. Chairman of the committee sponsoring the dinner was Donald Ogden Stewart, author and Hollywood scriptwriter. Among the more than two hundred sponsors were Orson Welles and Grace Moore, the opera star.

On the twenty-fifth we rejoiced to see in the *Detroit Free Press* the following article by James C. Haswell, whom we knew in Lansing:

> His is the unwelcome voice of the consumer, the employee, the welfare client, the pedestrian. His counsel is the counsel of the Little Man, the fellow about whom all the laws—in the last analysis—are made.
>
> . . . It is a fact that Nowak never has preached revolution or anything approaching revolution in the state senate. He never has expressed dissent with the principles of American government. He *has* preached a gospel of giving the victim a better break.
>
> He has argued for more liberal compensation for injured workmen, larger benefits for the unemployed, more adequate pensions for the aged, minimum wages and maximum hours, regulation of working conditions for children and women, and he has argued against using welfare to drive wages down.
>
> . . . He is a labor organizer, he is foreign-born, he's a Democrat, he comes from the big city's working class, he's not a business man, nor a property spokesman.
>
> By insistence and repetition he has hammered home his philosophy until when he rises to speak in the senate today most of his fellow-members well know what he's going to say. He's told them until it hurts.

16 A Race Riot and a Graft Grand Jury

In the spring of 1943 Stanley began working for the State, County, and Municipal Workers Association (SCMWA) and continued through that summer, along with his work in the UAW Polish Trade Union Committee and the Slav congress. I worked as secretary-receptionist for a physician in the General Motors Building. Each morning I walked with Elissa to Sherrill School, about three blocks away, where she stayed in the day-care center established for working mothers during the war. Then I boarded the Tireman bus to the GM Building. After work, I walked to the school from the bus and brought her home.

On the morning of 21 June Stanley left early for his office without reading the morning paper or listening to the radio. He had noticed nothing unusual on the way but found the office in turmoil.

"What's all the excitement about?" he asked.

"Stanley! Where have you been? Didn't you hear the radio this morning?"

"No, I left too early and had no time."

"Well, we have a race riot in Detroit!"

As substantiated by later press reports, Stanley learned that a fight had erupted the night before between a Black and a white man at the Jefferson Avenue end of the Belle Isle Bridge. Belle Isle is one of Detroit's oldest parks, on an island in the Detroit River. The fight had spread through Gabriel Richard Park and then to the north, east, and west sides of Detroit. Stanley immediately phoned me to stay home and keep Elissa out of school. Although all was quiet in our neighborhood, I did so.

The State, County, and Municipal Workers Union, for which Stanley worked, was vitally concerned because many of its members were Black. As a legislator and labor man, Stanley was invited by Mayor Edward J. Jeffries to an emergency meeting at the Lucy Thurman Branch YWCA, and the union sent both Stanley and his coworker, Mort Furay, to attend the mayor's meeting. Others present were Rev. Ellsworth Smith of the Detroit Council of Churches, Senator Charles C. Diggs, Sr., UAW president R. J. Thomas, Jack Raskin of the Civil Rights Congress, and representatives of other local unions, both Black and white. At the mayor's request, Rev. Mr. Smith took Stanley, Rev. Owen Knox, and other ministers with him in his car to see what was happening and report back. They drove up and down Woodward Avenue, the main thoroughfare dividing the city into east and west. It was thronged with thousands of white people watching like beasts of prey for any luckless Black person on streetcars or in private automobiles.

Near the Detroiter Hotel, Stanley's group saw a mob halt an old touring car driven by a Black, overturn it, remove the cap to the gas tank, throw a match into the gathering pool of gasoline, and gleefully watch the flames devour the car. The driver had disappeared somewhere. Within a few blocks at least six overturned and flaming cars lay in the street. Fire trucks came to put out each fire and then left. "Oh!" said Stanley bitterly. "If just once the trucks would turn their hoses on the mob, they would disperse. Why don't they? Why?" The press later reported about twenty cars left burning in the street along a six-block stretch of Woodward north of Peterboro and on adjoining streets and alleys.

Stanley's group turned off Woodward into a side street to encounter a crowd of frenzied whites spilling into the street from the sidewalk, shouting and gesticulating excitedly. "Catch him! Kill him, the nigger bastard!" they cried out as an elderly man dashed across the street in front of a car and was knocked to the ground. Before Rev. Mr. Smith could stop the car to aid him, the victim managed to pick himself up and drag himself into an alley, the crowd in pursuit. Evidently he escaped, for they moved aimlessly about and soon returned in search of other prey.

All afternoon, Stanley's group moved through white sections of the city just west of Woodward. They saw such scenes of hysterical, vicious hatred and violence as they had never dreamed possible in our city, particularly at that moment when unity was so desperately needed in the war effort. Anyone trying to assist a victim was also set upon and clubbed. The most horrible part of it was the sense of helplessness and frustration at not being able to help anyone or do anything.

Stanley's group sometimes found a quiet place where they could stop for coffee and listen to the latest radio reports. They heard accounts of pawnshops broken into and looted of guns and ammunition. The mayor at once ordered all pawnshops and hardware stores to remove firearms and knives from windows and lock them away. Mayor Jeffries appealed by radio for the UAW-CIO to order workers in all plants to stay home. He closed all liquor stores on the east side. Transportation through near-east side areas halted after streetcars had been stopped there. After more than twelve hours of rioting, news came that patients were arriving at hospitals at the rate of one every two minutes and the already overcrowded emergency centers had to convert storage rooms and extra space into additional emergency quarters. The call went out for more nurses and medical volunteers. The radio reported state troops and auxiliary police mobilized by afternoon, and in some cases their cars were surrounded and officers attacked. Afternoon shifts were reported as minimal in some plants engaged in war production. Hundreds of Ford workers reportedly left for the day as they received calls from harried families.

Sick from what they had seen, Stanley and his companions returned to city hall around 4:00 P.M. to report to the mayor. There they found Cadillac Square, between the old city hall and the old county building, packed with milling, murderous thousands—estimated later by the press to be around ten thousand—and vicious anti-Jewish pamphlets were being passed among the rioters. Trolleys were pulled from streetcars bearing Ford workers from the Rouge plant, the doors forced open, and Black workers dragged out and set upon as the police stood and watched. Stanley and his friends had never before experienced such horror and utter helplessness as they looked on in the face of that mad mob and police indifference.

Near the old city hall, someone spotted a Black man leaving the building, and the white mob immediately started for him. A Black deputy sheriff emerged from the doorway of the building, drew his revolver, and faced the bloodthirsty rabble. "I'll shoot the first one to lay a hand on him," he shouted as he approached the intended victim. Seeing the gun the crowd gave way. He waved them away with his revolver: "Now get out of here, all of you, before I turn loose with this thing." The deputy sheriff took the intended victim into the building for safety.

Stanley's group couldn't reach the mayor, so they continued to tour the city until the National Guard began to arrive about 9:00 P.M. Then they disbanded and went home. Although quiet had prevailed in our neighborhood, I was heartsick and tense from the radio reports to which I had listened all day. Stanley's account of the viciousness and diabolic hatred he had witnessed did not help me. We could only continue to listen to the radio reports and await developments. By 11:00 P.M. federal troops had things generally in control, and quiet began to settle.

On 22 June six thousand federal troops were bivouacked at strategic points in the city, such as high school grounds and public library lawns. The *Detroit Free Press* for 22 June reported 30 of Detroit's 176 elementary schools closed since noon of the day before. Sherrill School was closed and I stayed home from work with Elissa.

By the twenty-third, the press reported absenteeism among the sixty thousand Black workers in war plants, ranging from 50 percent to 90 percent, and an exceptionally high rate of 25-percent white absenteeism. The War Production Board pleaded with the UAW-CIO to persuade members to return to work, as war production had dropped 15 percent to 50 percent with absenteeism still soaring.

At the mayor's office that morning Stanley and Rev. Messrs. Smith and Knox, with leaders from the Black community—Rev. Charles A. Hill, Rev. Horace White, Senator Charles C. Diggs, Sr., and others—met to assess the situation. That morning's *Free Press* had reported more than seven hundred wounded and more than half a dozen near death. The total number of dead was reported as twenty-nine, and property damage not yet estimated. Stanley and his group reported what they had witnessed the day before. Bitter complaints were made of police indifference or brutality against Black people. It was said that many Blacks were shot, and some killed, by police. Rev. Mr. Smith and Stanley took several people with them to the morgue to view the bodies of victims. There were about twenty-one Blacks and only one white person. The latter had been hit by a stone while passing through a Black area, but all the Black victims had been shot from the back, their bodies riddled with bullets. A delegation went to see the Wayne County prosecutor, William E. Dowling, to demand an investigation of police conduct, which he promised.

By 24 June Governor Kelly eased curfew restrictions and reopened Belle Isle. He also appointed a fact-finding committee of public officials and called for an early report. Congressman Dies was threatening to come to Detroit to start an investigation, and Detroit newspapers and civic leaders joined in asking him to stay away. Mayor Jeffries appointed a twelve-member interracial committee to study the situation. Funerals were being held for victims. All these things were fully reported in the three Detroit dailies.

By the twenty-seventh the city was abnormally quiet, but it was reported by the press that only three hundred white and two hundred Black families had visited Belle Isle, compared to 100 thousand the week before. By the twenty-eighth Governor Kelly had lifted virtually all restrictions. Federal troops were to remain another week but had not withdrawn by

5 July; they were reportedly training and organizing Michigan state troops. By the tenth only about fourteen hundred of the four thousand federal troops were reported remaining. The furor gradually died down. I had stayed home from work for a few days; and as I returned to the office and walked with Elissa to the day-care center, I found other anxious-faced mothers of both races walking their children to school. There had been no trouble in our neighborhood, although we were only one block from the Black residential area. By 19 August the riots were virtually over and everyone seemed ready to let the matter rest, as evidenced by a statement in the *Detroit Times* that day: "Without even taking a formal vote, common council denied a new request from Mayor Jeffries for a grand Jury to investigate the race riots."

Meanwhile, the war in Europe raged on. On 18 July at Keyworth Stadium in Hamtramck, in the broiling heat, almost five hundred people gathered to demonstrate the unity of Michigan Slavs and to celebrate the allied invasion of Italy's Nazi-occupied mainland, the Balkans, France, and northern Europe. A huge thirty-ton tank, purchased by the Michigan Slav Congress and christened *The Michigan Slav* rumbled out of the stadium to wild cheers from the audience; and $130 thousand worth of war bonds were sold, according to *Glos ludowy.* Officers of the Michigan Slav Congress, including Stanley, spoke, and Shelton Tappes, secretary of Ford Local No. 600, brought greetings of solidarity from 50 thousand Ford workers and 250 thousand Blacks in Michigan. He received a standing ovation. John Yaksich, a young Croatian-American hero of Guadalcanal, said that soldiers at the front had been concerned about the riots and that on his return to the front he would tell the boys that all was well and that the U.S. Slavs were behind them. Colorfully costumed Poles and Ukrainians danced and sang spirited songs, and it was a great day for Hamtramck and Michigan Slavs.

The *Detroit News* of 21 August carried an item that interested both Stanley and me but that posed no threat to us—or so we thought at the time. Attorney General Herbert J. Rushton had drafted a petition for a one-man grand jury to investigate alleged corruption in the legislature. Rushton was quoted as saying, "I hope to present the petition Monday to Judge Leland W. Carr, presiding in the Ingham Circuit Court. When it is approved I will make up a list of persons I want to subpoena and will start work as quickly as possible, perhaps Wednesday."

Subsequent news articles revealed that by the twenty-eighth several legislators had been interrogated, and that the state police would be serving subpoenas to witnesses to appear on the thirtieth.

On the evening of 8 September a subpoena was served to Stanley at our home, ordering him to be in Lansing the next morning. To his surprise, it was Wayne County prosecutor Clarence Dowling who interrogated him in a routine manner concerning the date of our marriage and where it had occurred and about our income. Stanley was released, and we assumed that was the end of the matter.

Thus far, 1943 had been exhausting for both Stanley and me. It had begun with the fight to dismiss the indictment threatening his citizenship. Then had come the excitement and anxiety of the race riot, and Stanley's organizing work. A friend offered the haven of a cottage on a lake not far from Detroit, which we gratefully accepted. We left 12 September with four-year-old Elissa. My mother preferred to remain at home with her city comforts. My sister was to keep close track of her as always. Only my mother and the owners of the cottage knew where we would be and how to get in touch with us.

That night we were roused from sleep by loud knocking at the cottage door. Stanley got up and opened it to find two state troopers with flashlights. "Are you Senator Stanley Nowak?" asked one.

"Yes, what can I do for you?"

"I have a grand jury subpoena for you," the officer said, handing it to Stanley. "You are to be in Lansing tomorrow morning at nine o'clock."

"But how can I?" Stanley protested. "We just got here. I can't leave my family alone here without transportation. Can this be postponed a week?"

"I'm afraid not," said the officer. "The subpoena says you are to be in Lansing tomorrow morning. If you are not, then we will have to come and get you."

"Okay!" grumped Stanley.

Neither of us slept much that night. We were up by daylight, breakfasted hurriedly, and headed for Detroit. At home we found a telegram announcing that Stanley's sister, Connie, was dying of cancer in Chicago. She was the sister who had mothered and comforted him after his mother's death in Poland and who had brought him to the United States at the age of ten. He knew he must get to Chicago. He took the telegram with him and left for Lansing. Later, he related to me what happened.

When he arrived at the court house in Lansing, newsmen we had known since his first Senate term in 1939 gathered around him in surprise! "Nowak! Why are you here?"

"I haven't the slightest idea," Stanley replied. "I have to wait and see."

Kim Sigler emerged from the grand jury room and took Stanley into one of the smaller offices. He was an attorney from Hastings and Battle Creek, Michigan, a law partner of Judge Leland W. Carr, and apparently assisting in the grand jury proceedings. He was a dashing, colorful figure, commanding immediate attention with his flamboyant dress and speech. In the little office where he took Stanley, he wasted no time on preliminaries.

"Senator," he began, "we have investigated you thoroughly, and your record is clean as a whistle."

"So what am I doing here?" Stanley asked.

"I need your help, Senator."

"For what?"

"To clean up this mess in Lansing. Surely you must know who was taking bribes and who was handing them out. You could render a real service to Michigan by telling us what you know."

"Well, first, Mr. Sigler, one has to be on the inside to know about such things. Since, as you have stated, my record is clean, you should know that I have had no dealing with the lobbyists and therefore no knowledge of who offered what to whom. I don't know anything that would be of any value to you in your investigation. And second, I am not an investigator or prosecutor. That is not my function or responsibility."

Frustrated and angry, Sigler immediately put Stanley on the witness stand and grilled him mercilessly for several hours. Stanley said later that the questions seeming most important to Sigler were those concerning the year and place of our marriage and that Sigler was unhappy with the answers Stanley gave him. He finally gave up and told Stanley to remain in Lansing for possible future questioning.

Stanley handed Sigler the telegram from Chicago, with the words: "You know, Mr. Sigler, that I am not about to run away; and I would like to see my sister while she still lives. On my return, you know where you can reach me." Sigler's manner changed as he read the wire, and he became all solicitous concern: "I am very sorry about this, Senator. Of course, you must go see your sister. As a matter of fact, there is a train for Chicago this afternoon. I will have someone drive you to the station immediately." Surprised at Sigler's sudden change, Stanley soon found himself aboard the train for Chicago. He had phoned me before leaving, so I would know where he would be.

After making sure that Stanley was on that train, Sigler issued a subpoena for me, which the state police delivered that evening. I was to be in Lansing at 9:00 A.M. the next day. Apparently Sigler wanted to make sure that Stanley and I would have no opportunity to compare notes on the interrogation before I would arrive in Lansing. Josephine Polityka, treasurer of the Senator Nowak Club, phoned and told me that she and another club member whose name I cannot recall had been subpoenaed. We agreed to meet at the railroad station in the morning and travel together to Lansing. She had been instructed to bring with her the financial records of the Senator Nowak Club. Much perturbed, I phoned Stanley at his sister's home in Chicago. He laughed, for he now understood Sigler's concern that he should get to Chicago. I was terrified at the prospect of being interrogated in court. "What shall I do, Stanley?" I asked.

"Just tell them the truth, Margaret, no matter what they ask. We have nothing to fear from the truth."

This didn't comfort me greatly, and I didn't sleep much that night. I met Mrs. Polityka at the train in the morning, and she had with her the receipt books and check stubs of the club. I told her what Stanley had said and tried to make her feel at ease in spite of my qualms.

Clarence Dowling interrogated me. I noticed, as had Stanley (so he told me later), that the date and place of our wedding was of concern to the grand jury. Dowling was unhappy with my answers and seemed puzzled. From questions he asked, I gathered they found it incredible that we lived on such a small income; and when Dowling dismissed me from the witness stand he said a state trooper would drive both Mrs. Polityka and myself home and that I should give the officer our income tax records and check stubs. I was glad I had paid for everything by check, which made it simple to trace our financial records, both deposits and expenditures. The records of the Nowak club were left with the grand jury until the staff could go over them.

In the meantime, in Chicago, Stanley contacted a physician we knew and respected. She confirmed the medical diagnosis and helped bring comfort and relief to Connie before her death on 9 November.

We heard no more from the grand jury, although it would continue its work through 1945. We later learned there had been some confusion over the name *Nowak.* There was a Francis J. Nowak elected to the House the same year Stanley had been elected to the Senate. There were rumors that a Nowak was married during the legislative term and that his home had been furnished by unknown sources. As far as the grand jury and the legislature were concerned, the Nowak that immediately came to mind was Stanley. However, the date and place of our marriage did not fit the other information they had, and neither did our finances or lifestyle. The other Nowak was later indicted, tried, and convicted; and served time in prison. Naturally, no one ever apologized over the mix-up, but there must have been some red faces and some disappointed people who would have been delighted to catch Stanley in their net. During the next two years, forty-one people were tried and went to prison as a result of the graft grand jury, and twelve others walked into court and pleaded guilty. A number of those indicted suffered strokes and several died.

The year 1943 had been one to remember, not necessarily with pleasure; but the holidays found us free from personal anxiety, with no threat hanging over us; and we were able to enjoy the season as we had not done for a long time. My brother Dan, home on furlough, brought his banjo, and brother Harry brought his guitar when we gathered on Christmas eve. We had a bass, baritone, tenor, soprano, and alto. Apparently we sang with all our hearts that night, for our next-door neighbor phoned to ask us to open a window so they could hear us better. Instead, we invited them over for a drink and to sing along. For once, the year ended happily!

17 A Visit to Poland

> Warsaw, in the past regarded as the "Paris of Eastern Europe," today is its Pompeii. . . . Never have I imagined such destruction possible. . . . All of Warsaw is a vast cemetery. It is estimated that the city's ruins still hide some 100,000 dead.
>
> —Philip Adler, *Detroit News,* 11 Dec. 1944

Stanley's work in the UAW Polish Trade Union Committee, the American Committee for Protection of Foreign-born, and his occasional organizing assignments continued. The main focus of his attention and effort through these channels was directed toward winning the war. The increasing tempo of the war, the growth of reactionary and fascist elements in the United States, along with the vigorous resistance to his trend by democratic and liberal organizations—all gave us little time to take note of events in our personal lives.

Late in 1943 in Springfield, Massachusetts Fr. Stanislaw Orlemanski had founded the Kosciuszko League to provide moral and financial support for the heroic Kosciuszko Division of the Polish Army in the USSR and for the Polish underground. Stanley participated in founding a branch of the Kosciuszko League in Detroit, as announced in *Glos ludowy* on 8 January 1944. On the fifteenth *Glos ludowy* announced the formation of the Dąbrowski Division of the Polish Army in the USSR, which left for the battlefront to join forces with the Kosciuszko Division in the fight for Poland's liberation.

When Poland was crushed in September 1939, the Polish generals and government officials had fled to England to form the Polish government-in-exile. The remnants of the military forces in Poland had found themselves without an airforce or weapons and unable to continue their fight. Large numbers of them had made their way to that part of Poland taken over by the Soviet Union, where they had been received and taken to safety deep within the Soviet Union. During the Nazi occupation, Polish males were executed or consigned to slave labor within Poland or taken to Germany as slave workers on German farms or work establishments. Many Poles went underground to fight the Nazis within Poland, but large numbers continued to escape into Russian-occupied Poland to safety. These Polish refugees were trained, armed, and organized into the Kosciuszko and Dąbrowski divisions within the Soviet Union, as previously mentioned. They marched beside Soviet soldiers to liberate Poland in 1944. When Stanley visited Poland later, in 1945, he met and talked with some of these Polish veterans of the Kosciuszko and Dąbrowski divisions and learn how they had fled to the Soviet Union and how the Soviet Army had fought beside them in Poland's liberation. When I visited Poland with Stanley much later, in 1958, we learned that 600 thousand Russian soldiers lie buried in Polish soil and visited a huge cemetery where Russian and Polish soldiers lay next to each other on the site where they fell in the battle to free Poland. But I am ahead of my story.

At Chadsey High School in Detroit on 30 January 1944 Stanley chaired a meeting and introduced to the overflow crowd Rev. Fr. Stanislaw Orlemanski, founder of the Kosciuszko League. Together they spoke at another rally at Dodge Local Hall in Hamtramck. At both meetings, Orlemanski spoke for a new Poland free from aristocratic repression. The eastern front was still the center of the war. After Germany's defeat at Stalingrad, the Red Army launched a new offensive and, with the Polish legions, liberated the Polish city of Lublin on 21 July. There the National Committee of Liberation came into existence, consisting of the Polish Workers party, the Polish Socialist party, the Peasant party, and the Democratic party. By 29 July, according to *Glos ludowy,* the Red Army and the Polish legions were within fifty miles of Warsaw, and a fusion was formed with the Polish underground and Polish refugees from Russia. The United Polish Army was established under the command of General Rola Zymierski, incorporating the Polish Army of General Zygmunt Berling, 100-thousand strong, with the underground army. This guaranteed that no profascist government would be established with the old aristocratic elements. The struggle would continue between the people in Poland and the London government, reflected in the United States among the Polish-born.

The July primary election in Detroit gave Stanley a vote of 11,468 compared to a total of 7,325 for all his opponents combined. The November election gave Stanley a total of 95,944 votes compared to the combined total of 59,982 for his four opponents. On 12 April 1945 President Franklin Roosevelt died, and we mourned his passing along with millions of others who felt his loss. He had restored Stanley's and my faith in the political process, and there were changes in our lives and in society that we recognized as due to his leadership. On the twenty-first, in Lansing, Stanley's colleagues elected him Democratic floor leader.

Perhaps the most momentous event in human history occurred on 6 August with the dropping of the atom bomb from a U.S. B-29 bomber upon the Japanese city of Hiroshima. Although Japan was already on the verge of surrender, a second bomb was dropped on Nagasaki on the ninth. The horrible and devastating effects of the second bomb rivaled those of the first. On the 14th the Japanese government surrendered.

Following the recognition of Poland's provisional government on 5 July by the U.S., and the establishment of relations with Warsaw, the new Polish embassy opened in Washington on 15 September. Oskar Lange became Poland's ambassador to the United States. He had been a professor at the University of Chicago, where we had met him, active in Polish affairs in the United States.

In Detroit on 23 September Stanley and I attended a conference at the Book-Cadillac Hotel where fifty-five delegates representing thirty-three organizations, along with over two hundred observers, came to hail the recognition of Poland's new government and explore ways to aid the Polish people. Stanley was one of the speakers. Full support was given the conference by the Wayne County CIO council and local unions, both AFL and CIO. Philip Adler, foreign correspondent for the *Detroit News*, announced at the conference that his paper would help promote a broad campaign to obtain clothing, shoes, soap, food, and other needed items for Poland and to help establish a national committee for that purpose. John Lovett, executive secretary of the Michigan Manufacturers Association, sent a wire pledging the aid of his organization in Poland's reconstruction.

Stanley was elected national chairman for 1946 at a conference of the American Committee for Protection of Foreign-born on 20 October in New York City.

The weekend of 10 November was a busy one for us, when Poland's new vice minister of agriculture, Michael Szyszko and his wife, Sofia, visited Detroit. As a state legislator, Stanley accompanied the pair throughout the weekend. It was typical of the new Poland that Szyszko, son of a poor Polish peasant, now held at the age of thirty-three an important government post. He had been a colonel in the underground resistance army during the Nazi occupation, then later organized the Workers Militia of the Socialist party, a section of the Polish People's Army.

There was a press conference that morning, followed by a conference with leading trade union figures and outstanding Polish-American leaders. A reception was held that afternoon for the vice minister and his wife at the Slavonia club, and this I attended. Sofia Szyszko, the twenty-seven-year-old wife of the vice minister, was a colorful and dynamic figure in her own right, with her dark, magnetic beauty and a commanding presence. She had been a lieutenant in Poland's underground army and now worked with Poland's youth, of whom she proudly said,

> Young people played a large part in the fight against the Nazis. Even 10-year-olds distributed illegal leaflets. Our youth organizations—Catholic, peasant, socialist, communist, scouting—all united in a co-ordinating council. Now they are fighting all the remnants of fascism. Young and old help out in Poland's reconstruction. Children nail their shattered schoolhouses together. Youth battalions help gather the harvest. The government sponsors special co-operatives where young people can become self-supporting. . . .
>
> We need textbooks, as sometimes there is only one book for a whole class. We need laboratory and school supplies, sport and scouting equipment, vitamins, calcium, shoes, sweaters, and wool underwear.

This was fully reported in *Glos ludowy.*

That same evening, Stanley chaired a meeting of more than two thousand people at Detroit's Class Technical High School and introduced to the audience the new Polish vice minister of agriculture, who spoke of conditions under the Nazi occupation and what gains were now being made under the new Polish government.

Among the many Polish-American organizations there was a growing desire for first-hand reports on conditions in Poland. Several conferences were held and a delegation selected to visit Poland, consisting of Stanley; Anthony Karczmarczyk, president of the Kosciuszko League of Detroit; state representative and UAW-CIO leader Vincent Klein; Thaddeus Kantor, writer and actor; and Henry Podolski, a Polish editor of *Glos ludowy,* who was to serve as secretary of the delegation. Before leaving Detroit around 12 November, they held meetings throughout the city where people could indicate what information they most desired to hear about Poland. Philip Adler, already in Warsaw, sent dispatches to the *Detroit News* describing the incredible devastation and the desperate plight of people of all ages.

Michael and Sofia Szyszko were returning to Poland, and they sailed on the *Queen Elizabeth* to London with Stanley and the delegation. Once in London, the problem was to get to Poland. After a week of tedious waiting, space was found aboard the Polish ship *Slask,* which had served in the English fleet during the war and was now homeward bound with a cargo of United Nations Relief and Rehabilitation Administration supplies. The Detroit delegation and the Szyszkos would be the only civilians on board, and the trip across the Baltic Sea to the Polish port of Gdynia was expected to take three days. The second day out, the ship halted for several hours for the crew to repair a broken pump. Later they discovered mines in the water, placed by the Nazis. At that moment Poland had neither the equipment nor the time to remove them, and the ship had to move at a snail's pace to avoid them, particularly at night.

After about five days, the ship arrived in Gdynia, 3 December. The harbor was littered with sunken battleships. Members of the delegation had been told of the destruction in Gdynia, but nothing had prepared them for the awesome sight of a city reduced to rubble. The Nazis had held out here until forced to retreat. Building by building, house by house, the town had been taken in grim battle by the Red Army and the Polish legions. The city was almost 90-percent destroyed; but somehow, somewhere, among the ruins, people had found spaces to exist, sometimes a room or a corner of a room still clinging to a wall, in basements, or buildings half-buried in the rubble.

A car without windows or heat took the delegation to Warsaw in the bitter Polish winter, wrapped with warm blankets and with a good supply of vodka to help them fight off the freezing cold. They arrived at night. In the moonlight, mountains of rubble again greeted the delegation. Steel girders of what had been tall, substantial buildings rose in fantastically twisted forms above the ruins like creatures writhing in pain. The delegates were told how the Nazis had bombed the city by air, then sent special detachments from block to block, building by building, to dynamite, burn, and destroy. People also described how the Nazis had cut off power and telephone lines and dynamited sewers and water lines, to leave the city without light or heat or water.

Only one hotel, the Polonia, was left standing, for it had served as headquarters for the Nazi officers until they fled with no time to demolish the building.

The delegates had no heat in the room to which they were all assigned. They undressed in the cold and snuggled under feather mattresses, which made them perspire. When they left the warmth of their beds in the morning, the icy cold bit into them. They splashed themselves with the frigid water from the lavatory in the room and dressed with shaking fingers to dash down to the warm kitchen, where the old, experienced waiter brought each a tall glass of vodka.

"Vodka? So early in the morning?" protested Stanley. "I seldom drink alcoholic beverages and never this early in the day."

"My dear young man," the waiter said gently, "we have so little heat, and you must keep warm. Drink this and I'll soon bring some hot breakfast. This is the way we have kept warm all through the war and stayed healthy."

Stanley drank it without further protest. He fully expected to be staggering around, half conscious, but nothing happened except he got warm and stayed that way. All the delegates had the same experience.

They found that all foreign embassies were quartered in this hotel, also all foreign correspondents and delegations. Some shouting brought the delegates to the hotel window, where they saw people emerge from the piles of rubble to race to an army truck standing in front of the hotel. It turned out that with no streetcars and with most streets impassable, the army truck was the only means of getting to work for anyone who could climb in, hang on, or sit on top of someone else.

The delegates had with them the names of people to try and locate, and envelopes containing money and letters from people in Detroit to relatives in Poland. The names were given to the press and radio to be announced with instructions to contact members of the delegation at the hotel.

As the delegates left the hotel that morning, an awesome sight met them, much worse than what they had been able to see by moonlight the night before. Philip Adler's dispatch from Warsaw to the *Detroit News* of 11 December gave what Stanley says was a realistic description of what he and the delegates saw as they emerged from the hotel the morning after their arrival in Warsaw:

> Warsaw, in the past regarded as the "Paris of Eastern Europe," today is its Pompeii. . . . Never have I imagined such destruction possible.
>
> Over the entire distance of about two miles from Hotel Polonia . . . I have not found a single habitable house. . . . This entire stretch . . . is in ruins: empty shells of buildings with their entire interiors gutted out; heaps of rubbish many stories high from which project fantastically twisted girders, misplaced portions of buildings—roofs, colonnades, stairways and balconies. . . .
>
> All of Warsaw is a vast cemetery. It is estimated that the city's ruins still hide some 100,000 dead. . . . Closer examination revealed many families living in the debris, existing only God knows how.

As Stanley and his delegation walked that same street, apart from it they found only one street—a crossing street near the hotel—cleared of rubble, and that not for a great distance. In the bitter cold, inadequately dressed against the severe Polish winter, men and women stood atop the huge mountains of rubble where streets had been, passing hand to hand such rocks and bricks as they could handle to be loaded on conveyances of whatever kind could be mustered to carry them away. There was no equipment to help them. Bit by bit, that was how the one long street and its cross street near the hotel had been sufficiently cleared for vehicles to get through.

Walking alone near the hotel, Stanley encountered a group of people, a military band, and some soldiers. He approached and asked what it was all about.

"The Polish Sejm [Parliament] is meeting here," an officer replied.

"I am with a delegation from America," said Nowak as he introduced himself. "I am a state senator from the state of Michigan and would be interested in seeing how your government proceedings are conducted. Do you think I might be allowed to be present as an observer?"

"Let me take your passport, Sir," said the soldier, "and I will go in and see. I'll be back in a moment."

He returned with a delegation to welcome Stanley and escort him to a large room in a building hidden under the rubble and only partially destroyed. Poland's president, Boleslaw Bierut, was chairing the meeting. He interrupted proceedings to invite Stanley directly to the platform, shake his hand warmly, introduce him to the Sejm, and ask him to speak.

Surprised by the swiftness of events, Stanley soon collected himself and told the audience of the various organizations in the United States that were organizing help for Poland. He received a cheering, standing ovation, and tears rained freely down the cheeks of his listeners, old and young. To them he was the visible evidence that people beyond Poland's borders knew of their plight and cared. Deeply moved by his reception, he found his own face wet with answering tears.

The meeting no sooner ended than Stanley was surrounded by a group of veterans of the Kosciuszko and Dąbrowski divisions that had marched into Poland with the Red Army to liberate Polish cities in July of the previous year. They were delighted to see someone from the United States who could speak Polish, and they bombarded him with questions. They also told him of their experiences in the Soviet Union during the Nazi occupation of Poland, and how they had been trained and armed and participated in Poland's liberation with the Red Army. Stanley left this meeting deeply grateful that he had seen and talked with these brave veterans many of whom bore visible evidence of their battle experiences. They were now participating in Poland's new government, trying to solve the many problems of rebuilding their country.

He had scarcely arrived back at the hotel when he heard his voice through the overhead loudspeakers on the street, as the radio broadcast the speech that he had just delivered. His fellow delegates, vastly surprised, said, "Why didn't you tell us you were going to do this? We would have liked to have been there, too."

A few days later Stanley addressed a meeting of trade unionists in the shell of a building, consisting of four walls still standing but without a roof. As he spoke, snow fell on both him and his audience as people huddled together in the cold, excited and happy to hear someone from the United States.

Within a few days, numbers of people were waiting for the delegation each evening on their return to the hotel from the day's activities. After properly identifying themselves, these people received the letters and money from families in Detroit. Such happiness and tears! Most were dressed in forlorn rags, and their joy at hearing from loved ones and knowing they were not forgotten was truly rewarding.

A few days after Stanley's delegation had reached Warsaw, another led by his old Detroit acquaintance, Bishop Stephan Woznicki, arrived. The two groups met over dinner almost every evening to compare notes. They agreed not to raise controversial issues on their return to Detroit, but to concentrate on seeking help for Poland. Stanley also saw Philip Adler almost every day and they, too, exchanged impressions of what they had seen and heard.

Stanley's delegation visited Krakow and the coal miners in Katowice, and were told the miners had been for three days without bread, the main staple of their diet. The delegation visited Oswiecim (Auschwitz), the Nazi death factory where so many thousands had perished. It was a gruesome sight, still much as it was when the Nazis had fled, leaving piles of human bones and ashes everywhere. There were mounds of human hair, sheared from the heads of victims, and, most touching of all, piles of tiny shoes and toys that had belonged to the most defenseless ones. Stanley stood a long time looking at all this and trying to understand how human beings could become worse than animals in inflicting cruelty and torture on innocent and helpless people.

The delegation twice interviewed President Bierut and all cabinet members. They learned that while our U.S. Congress had been debating the matter, the Soviet Union had come to Poland's aid. Russian technicians had reestablished power and telephone lines, water stations and pipelines to carry it, and were working on the sewers. There was still a very real danger people would not survive the winter, lacking adequate food and medical supplies, as well as other desperately needed items. Dispatches came to *Glos ludowy* from the delegation and were relayed to me. The *Detroit News* published some of the dispatches. I would not hear from Stanley directly until his return.

In the meantime, things were happening in Poland's behalf in Detroit. At the downtown YWCA, on 28 November, a committee of prominent citizens from organized labor, business, the clergy of all faiths, and political and civil leaders was formed to provide aid to Poland. Under the heading, "Help the Poles!" the *Detroit News* published an editorial on 9 December, calling attention to the committee, telling of the desperate plight of Poland's people, and calling for assistance to Poland.

Press dispatches continued to arrive from Adler and Stanley's delegation, and finally word came that Stanley's group was on a plane over the Atlantic Ocean. Then for four days, silence! In view of the reported storms over the Atlantic, all of us here were uneasy. At last, on 26 January 1946, Stanley phoned me from Chicago that they were going through customs and would soon be in Detroit. Although it was late at night, there was no further sleep in our house until Stanley was back home and safe. He arrived in the early morning hours, but we were all too exhausted from the long strain of uncertainty and anxiety to do much talking. We slept the sleep of exhaustion and began that afternoon to catch up on events that took place while we were apart.

Our home was soon swamped with people anxious to know whether their letters had been delivered and whether Stanley had news of relatives in Poland. The phone rang incessantly, and Stanley's days and evenings were soon filled with speaking engagements, locally and nationally, about Poland. His very first report was at my church, First Church of the Brethren, then located on Seyburn at Lafayette, on 2 February, to tell of a shipment of heifers from the Brethren that had arrived as Stanley reached Poland and to deliver a message of thanks from the Polish government.

Long before this, I had rejoined my church, for it had reached out to embrace my social concerns for which I was now able to work within the church structure. The National Brethren Service Committee had been established at an annual conference of the Churches of the Brethren, with a subcommittee titled the Heifer Project Committee. Hundreds of heifers (all ready to calve shortly after reaching their destination), horses, and tons of food and clothing were collected at a central point in Windsor, Maryland and sent on United Nations Relief and Rehabilitation Administration (UNRRA) ships to war-torn countries after the war.

A crew of Brethren men, dubbed "cowboys," always accompanied the heifers to care for them and oversee their distribution by the designated government, remaining several weeks to see that the cattle were well placed and cared for.

The first shipment of 225 heifers arrived in Poland while Stanley and his delegation were there. Much surprise and curiosity were aroused, and Stanley had to explain my church and what it stood for. The only requirement of each family receiving a heifer was to sign an agreement to pass on to another needy family any heifer calves and any extra milk.

On the twelfth the Michigan Senate suspended proceedings to hear Stanley report on Poland and answer his colleagues' questions. He and others of the delegation would be reporting all over Detroit and in other cities on what they had seen and learned.

Activities in Poland's behalf would continue through 1946. Mayor Edward J. Jeffries proclaimed the week of 21–28 February "Books for Poland Week." A drive launched by the American Friends for Poland, headed by Rev. Ellsworth Smith, received an initial donation of several thousand scientific and technical journals by the Detroit Public Library. More than a thousand had previously been collected by the University of Michigan from faculty members and others. On 14 April we attended a meeting at Cass Technical High School in which Stanley participated, along with Jan Stanczyk, Polish minister of labor and social welfare, and Leo Krzycki, recently arrived from his tour of Poland and the USSR. We were inspired by the reports of progress in spite of lack of technical help and goods and material. *Glos ludowy* of 4 May reported that Bishop Stephan Woznicki, newly arrived from Poland, gave an impassioned radio plea for the intensification of Polish relief activity if thousands of Poles were not to die that year.

And so it went with us throughout the entire year. Stanley would be reelected in November and again return to the Senate in 1947.

18 McCarthyism and Deportation Hysteria

Early in 1947, Jozef Winiewicz succeeded Dr. Oskar Lange as the Polish ambassador to the United States, and Lange became Poland's UN representative on the security council.

In Lansing on 19 March Stanley attended a conference on fair employment practice legislation, with two hundred delegates from fourteen Michigan cities. After the conference, the delegates lobbied in the Senate for a fair employment practice bill that Stanley had introduced jointly with senators Charles S. Blondy and Joseph A. Brown. Stanley took a group of eight conferees to visit Governor Kim Sigler and seek his support for the bill. His response was that the bill was sponsored by Communists, who would have to withdraw their sponsorship before he could support it.

Sigler had used the graft grand jury as a vehicle to reach the governorship. He had created quite a splash and defeated Pat Van Wagoner decisively at the polls the previous November. Sigler frequently held joint meetings of the House and Senate finance committees in his office, often calling in others not on the committees but whose help he needed. Stanley was one of these since he was the Democratic floor leader. Because of his influence with Democratic legislators and some liberal Republicans, Stanley was often consulted by Sigler on issues of vital concern to him. Stanley frequently differed with him and frankly told him so, refusing to use his influence to persuade Democrats to vote for measures he did not approve. Governor Sigler made a terrific impression in the very early days of his term, but it soon became evident he knew little about the complex problems of government. When his proposals came before the Senate, none of the Republicans dared take the floor and speak against them, but with a little encouragement they would often vote against them. Stanley provided the encouragement. He spoke against measures he deemed worthless and, in most cases, was able to swing the Democrats and some Republicans against them.

A ballot proposal had been won in 1946 to earmark a percentage of the state's income for schools. Governor Sigler sought to repeal that measure in 1947. A resolution for this purpose had carried in the House, but was opposed in the Senate by the Democrats and some Republicans on the grounds that the people of Michigan had already expressed themselves on the issue. Sigler's resolution required a two-thirds majority vote and would not win without Democratic support. Knowing that Stanley and Republican senator G. Elwood Bonine were on good terms, the governor sent Bonine to ask Stanley's help.

"But how can I ask the Democrats to vote for something for which I, myself, have no intention of voting?" Stanley asked.

Within a few moments the resolution was on the floor for a vote but failed to obtain the necessary majority. Stanley not only spoke, but also voted, against it. Furious with the senators, particularly Stanley, the governor found an opportunity to get even that very day. He left that afternoon for Washington to appear before the House Un-American Activities Committee (HUAC). This was reported in the 29 March issue of the *Detroit Free Press*. Sigler named twenty-two organizations as subversive and branded as reds UAW's R. J. Thomas, George Addes, and Richard T. Leonard. The ariticle said in part, "Sigler told the committee that Michigan has at least one communist sympathizer in its legislature, Senator Stanley Nowak, Detroit Democrat. . . . The colorful Michigan Governor, with his white hair, sharp, commanding features, his pearl-gray waistcoat, black-ribboned pince nez glasses, made a tremendous hit with the committee."

When Stanley and I went to Detroit's city hall that spring to enter his name in the race for common council, among the many who accompanied us were attorneys Ernest Goodman; Dean Robb; George W. Crockett, Jr.; Wallace McLay (nephew of Henry Wallace); Robert Wolpe, state chairman of the American Veterans Committee; Rev. Charles A. Hill, himself a candidate; Rev. Arthur Bily of Dodge Christian Community House; Polish unionists Frank Danowski and Jim Cichocki; and the UAW figures Sam Sage and Tracey Doll, the latter also a candidate. Hundreds of volunteers of both races staffed the several campaign headquarters for the team of Nowak and Hill, who appeared together in their respective districts to campaign.

On Labor Day, 1 September we found 125 thousand observers lining Woodward Avenue in Detroit to watch 40 thousand paraders. The *Detroit News* of that date reported that the AFL contingent of 18 thousand marched from 10:00 A.M. to 1:30 P.M., and the CIO's 22 thousand from 2:00 P.M. to 3:00 P.M. Of the many bands and floats, an old, horse-drawn streetcar, representing the DSR (Detroit Street Railway) Union, drew the most attention. Floats depicted workers driven along in Taft-Hartley bondage, and one of the most popular placards read, "Heil Sigler!" Vice President Henry Wallace, R. J. Thomas of the UAW, and Coleman Young, then director of organizing for the Wayne County CIO council, spoke. According to *Glos ludowy*, Wallace declared Thomas's speech the best he ever made and said further, "I'm surprised that to the smear list published by Hearst's Detroit Times your name was not added. This is really an honor list, with my good friend the Rev. Charles Hill; that progressive union leader George Addes; and that outstanding worker for the people, Senator Stanley Nowak."

On 7 October both Hill and Stanley were nominated to the Detroit City Council along with Tracey Doll. However, in the 4 November vote, the three labor-sponsored nominees failed to make it among the first nine to be elected. Eugene I. Van Antwerp replaced Mayor Edward J. Jeffries.

The birth of the Progressive party and the candidacy of former Vice-President Henry Wallace for President on the Progressive Party ticket brought a wave of enthusiasm among liberal and leftwing forces.

Throughout our district and around the city, our campaign workers and supporters insistently urged Stanley to run for Congress that summer of 1948. Each time he had been reelected to the State Senate his votes had climbed to equal and sometimes even surpass the number of Congressman Lesinski's votes, in the same district. Even Stanley became caught up in the enthusiasm of the moment, and though he had some misgivings, he decided to run against Lesinski. It turned out to be the wrong moment, as the political climate was moving to the right.

Glos ludowy announced Stanley's candidacy on 26 June 1948 and published a call for a citywide meeting of union and mass organizations. The call was issued jointly by Professor Russell Broadhead of Wayne State University as acting chairman of the Nowak for Congress Committee, and by Percy Llewellyn, Ford Local leader and chairman of the Sixteenth Congressional District Wallace Committee. Attorney Maurice Sugar added his voice to the growing demand for Stanley to run for Congress and was quoted in *Glos ludowy* of 3 July. "Nowak was always the one Senator the union could rely on for support for labor measures. Not only could we go to Senator Nowak, but he would come to us to warn us of legislative plots against the people." The candidacy of Henry Wallace and the emergence of the Progressive party met with division in both the Democratic party and organized labor. In spite of the enthusiastic and energetic support of many people and organizations, this division cost Stanley the forces needed for victory. In the primary election of 14 September John Lesinski was renominated for Congress by a decisive vote of 18,971 to Stanley's 13,207.

A new candidate was nominated for Stanley's senatorial district on the Democratic party ticket and elected in November. This was Robert A. Haggerty, financial secretary of Local No. 946 UAW, also Political Action Committee coordinator for the Wayne County council. He would, in turn, be succeeded by a man with the same name as Stanley's who would win with very little campaigning. Many people thought they were still voting for their senator of the past ten years.

The American Slav Congress and the American Committee for Protection of Foreign-born were now on the subversive list of U.S. attorney general Tom Clark. A large conference of the Slav congress in Chicago on 24–25 September called for the election of Henry Wallace as president and U.S. Senator Glen Taylor as vice president. George Pirinsky, recording secretary of the Slav congress, had been arrested for deportation and later released on bail. He called his arrest "a deliberate attempt to intimidate Slavic Americans from attending the conference." At the Chicago conference, Wallace brought down the house when he grasped Pirinsky's hand and shook it warmly, saying, "Truman and Attorney General Tom Clark have slandered the American Slav Congress, but I consider it an honor to speak before this gathering." In the November election, Harry Truman was reelected president of the United States, and Alben W. Barkley vice president.

That summer I went to work in a downtown office as a bookkeeper. My mother and nine-year-old Elissa looked after each other after school. On the bus to and from work I began studying for my general insurance solicitor's license and would continue this through the year. Early in 1949 I passed the examination, obtained my license, and sent out an announcement to all our friends and associates. Our large living room now became my insurance office, and by June I was advertising in *Glos ludowy*. My clients were largely people with whom we had worked in labor and political circles. I did my insurance work in the evenings and on weekends and continued working in the downtown office. Stanley sold printing on commission for Chene Printing Co. which printed *Glos ludowy*. He also had many out-of-town speaking engagements, for which he was paid by the ad hoc committee that had invited him.

Resistance to repression was growing locally and nationally, as evidenced by a conference in defense of the Bill of Rights in New York City,

16–17 July 1949, with over thirteen hundred delegates from thirty-three states; and on 23 July *Glos ludowy* reported that Ford Local No. 600 was calling for the immediate abolishment of the House Un-American Activities Committee. Twelve Communist leaders were on trial in New York in the famous Foley Square trial; and Vito Marcantonio, the fighting congressional representative from New York, declared the first line of defense was the defense of the twelve. Waiving congressional immunity, Marcantonio further declared that the indictment of the twelve was planned as a vote-getting maneuver to elect Truman. By July's end, George Pirinsky had been arbitrarily arrested and his bond canceled; and he was imprisoned before any deportation order was issued. Abner Green, executive secretary of the American Committee for Protection of Foreign-born, stated in *Glos ludowy* of 3 September, "It appears that the pledge of the Attorney-General Tom Clark to arrest 3500 non-citizens and intimidate the foreign-born is well on its way to accomplishment. Up to this time, the arrests include 29 nationalities, thereby spreading fear among foreign-born groups and preventing them from voicing any protest against the anti-democratic and pro-war policies of the administration, . . . but the foreign-born in the U.S. will not be intimidated; . . . they are speaking out and will continue in even grater numbers."

That summer, Stanley had again campaigned with Rev. Charles A. Hill for election to the city council. Both had been nominated in the September election. Then, early in October, all three dailies carried headlines announcing possible federal action to denaturalize and deport Stanley. The 4 October banner-headlined article of the *Detroit News* read, in part, "Nowak, a candidate for City Council and a former State Senator, was recommended for 'denaturalization proceedings' about a year ago by E. E. Adcock, District Immigration Director. Nowak was an important factor in the organizing here of the American Slav Congress, according to the House Un-American Activities Committee. The American Slav Congress is on the U.S. Attorney-General's list of subversive organizations."

The *Detroit Times*'s banner-headlined article of 4 October stated, "Five months after Nowak was naturalized, Zygmund Dobrzynski, a former UAW-CIO official, told the Un-American Committee that he was solicited for membership in the Communist Party by Nowak. The Congressional Committee was given even more definite information on Nov. 30, 1939, in testimony by William Odell Nowell, a leader in the Communist Party from 1929 through 1936. Nowell is now employed by the Immigration Service and was a witness in the Communist trials." Dobrzynski and Nowell had been expelled from the UAW as company agents and tools of Harry Bennett in sabotaging the fledgling Ford Local No. 600. After their expulsion from the UAW, both apparently tried to even the score by offering testimony before the Dies Committee, predecessor of HUAC, naming many UAW pioneers as Communists.

The *Detroit Free Press* article of 5 October also under banner headline, had this to say: "Stanley Nowak declared in Detroit. . . . 'I'm a liberal and I challenge anyone who questions my loyalty to the United States to provide proof.' Attributing the revival of charges to political enemies fearful of his election to the Detroit City Council, he said he did not intend to apologize for his liberalism." Nowak branded the announcement of possible federal action at that moment as "direct federal intervention in the Detroit elections," and said further in the 5 October edition of *Glos ludowy*, "I consider this attack . . . a threat to all foreign-born naturalized citizens . . . to intimidate them from exercising the rights guaranteed to them by the Constitution. The campaign was first started against non-citizens and now has been extended to include naturalized citizens, and next will involve native-born Americans who may hold liberal or progressive views or opinion." Henry Podolski, an editor of *Glos ludowy* had been arrested and released on bond. *Glos ludowy* of 15 October reported that deportation proceedings were instituted against him, and that George Pirinsky was still held on Ellis Island. He was later released on 22 October after ninety-one days in solitary confinement.

In the meantime, Stanley and Rev. Mr. Hill were campaigning together throughout the Detroit area to present election issues before various language and ethnic groups. Wide support from labor was shown in the campaign, both financially and in campaign work. In the November election, neither Hill nor Stanley placed among the nine to be elected, but Hill did make it to the fourteenth place with 116,637 votes, and Stanley placed seventeenth with 100,015. A careful analysis of the voting revealed that Hill had received 60 percent of Stanley's vote in the heavily Polish precincts, something never before achieved by a Black candidate. Albert Cobo became the new mayor.

Regarding Adcock's announcement of possible federal action against Stanley in early October, the 26 November edition of *Glos ludowy* had this to say: "Immigration Director E. E. Adcock, when confronted with the demand to produce proof, admitted he had none. His irresponsible charges, he lamely told a sub-committee of the Senate Judiciary Committee, meeting in Baltimore, were just 'impressions.' . . . Nowak, who has served five consecutive terms in the Michigan Senate, and who has established himself as a fighter for the rights of the working man, labeled this as a shabby trick, but it helped to defeat him."

I went with Stanley to participate in a conference of the American Committee for Protection of Foreign-born in Detroit on 2 April 1950, at what was then Hotel Park Avenue. Attorney George Crockett, Jr. was the main speaker. He had been one of the defense attorneys in the Foley Square trial of Communist party leaders, and was facing a possible jail sentence on charges of contempt of court for his protests against the bias of the trial judge. At the conference we watched as certificates were presented to Detroit-area victims of the deportation hysteria. Most were old and dear friends with whom we had worked in labor and Democratic circles on various issues. Chairperson of the conference was Erma Henderson, later to become president of the Detroit City Council.

The McCarran omnibus "anti-alien" bill had been introduced in the U.S. Senate on 12 March. The United States had become involved in the war in Korea, and the atmosphere of fear and hysteria was growing.

Glos ludowy reported on 9 September that editors of progressive publications and leaders of local Slav committees had their homes smashed and their families threatened in Pittsburgh and Akron. Arrests were made for circulating peace petitions, and letters containing death threats were reported almost daily. Some of the most outstanding fighters for peace, among them Howard Fast and Harry Bridges, were already in prison and more arrests planned. Peace demonstrations met with police brutality in New York's Union Square on 2 August.

In the face of all this, American Slav Congress secretary George Pirinsky planned a national conference in New York on 6–8 October. At the same time Abner Green, executive secretary of the American Committee for Protection of Foreign-born, undertook a national tour to defend the Bill of Rights and planned a conference for 2–3 December. At all these conferences, Paul Robeson used his magnificent voice in the cause of peace and freedom, speaking and singing.

Henry Podolski was still in jail, where he had been confined after deportation proceedings had been initiated against him but was released on 11 November. James Papandreau, Greek activist in Democratic and progressive circles in Detroit, was also released after his arrest on charges similar to those against Podolski. Such arrests were occurring around the nation.

From 16 to 29 February 1951 Stanley was on a speaking tour in opposition to rearming Germany, covering ten cities in the east. An ad hoc committee in each city invited him, arranged the meetings, handled the expenses, and paid him a fee.

In the 24 March issue of *Glos ludowy*, Rev. Charles Hill denounced the listing of the American Committee for Protection of Foreign-born as a subversive organization by the U.S. attorney general. Hill declared, "The same forces that are anti-Negro are also anti-foreign-born" and asked, "Is to oppose segregation, discrimination, and injustice subversive?" *Glos ludowy* of 26 May carried an interview of Stanley by Harry Fainaru of the *Romanul American*. Stanley described twenty-five meetings in textile, mining, steel, packing, and auto in New England and the Midwest, with attendance varying from fifty to one hundred despite the denial of access to press and radio and in the face of attacks by the press. In Buffalo, a young steelworker reportedly said to Nowak after a meeting, "I struggled in my mind whether I should come to the meeting. If I should come I would endanger my job which I need very badly. If I keep away from peace activities I endanger the lives of my two sons. Here I am, and I am glad of it, for unless we are able to save the peace, neither my job or that of others will be worth anything."

Glos ludowy of 11 August reported the Justice Department continuing its campaign of intimidation by canceling bail that had been provided for thirty-nine aliens by the Civil Rights Congress and ordering them rounded up. Of these, twenty-two were ordered to appear within an hour to post new bail in amounts of five hundred to ten thousand dollars. Persons offering bail were questioned mercilessly as to political beliefs and sources of their bond money, and in some cases bail was denied. As of the eleventh, most of the thirty-nine were either on Ellis Island or in local jails, and Abner Green himself was in prison.

On 15 September *Glos ludowy* reported George Pirinsky was the first deportee under the McCarran Act, aboard a Danish freighter bound for Copenhagen whence he would proceed to Bulgaria, his homeland. Abner Green was reported still in jail; and on 11 October *Glos ludowy* reported our old friend Henry Podolski and his U.S.-born wife, Dolores, had left for Poland to become permanent residents.

On the twenty-seventh and twenty-eighth the press reported that a thousand delegates from around the United States had formed the National Negro Labor Council, with Secretary William Hood of Ford Local No. 600 as president; Maurice Travis of the International Union of Mine, Mill, and Smelter Workers as vice president; Coleman Young, former organizational director for the Wayne County CIO council (later to become Detroit's first Black mayor) as executive secretary. The conference called for unity of Black and white in opposing discrimination and oppression in the current hysteria.

It was in this mood that 1951 ended. As more and more valiant fighters for civil and democratic rights were indicted on one pretext or another, Stanley and I could not but wonder when our turn would come. We could only continue to work for what we believed to be right and just and face whatever the consequences might be.

19 HUAC Hearings and Another Indictment

Dark storm clouds gathering overhead,
Layer on layer, awesome with dread,
Blotting out sun like snuffed out hope.
Hardly a glimmer of light to cope.
When will the thunder and lightning bolts flash
Round and about us with deafening crash?

Facing the storm and its rumbling roar;
We work and we wait for what is in store.

—Margaret Collingwood Nowak

On 24 February 1952 Elissa and I went with Stanley to a banquet that he chaired in honor of Poland's ambassador, Jozef Winiewicz, and his wife at Danish Brotherhood Hall at Forest and Twelfth Street. The division then between reactionary and democratic elements in the Polish community was so sharp that no Polish hall could be obtained for the affair. Even the use of the Danish Brotherhood Hall had been granted reluctantly. Board members of the organization owning the hall had been terrorized by the FBI, the manager said, and in the future they would not permit its use by any controversial labor or political group. The ambassador and his wife described the horrors of the Nazi occupation. Our twelve-year-old Elissa presesented flowers to Mrs. Winiewicz, who embraced her and burst into tears. Elissa had brought back the memory of Mrs. Winiewicz's own beloved daughter, killed in the bombing of Warsaw.

While Stanley chaired the banquet, he was troubled with what loomed ahead of us. He had been subpoenaed three days before to appear before the House Un-American Activities Committee, which was to begin hearings the next day, the twenty-fifth, in Detroit. Attorney George W. Crockett, Jr. would represent him. Although he was not yet scheduled as a witness, Stanley and I attended the hearings on Monday, Tuesday, and Wednesday to observe committee procedures. Repeatedly, witnesses were questioned about their sponsorship or participation in organizations now on the U.S. attorney general's subversive list. A witness would be handed a program or brochure evidencing his or her participation; yet the witness dared not acknowledge this, for the next question was always, "Who obtained your sponsorship?" or "Who influenced you?" This placed the witness in the position of having to become an informer, naming names. Having once acknowledged the activity, the witness was obliged to answer subsequent questions or possibly be charged with contempt of Congress. The only recourse was to refuse to answer under the constitutional protection of the fifth Amendment. Apparently the witnesses had been so advised by their attorneys, for they followed this procedure.

Our good friend, Dave Miller, the grand old man of the UAW, was one of the witnesses on the twenty-sixth and gave a good account of himself in his thick Scotch brogue. He was represented by attorney Ernest Goodman. On the twenty-seventh Rev. Charles A. Hill testified, with Crockett representing him. Hill was confronted with evidence that he had participated in and served as a sponsor in many affairs or conferences of organizations now branded as subversive. Both Representative John S. Wood of Georgia, chairman of HUAC, and Frank S. Tavenner, Jr., counsel for the committee, pressed Hill repeatedly to say who had influenced him and obtained his support. Hill steadfastly refused to answer on constitutional grounds, even though it must have gone against every instinct to do so, for he was a very forthright, honest person. He did manage to get a statement into the record: "I have been interested primarily in one thing, and that is discrimination, segregation, the second-class citizenship that my people suffer, and as long as I live, until it is eradicated from this American society, I will accept the co-operation of anybody who wants to make America the land of the free and the home of the brave." Coleman Young was before the committee the next day. The hearing's record show that he was aggressive and repeatedly put committee members on the defensive. He refused to answer incriminating questions and yet got points across.

Released from prison, Abner Green was honored in Detroit on 2 March at the Jewish Cultural Center on Joy Road (now a Black church) at a banquet. He was scheduled to speak on the university campus in Ann Arbor, but university officials canceled the meeting at the last minute on the grounds that his speech might be subversive. Attempts to secure a hall off campus failed, so several smaller meetings were arranged. In a statement to the *Michigan Daily,* Green said, "I know of no one who would overthrow the government but the Ku Klux Klan, the Un-American Activities Committee, and the Smith and McCarran Acts if carried out completely. I had intended to speak on the 3500 non-citizens threatened with deportation and separation from their families and the 1200 naturalized Americans facing loss of citizenship on political grounds. If the defense of democratic rights is subversive, then I would be making a subversive speech."

The tenth found us at the hearings, with Stanley on the witness stand before HUAC all day. He, too, was presented with programs and booklets from affairs and conferences of the American Committee for Protection of Foreign-born and the American Slav Congress, both now on the subversive list. It was obvious he had served as an officer of these organizations and had sponsored and participated in their programs and conferences; yet he had to refuse to admit this and to rely on the protection of the fifth Amendment. At certain stages in the questioning, however, in spite of a warning kick under the table from attorney Crockett, Stanley did some talking back and put some information in the record. Crockett was uneasy, fearing Stanley might go too far and be charged with contempt; and I sat anxiously with fingers clenched in fear.

Stanley was told of William Nowell's testimony against him before the committee and was asked if it were true. Even though Nowell's testimony was sheer fabrication, Stanley had to take refuge in the fifth Amendment; for if he denied it, he would be charged with perjury, since Nowell's testimony was accepted by the committee as "gospel."

Toward the end of the day, when it seemed the committee might adjourn, a man came from the back of the hearing chamber, surrounded by newsmen with cameras and lights. He came to stand in front of Stanley, and Tavenner asked if he knew this "Mr. X." Stanley looked long and hard at the face before him but could find nothing familiar about it. He was opening his mouth to say no when a kick from Crockett and an urgent whisper warned, "Stanley, don't answer!" "But I never saw this man before in my life!" protested Stanley in an equally loud whisper, which I heard. A lighter moment in the proceedings occurred when Tavenner cautioned Crockett to please advise his client in a lower undertone, as it was coming over the speaker system; and laughter eased the tension for a moment or two. Stanley heeded Crockett's warning and took the fifth Amendment, but his curiosity was aroused. "Who is this man?" he wondered. He was positive he had never seen him before. The man identified himself as

Casimir Rataj but was on the witness stand for only about ten minutes when the committee adjourned for the day.

Stanley was exhausted after almost eight hours of interrogation, and I, too, from the tension of watching him. Crockett and his family lived only a couple of blocks from us, and he drove us home. On the way, Stanley stretched, relaxed, and said, "Well, George, what do you think?"

"I think you probably will not be charged with contempt of Congress, Stanley."

George had troubles of his own at that moment but probably realized Stanley had enough to handle just then, so he did not mention that he himself had been notified that day that the U.S. Supreme Court had upheld his conviction for contempt of court, a charge stemming from his role in defense of the twelve top Communists in the famous Foley Square trial of 1949. George would have to serve his four-month prison sentence.

At the next day's hearing, 11 March, Rataj stated he was formerly a Communist party member and had seen Stanley at Communist meetings and affairs. Stanley still could not recall anything about Rataj or any such meetings as he mentioned, but the name Rataj seemed familiar somehow. Among Polish circles, after the hearings were over, Stanley made inquiries and came up with information that proved the wisdom of Crockett's counsel.

When Stanley had edited a Polish paper, *Glos robotniczy* (Voice of the workers) in Detroit in 1924, it was the father of Casimir Rataj who had come to him and to the paper for help in a family tragedy. The family lived near Bay City, where three of his small children had died in trying to cross a frozen river on the way home from school. The father, member of a fanatically anti-Catholic religious group, accused the local priest of the children's death and charged that the local sheriff had hushed up the matter. Already unpopular in a predominantly Catholic community, Rataj only aroused further antagonism. At length he came to Detroit to seek help from Polish organizations and newspapers. The *Dziennik Polski* (Polish daily) spearheaded a fund drive to bring the family to Detroit. Eventually, Mr. Rataj sought help from *Glos robotniczy*. Stanley and the staff did considerable investigation and concluded that the father's suspicions were groundless and the death of the children a tragic accident.

Stanley heard no more from the family until 1935 or 1936 when he spoke at a meeting of the Unemployed Council in Hamtramck. After the meeting, the young chairman came and introduced himself as Casimir Rataj, son of the man Stanley had tried to help in 1924. His father's mind had become unbalanced, he said, from brooding over the children's death, and he had died in a mental institution. Casimir mentioned with gratitude Stanley's efforts in the family's behalf. The man who confronted Stanley in the HUAC hearings of 1952 bore no resemblance to the young chairman of that 1935 meeting. He had aged, was gaunt, broken in spirit, confused and uncomfortable in the flurry of excitement surrounding his appearance in the hearing room. Stanley wondered what had happened to so alter the man's appearance and bring him to testify against the person who had spent so much time on the family's behalf.

On 12 April 1952, Stanley was in Washington, where nearly eight hundred delegates from Black and nationality groups from thirty states had come to lobby for peace. They brought 500 thousand signatures asking for a five-power peace pact. State delegations broke up into congressional districts to lobby their congressmen and present signatures. Labor delegations visited Labor Secretary Maurice Tobin's office. Another went to the Justice Department. Stanley visited the State Department along with Dr. Willard Uphaus of World Fellowship and Mrs. Charlotta Bass, for over forty years the publisher of the *California Eagle.* Stanley also visited the Democratic National Committee.

The Department of Justice celebrated Constitution Day, 17 September, by arresting eighteen more people in the Midwest and Pacific coast area, including six from Michigan—leaders in what were considered subversive activities, such as the Progressive party, civil rights, peace, and labor. All would be aquitted eventually after lengthy and expensive court proceedings and appeals, even though national leaders of the CPUSA and several others had served two to eight years in federal prisons and paid large sums in fines.

The press reported growing resistance to the continued harassment and arrest of victims under the Smith Act. By 4 October, as reported in *Glos ludowy,* millions of citizens, individually and through their organizations, were on record against the Smith Act, irate over the eighteen new arrests of 17 September.

During this period I ran for office of state senator from our Twenty-first District on the Progressive party ticket, while Stanley ran for Congress on the Democratic party ticket. We both knew there wasn't a chance of winning, but it gave us a platform for fighting the growing repression. People equated war with jobs, and many who had loyally supported Stanley through the years now said they could not support a position against the Korean War, as it would mean unemployment. Much of our political base was already gone with the intimidation of the nationality groups by threats of denaturalization and deportation, under McCarthyism. The election of November gave us Dwight Eisenhower for president and Richard Nixon for vice president.

The American Committee for Protection of Foreign-born began a series of public hearings on the Walter-McCarran Act with a two-day conference in Detroit at the Jewish Cultural Center on 13–14 December, in which Stanley and I participated. More than eighty-five nationally prominent citizens had signed the conference call.

Each day, the circle drew closer around us as denaturalization and deportation proceedings were stepped up, affecting many dear friends. Then on Christmas eve the expected blow fell when our thirteen-year-old Elissa raced happily to answer the doorbell, expecting some of the family or perhaps a Christmas package. Instead, a stranger stood there asking for her father. He handed Stanley a paper, turned to go, then hesitated. "I'm sorry," he apologized. "This is only my job, you know. I don't issue these, I just deliver them. I'm sorry."

The paper was a notice of action in the federal court to revoke Stanley's citizenship. Soberly we read it through. The charges were similar to those ten years earlier, but this time a civil, instead of a criminal, action (see pp. 191, 236).

"Well, Margaret, this is what we've been expecting, isn't it?" Stanley said with a rueful smile.

"Yes," I answered, "but not on Christmas eve!"

We had expected this sooner or later. It had happened to so many with whom we had worked. Why not to us? And yet, even a long-expected blow carries an element of surprise. Stanley, Elissa, and I discussed what this could mean to our personal lives. We knew the fight this time would be much more difficult than the one ten years earlier, when the New Deal was at its height and Stanley had the support of a united and growing labor movement. In 1952 we were not sure of any support at all from organized labor, riven as it was with factionalism and cowed by the Taft-Hartley Law and other repressive legislation. We felt that the case could not be won by the legal process only, for the courts at that moment reflected the current hysteria. Sufficient support and pressure must be rallied in the state and nation to change the political climate and bring more reasoned and liberal decisions by the time Stanley's case would be decided. Finally, Elissa dared ask the question uppermost in all our minds: "Daddy, what if people are afraid to come out and support you? What if we lose in the courts? Will we all have to go to Poland?"

"Would you go with me?" Stanley countered.

"Daddy! How could you even ask such a question! After all, we *are* a family, aren't we?"

She had answered for both of us. We discussed the possibility of having to go to Poland. It would be difficult for Elissa and me to learn a new language and adjust to a very different culture and environment. It would not be easy even for Stanley, with his fluent command of the language; for he had grown up here and regarded himself as an American. He did not allow us to pursue this idea for long. "Look," he said. "The people who settled and built this country were all immigrants, whether they came early or late. They became part of this nation and consider themselves American. This is *my* country, and I intend to fight to remain here just as any other American would."

Our tasks in the months ahead would be to spearhead the fight against McCarthyism and work for the repeal of the Walter-McCarran Act. We wondered how many others had received a Christmas gift like ours that night as that law had gone into effect. After the holidays we would call our friends and make plans for Stanley's defense.

The *Detroit News* of 4 January 1953, reported an interview with John C. Lehr, former U.S. district attorney here, concerning the denaturalization proceeding instituted against Stanley:

> "Pressure of 'organized minorities' upon the Department of Justice prompted dismissal 10 years ago of a criminal indictment against former State Senator Stanley Nowak," said John C. Lehr. . . . After the indictment was issued, Lehr said, his and Biddle's office were "flooded with scores of protests from various left-wing organizations." . . . Biddle asked him to drop prosecution. . . . "I declined," Lehr said.
>
> "But at that time," he pointed out, "the Attorney-General had the right to dismiss any indictment which had been returned, and Biddle did so. By a Supreme Court ruling, indictments can now be dismissed only by a proper showing before the court."
>
> "I am glad that even at this late date some action is being taken in this matter," said Lehr. . . . "A decided change has occurred within the Government within the last year or two."

The change Lehr referred to was the campaign in full swing on the part of reactionary, repressive elements to brand as "twenty years of treason" the social and labor gains made during the depression and World War II. It was in this atmosphere that Stanley and I prepared to fight for his citizenship.

Within the first week of 1953, we called together our friends, and the Stanley Nowak Defense Committee came into existence. Carl Haessler, long-time friend and newspaper man, editor of the *Federated Press,* would serve as secretary-treasurer, as he had in 1942. Ben Okshea, also a long-time friend, pioneer in the insurance workers' union, and activist in progressive causes in both the Polish and non-Slavic communities, would serve as chairman. He had also been part of our 1942 committee. An unknown, Arthur Baker, a rank-and-file unionist from the Mechanics Education Society, was so outraged that he wrote the FBI protesting Nowak's indictment and was interrogated for his pains. He protested by volunteering his services to our committee.

Others rendering valuable services were Conrad Komorowski, labor journalist; John Novak of UAW Local No. 157; Harold Shapiro, business representative of the Fur and Leather Workers; Dave Miller, former president of Cadillac Local UAW and later the head of the UAW retiree department. There were so many whose names we cannot even remember. It was a source of strength and inspiration to find so many ready to brave the political climate of the time.

The new attorney general, Herbert Brownell, in the *New York Times* of 18 March, declared that the Department of Justice had ten thousand naturalized citizens and twelve thousand aliens under investigation for possible deportation as subversives. He could speak with confidence, because at midnight on 24 December 1952, the most sweeping of all immigration laws in our history, the Walter-McCarran Law, had gone into effect, the very night that Stanley had been notified of denaturalization proceedings against him. Passage of this act over the sharply worded veto message of President Truman had marked the launching of an intensive nationwide drive against the foreign-born. During the previous five years, the Justice Department had encountered many legal setbacks. The Walter-McCarran Law was specifically designed to negate or circumvent these legal obstacles. To this day that law has never been repealed. It is still there to be used whenever an administration sees fit. Senator Pat McCarran had publicly espoused the cause of Spain's Fascist dictator, Franco, and repeatedly attacked organized labor. Representative Francis Walter delivered on the floor of Congress a series of anti-Semitic tirades and labeled opponents of the Walter-McCarran Law as "professional Jews" (see *Congressional Record,* 13 January 1953, p. 380).

Long before this, our front room had been converted into an office for my insurance work and Stanley's political work. Here we carried on our defense activities as well. Volunteers got out thousands of letters and leaflets for distribution at churches, factories, and clubs. Stanley again toured the country, appearing before union locals, churches, clubs, language groups, and other organizations. Ernest Goodman, our attorney in 1942, again undertook Stanley's defense, ably assisted by George W. Crockett, Jr.

In June 1953 friends in Los Angeles sent plane tickets for Elissa and me to join Stanley in his tour of Pacific coast cities. We met tremendous response and fighting spirit wherever we went. More than three thousand people came to hear him at the Festival of Nationalities in Los Angeles.

On our return he reported at dozens of meetings, house parties, and picnics to raise funds for travel, extensive mailings, and literature distributions. In March 1954 a banquet arranged for three hundred people was swamped by an attendance of over six hundred.

Finally, the trial date was set for 13 July 1954, and we began intensive preparatory conferences with our attorneys in their Cadillac Tower offices, some of which I attended. Stanley sat on one side of Ernie Goodman's big desk, facing him and a huge window overlooking the Detroit River and Canada. George Crockett sat in a corner chair by the window, facing Stanley and Ernie. One of the best legal minds in the nation, Crockett's contribution would be the drafting of briefs and other legal papers for the defense. Ernie would represent Stanley in court.

Together they studied the charges and the list of witnesses called by the government. It was evident the government would try to prove

1. that both in his petition for naturalization and in the oral examination on his petition, Stanley denied membership in the Communist party, which constituted, in the government's opinion, fraud
2. that he had been a member of the Communist party prior to or at the time of his naturalization in 1938
3. that the Communist party advocated force and violence and that Stanley was aware of this and personally advocated such policy
4. that such membership and advocacy was in violation of the Immigration and Naturalization Law in effect in 1938

With papers spread out on Ernie's big desk, they next tackled the list of government witnesses, many of whom were being used in other denaturalization cases around the country. With one exception they fell into the following categories:

1. government "experts" or "consultants"
2. renegades from the left-wing movement
3. disgruntled people, failures due to some weakness
4. psychopathic or confused types of unstable personality
5. people whom the IRS or FBI had some hold over or something attractive to offer to them

The one exception was William Hewitt, a complete stranger, about whom we knew absolutely nothing. Investigation by us and by our attorneys' investigators failed to produce any information. "How can I cross-examine this man Hewitt or do anything with him unless you know something about him, Stanley? Isn't his name at all familiar? Can't you recall him at all?" Ernie pleaded hopefully.

"Sorry, Ernie, I have never seen or heard of him before."

"All right, we'll just have to do the best we can."

We knew the political forces behind this second proceeding against Stanley and were somewhat apprehensive as the trial drew near. The long wait from the 1952 indictment to the trial date in 1954, filled with exhaustive work and anxiety, had taken its toll of us as a family. We had often wondered how it would all end.

Stanley had fulfilled organizing assignments as well as handling the burdens of his defense committee and traveling. Immediately after the indictment in December of 1952, I had begun a grueling program of sitting at my typewriter not later than 5:00 A.M. daily, while the family slept and I was free from interruptions, to prepare a mailing list of five thousand names from our legislative, political, and labor contacts. Upon my shoulders fell the tasks of recording and typing the minutes of our defense committee meetings, calling the subcommittees together for reports, handling correspondence, and many other things, besides taking care of my insurance business and home responsibilities. However exhausting all this was for me, it was being thus involved in Stanley's defense that saved my sanity. The uncertainty of the outcome and the fear of what might lay ahead were always in the back of my mind by day and in my thoughts at night as I sometimes lay sleepless, wondering what would come of it all. The crowded, hectic days kept it in the background most of the time; and both Stanley and I shared a common faith in the people of our nation. We had to believe it would all come right, somehow.

Our relationship was a steadying factor. We were in complete agreement on the issues and values that had led to this period in our lives, and we would not have done anything differently even if we could have. The families of dear friends were destroyed in facing similar struggles. Men who had not fully shared their political beliefs and activities with their families saw them alienated by the price demanded in unfavorable publicity, ostracism, and condemnation. Divorces and separations resulted, and children were hurt and bitter. Because Stanley and I fully believed in what we did, were committed, and shared our goals, we were able to weather the difficulties and be supportive of each other. Because we had shared our beliefs and goals with Elissa, without preaching, she also reacted in this spirit and was proud of what her father had done and the principles for which he stood.

It did hurt when some former friends stood aloof and avoided us, but we could understand their fears in this troubled time. It was more difficult for Elissa; but as she came to understand, she, too, was able to handle the situation and come out stronger for it. We had to remind ourselves and Elissa that all persons who had stood for real freedom and democracy in our history in time of crisis had to pay a price for it even though history vindicated them.

Already exhausted from the long battle, we now would be going into the trial, a period of intensive emotional involvement and strain. To add to our fears, Elissa lay seriously ill in Sinai Hospital with viral pneumonia. We spent the evening before the trial with her. In the large high-ceilinged room, windows wide open and bed curtains all pulled back for better air circulation, she looked so small and vulnerable. She was wan and apathetic, undoubtedly fearful about the trial. I was so torn between the wish to be with her the next day and the feeling that I should be in court with Stanley. As usual, Elissa's fragile appearance belied her great inner strength, as she sensed my conflict. "No, Mom, your place is with Daddy tomorrow," she said decisively. "You can tell me all about it in the evening."

And so it was settled. The doctor, a dear friend, came bouncing in, bringing an atmosphere of hope and reassurance. A big, rotund person, he radiated buoyancy and warmth. Dr. Robert Axelrod—or Dr. Bob as he was called affectionately by all—was a master of the art of kibitzing and soon had us laughing. He knew the trial was to begin the next morning, and he applied the most effective antidote of all—love, hope, and laughter. We left in a more hopeful mood, both for Elissa's recovery and for the successful outcome of the trial, yet neither of us slept much that warm, humid night.

We wakened to a smotheringly hot, airless morning and set out with heavy hearts for Goodman's office for a last-minute briefing before going to court. Together with Ernie, we walked from his office to the federal building where our future would be decided.

20 The Trial and Its Aftermath

Though the heel of the strong oppressor
  May grind the weak to dust,
And the voices of fame with one acclaim
  May call him great and just,
Let those who applaud take warning,
  And keep this motto in sight,—
No question is ever settled
  Until it is settled right.

Let those who have failed take courage;
  Tho' the enemy seems to have won,
Tho' his ranks are strong, if he be in the wrong
  The battle is not yet done.

—Ella Wheeler Wilcox, "An Inspiration"

On 13 July 1954, the courtroom windows were wide open. People were seated around the room. Others stood about, talking in groups. The government attorney was registering some documents with the court clerk. About thirty people, mostly old friends, sat in the spectator section. I saluted their courage for braving both the heat and the publicity, for photographers were snapping pictures of everyone coming in. As I seated myself in this area, guarded nods and smiles, or a wink here and there flashed messages of encouragement. More people came in, some placing a hand momentarily on my shoulder or nudging my arm in passing. Several slipped folded bills into my hand.

Assistant U.S. prosecutor Dwight Hamborsky approached Goodman to be introduced to Stanley. The two attorneys presented quite a contrast in appearance. Hamborsky was tall, broad-shouldered, possibly in his midthirties—the clean, young American type with a certain smoothness about him. Goodman, a little older, shorter, darker of complexion, small featured and slight of build, was self-possessed and at ease. This trial was important to Hamborsky. Ten years earlier, the government had failed to make almost the same charges stick. If he could do it now, it would certainly enhance his prestige. After introducing Hamborsky to Stanley, Goodman led the way to the defense table.

A hush fell as Judge Frank Picard emerged from the doorway behind the rostrum to take his seat. Throughout the usual quibbling between attorneys over procedure, he affected an air of impartiality, remarking once to Hamborsky, "You can't take away a man's citizenship on flabby evidence—you *shouldn't,* anyway."

Both Stanley and I watched this show of objectivity with reluctant admiration. How blatantly unreal it was we knew only too well from the role Picard was said to have played in Stanley's 1942–43 battle to retain his citizenship. Following the dismissal of the 1942 indictment, our friend, Mort Furay, had told us of a gathering he had attended just prior to that indictment on a farm owned by Picard. The guests, Furay said, had included Larry Davidow, attorney for the Ford interests; U.S. district attorney John C. Lehr; and other Democrats. Someone had brought up the question of what to do about this "upstart left-wing politician, Stanley Nowak," who showed such strength in Michigan political circles. In spite of opposition from most of those present, he had been reelected twice. How could they remove him from the political scene? Someone had suggested that since Stanley was a naturalized citizen, this might be his vulnerable point. This had been eagerly seized upon and plans had been hurriedly made to present material to the grand jury before the statute of limitations ran out, in five days. Furay swore us to secrecy. He could not testify in our behalf without jeopardizing his job and his family's security. If subpoenaed, he would have to deny all knowledge of the matter. "What good is it to know all this?" I wondered bitterly that July day of 1954, realizing that Stanley's case was being heard before that very man, now a federal judge, in whose home the indictment of ten years earlier had allegedly been hatched, with his participation. If that were true, he should have disqualified himself. We watched as he very artfully created an impression of fairness and impartiality.

Picard tapped his gavel, and the court clerk declared the court in session. The judge folded his arms on the desk: "All right, Gentlemen."

"I believe, Your Honor," Hamborsky began, "that the first order of business would be to quash the subpoena for the production of documentary evidence." Picard was already reading aloud from the subpoena in question, which Goodman had filed with the court earlier: ". . . bring with you all statements, affidavits, or memoranda in your files in connection with the indictment or trial in the case of the United States of America versus Stanley Nowak."

Asked by Picard on what authority he made such a demand, Goodman explained that the charges in 1942 and now in 1952 were substantially the same, except it was a criminal charge in 1942 and a civil charge in 1952. But, he said, there were two important differences that the subpoenaed documents would reveal: there was no claim then that the Communist party was an organization that advocated the overthrow of government by force and violence, nor was there a claim that the defendant had falsely denied to the examiner that he had been a member of the Communist party. Furthermore, said Goodman, he sought these documents in order to argue that the government, by instituting these proceedings based substantially upon the same grounds as the criminal proceedings of ten years before, was abusing the process of the court, violating the basic traditions and conscience of the people as embodied in the Constitution, and denying due process." He was instructed to give his authorities to the court clerk.

"At this time, Your Honor," began Hamborsky, "I would like to state [what] the government's position is on the grounds of fraud and illegality." He claimed fraud was committed when Stanley answered no to the naturalization examiner's question whether he had ever been a Communist party member, although Hamborsky admitted that that question does not appear on the naturalization petition. He claimed further commission of fraud when Stanley answered no to question no. 28 on the petition, whether he belonged to or was associated with any organization teaching or advocating anarchy or the overthrow of the government. With this statement of intent, the court was ready for the first witness.

Harold J. Hart mounted the rostrum and took the oath. He was tall, well built, appearing of middle age. Although he said he had interviewed at least fifteen hundred people during his six years as a naturalization examiner in the Detroit area, he recalled asking Stanley, during a twenty-minute interview in 1937, whether he were a member of the Communist party, even though this was not standard procedure and not even required. Stanley's original naturalization petition was produced in court. After careful scrutiny, Hart admitted it had no written notations indicating he had asked the question; yet he maintained he had asked it and that he remembered doing so. Finally Picard pressed him: "You have said there are no notes there that gave you that recollection. There must be some reason—and the court would like to hear it—why you can remember specifically seventeen years ago asking Mr. Nowak that question."

Further questioning provided no answer. After a recess and conference with attorney Hamborsky, and after further scrutiny of his handwritten notes on the naturalization petition and more prodding by Hamborsky, Hart finally produced a "reason": "There are notes here which indicate [to me] that I asked the question, and these notes refer to the fact that Nowak was an official of the UAW and that he had engaged in at least one sit-down strike and told the strikers to hold—to continue to carry on and hold the fort." Hart had been greatly disturbed by the sit-downs of 1935–36, he said, regarding them as unlawful invasion of property rights. He was convinced the Communist party was trying to gain its first foothold in the United States through control of the unions and that sit-downs were part of their tactic. It was his concern over this, he said, which prompted him to ask everyone appearing before him whether they were Communists, even though it was not required. The government now had what it wanted of Mr. Hart, and he was excused as a witness.

Stanton L. Smiley was called to the stand. He also seemed of middle age, not so tall or heavy as Hart. Smiled stated he was a naturalization examiner in Detroit when Stanley was obtaining citizenship. He estimated he had interviewed thirty-five to forty thousand people over the years, fifty-four besides Nowak on the day of his interview in 1938. Like Mr. Hart, Smiley stated he had asked Stanley about Communist party membership and received a negative answer. At this point the court adjourned with Smiley's testimony to continue in the morning. Stanley and I accompanied Goodman to his office to review the day's proceedings.

That evening we visited Elissa in the hospital where she anxiously awaited news of the day's testimony. There had been a brief mention of the trial on the television news. We described what had happened that day, and she seemed reassured by our lack of concern. Dr. Bob again cheered us on, and we were relieved to see Elissa looking better and in lighter spirits.

On 14 July Smiley again took the witness stand. Like Mr. Hart, he revealed a decidedly antilabor bias; and like Mr. Hart's, Smiley's amazing memory functioned in the absence of written notations. Under cross-examination he could recall only his interview with Stanley out of the fifty-five he had conducted that day. His answers were so pat he got them out before Goodman could finish his questions.

"Now, Mr. Smiley," said Goodman. "My last question was whether the first official inquiry made of you since 1938 on the Nowak case was three years ago or a year and a half ago or less?"

"I am unable to state that."

"In other words, your present recollection is not good enough to enable you to state whether the first official inquiry made in the Nowak case was three years ago or a year and a half ago?"

"That's correct."

"Yet you want the court to believe your recollection is good enough to independently remember your examination in the Nowak case sixteen years ago?"

Goodman ended his cross-examination and Judge Picard asked for the next witness. The court clerk called out the name of Casimir Rataj. Since Rataj's dramatic appearance at the hearings before HUAC in March 1952, Stanley had often wondered what had so drastically changed the man's appearance and brought him to testify against one who had spent so much time and effort on behalf of Rataj's father and the family many years ago. "Perhaps today we will find out," thought Stanley. The same rush of newsmen and popping of flashbulbs as in Rataj's 1952 appearance accompanied him this day in 1954. Hamborsky began his interrogation.

Rataj stated he had first met Stanley at a streetcorner meeting on Michigan Avenue near Third in 1926, was impressed by him, and took him home to meet his father. Goodman asked about this in cross-examination: "Do you remember, Mr. Rataj, an incident in Bay County where your brothers drowned?"

"That's right."

"Do you remember after that tragedy your father was trying to get help from people to try and put the blame on persons he thought were responsible for that? Do you remember that?"

"I don't know what my father was doing."

"Did you know at that time that Mr. Nowak was associated with a Polish newspaper in Detroit, about 1925?"

"No."

"Did you know that your father went to see Mr. Nowak at that time to get him to intercede to write articles on it?"

"Well, I wasn't home. I was on the farm at that time, and I didn't know exactly where he was."

"Now isn't it true, then, Mr. Rataj, that your father knew Mr. Nowak before you ever met Mr. Nowak?"

Judge Picard interrupted in surprise. "If that is true, he couldn't have introduced Mr. Nowak to his father, because he already knew him."

"That is right," agreed Goodman, and he continued with Rataj.

"Now do you remember you were chairing a meeting of unemployed, and you saw Stanley Nowak and reminded him of his relationship with your father? You remember that?"

"No."

Rataj stated the government learned of his party affiliation when he applied for citizenship in 1936, and told him to wait seven years. Then, he said, he was visited in his Marine City home in 1950 or 1951 by two men from the immigration service, who interviewed him for about three hours and then advised him to draw up first papers and apply again. Later, he said, he received a phone call from Detroit to report to the immigration service on East Jefferson Avenue, where he was interviewed at length about Stanley and asked to name Communist party members. Rataj had served the government's purpose and was excused as a witness. It is a matter of interest that he received citizenship shortly after Stanley's denaturalization hearing. At the end of Rataj's testimony, the court adjourned.

The next day's first witness was Mrs. Jean Herbster, a motherly looking woman, gray hair fluffed about her face. Neither Stanley nor I could recall ever seeing her. She said she had lived in Detroit in the twenties and thirties and joined the Communist party in 1937 and had seen Stanley at various Communist meetings. This was all Hamborsky wanted from her, and he turned her over to Goodman. The rest of her testimony was vague: "It is so long ago I can't remember." She was excused after Goodman's cross-examination.

Richard Eager was then summoned as a witness, and when he did not appear at once, Hamborsky went to find him. Both Stanley and I remembered Eager from the early organizing drive at Ternstedt's. He had been one of the first to join the union, and his Irish wit and humor soon won him the chairmanship of the shop committee. However, his fondness for the bottle and his lack of responsibility brought widespread criticism and he was defeated for reelection. Disappointed, angry, seeking something or someone other than himself to blame, he had turned on Stanley. In the factional fight then developing in the UAW, Eager went with the Martin group and was later expelled from Local No. 174 for disruptive activities. This is all a matter of record. His anger and resentment had led him to appear before the FBI and the Dies Committee in 1938 and the immigration service in 1940 to testify that he had heard Stanley speak at meetings of Communist party members of Ternstedt.

Stanley's reminiscing was interrupted when Hamborsky returned to the courtroom with Eager, a short, slender man with graying hair. Stanley regarded him intently as he seated himself in the witness chair, but Eager looked at the floor, the ceiling, the walls, anywhere but at that level gaze. Hamborsky sought testimony showing that Stanley believed in and advocated violent overthrow of the government; but Eager, either embarrassed by Stanley's constant scrutiny or suffering pangs of conscience, was not giving the desired answers. "I have heard him speak at several meetings," he said. "You can't keep it all in your mind. It is so long ago I can't remember him passing any particular remarks that would leave any indelible mark on my memory."

Over Goodman's fruitless objections, Hamborsky hurled suggestive and leading questions repeatedly until Judge Picard intervened: "Let this man testify what was said. If he doesn't recall, you certainly can't take the stand for him!"

Hamborsky modified his approach but finally threw up his hands in exasperation. After the luncheon recess he resumed his belaboring of the witness. Now, his merciless probing gouged from the reluctant Eager a new phrase: "He told us that we couldn't depend too much on the ballot to gain our objective, but that it would eventually resolve to bullets."

"That is all," said a relieved Hamborsky, mopping his brow. This was quite different from the morning testimony when, in reply to the repeated question, "Did you ever hear Stanley Nowak advocate such a revolution?" Eager had said, "I can't say if I did." What had happened during recess? Even Judge Picard wanted to know. Turning to Eager, he said: "Mr. Eager, you were asked the question as to what Stanley had said and you never mentioned bullets until after the recess. Now when did you get the idea of bullets?"

"Well," Eager stammered in confusion, "that is my impression of it."

"All right, all right, if that is your answer, that is your answer."

Goodman crossed-examined, reviewing several statements mentioned in the morning testimony; Eager said he had made such statements to somebody but couldn't remember where or to whom because, as he said, "I can't recall. That is a long time ago." Statements he could not recall were much more recent than those he said he did recall from 1938 and 1940. Goodman called attention to contradictions in Eager's testimony; then, since neither he nor Hamborsky had further questions, Eager was excused. As he left, he averted his face to avoid looking at Stanley and passed quickly out of the room.

The next witness was William Nowell. Stanley had seen him only once, when he had testified in the deportation hearing of Henry Podolski in 1949. Ford workers had repeatedly told us of Nowell's antiunion activities during the Ford organizing drive of 1937, when he was exposed as a company stooge. In 1938, before the Dies Committee, he had made statements about Stanley that were used by his political opponents in an unsuccessful effort to defeat his first bid for the Michigan Senate. After Ford had been compelled to sign a contract and desist from antiunion practices, people like Nowell were no longer useful; and he was discharged. Since then, the FBI had used him as a witness in many political trials, where he testified about his Communist party membership, of being sent to the Soviet Union to study Marxist theories, the use of firearms, and how to engage in sabotage and organize armed rebellion. In this day's hearing, Nowell was to show the ideology and aims of the Communist party and to claim that Stanley, as an alleged party member, subscribed to those ideas and aims. A Black man of medium height and build and distinguished in bearing, he took the oath and sat in the witness chair. Hamborsky began his questioning.

Nowell stated he had served as consultant to the immigration bureau from December 1948 to June 1954 and had testified in approximately forty denaturalization cases. He appeared nonchalant, yet was obviously aware of every eye as he carefully crossed his legs or placed his hands. His replies to questions were deliberate and lengthy; and he pressed his fingertips together in studied thoughtfulness, giving the impression of a very credible witness. His testimony followed the same pattern he used in other denaturalization proceedings; and Hamborsky's questions literally placed replies in his mouth, with Goodman repeatedly objecting until Picard was forced to intervene. Nowell continued his long recital until the court adjourned for the day.

On 16 July Goodman cross-examined Nowell, calling attention to contradictions in his testimony, and all vestiges of Nowell's composure vanished, revealing a nervous, harried man, caught in the web of his own fashioning. He was released from the stand to refesh his memory as to earlier testimony in 1938 and 1942.

Court adjourned until the following Tuesday (20 July). This was a busy weekend, as we met with several language groups and with Stanley's defense committee to report on the trial and to plan fund-raising. During the week we had seen Elissa at the hospital or talked to her by phone every day. Friends and relatives had visited her. She had read press reports quoting witnesses without contradictions or conflicting testimony and was full of anxiety. As we spent time with her Saturday and Sunday and described what had actually taken place, she became more at ease.

On the twentieth William Hewitt was the day's first witness. He was the man we had tried so hard to identify in pretrial conferences. He was about six-feet tall, trim and athletic in physique, with a brush haircut, well groomed, and appeared confident and at east. His testimony revealed an impressive academic background. Hewitt stated that, as a Communist, he had been sent from Chicago to Detroit in the early fall of 1938 to see Stanley, who, he said, was to be in charge of Hewitt's Communist activities as a teacher at Michigan State College. He stated that he paid dues to Stanley in the latter's apartment and received instructions on setting up a party unit in Michigan State College. To cover it both ways, Hewitt testified that Stanley paid dues to him later at a meeting of the unit in East Lansing. Hewitt's response to questions was crisp and definite, and he seemed positive and assured. Had we not known otherwise, we would certainly have believed him. We were later told he had impressed Picard more than any of the other witnesses, yet his whole testimony was sheer fabrication.

We were completely baffled. Why would this man, a total stranger, testify against someone he had never met and against whom he could not possibly have a personal grudge or animosity? Some illuminating facts came out of Goodman's cross-examination. Hewitt testified about a visit from FBI agents in 1949 at Howard University, regarding falsification on an application he had filed. He admitted it was about membership in organizations. He said he had failed to list the Communist party on a questionnaire but that he did advise them of it some six weeks later, under pressure, and then gave them information on his activities in the Communist party and on persons he identified as having been members.

Hewitt said he could not remember the names of the Chicago party members who sent him to Detroit to see Stanley in 1938, nor the names or addresses of his Detroit hosts. When it was called to his attention that we lived in one rented room of an upper flat in a two-family house in a working-class district where there were no apartment buildings, he still stuck to his story. He said he could not recall on what street or what part of Detroit we lived, nor in what room we met, whether other people came and went, whether it was afternoon or evening, or how he got to and from our so called "apartment." To every question, he gave an unequivocal, "I don't remember."

Asked how his memory could be so vivid regarding alleged details of conversation with Stanley and so blank about everything else, Hewitt replied, "That was important. That is what I came for."

At one point Hewitt, who had once worked for Wilmark Service System, a private detective agency, let slip a bit of hearsay: "The firm framed employees. I was told by other employees of the Wilmark Service System." Of course, the remark was stricken from the record, but Stanley and I have since wondered if Hewitt might have still been secretly pro-union and let this information slip out deliberately. We later learned he did not testify in any other denaturalization hearings. We concluded he apparently "paid his dues" by testifying for the government this once to get it off his back regarding the falsified document. After Goodman's cross-examination, Hewitt was excused.

Clayton W. Fountain was called to the stand. He was much as we remembered him: short, slight, small-featured, and with a swarthy complexion. We had known him in the early UAW drive in Chevrolet and had thought him a good union person. We had not heard of him for years and wondered why he was here this day in court. His testimony revealed he had authored a book, *Union Guy,* in which he set out to expose Communists in the UAW. He admitted that Stanley was not mentioned in the book. When it was published in 1949, Fountain said, he was approached by the Immigration and Naturalization Service and asked if he could identify Stanley as a Communist, and he said he could. His testimony followed the same pattern as other government witnesses, placing Stanley at closed meetings or in halls where Communists met. At this point, court adjourned, with Fountain's cross-examination to take place in the morning.

On 21 July, under Goodman's questioning, Fountain stated that the UAW's Unity Caucus, to which he, Stanley, Reuther, and others had belonged, aimed to unite all political elements within the union, including Communists. He admitted that the meeting hall he had described, where he had seen Stanley and where Communist classes were allegedly held, was also the union center for organizing activities for Chevrolet workers and for union classes. Confronted with contradictions in his testimony, Fountain became confused, unable to remember what his testimony had been. Goodman ended his interrogation and Fountain was excused.

The next witness, Charles Baxter, was a stranger to us. He was rather tall, approaching middle age. It was soon evident that his purpose was to show that the Communist party taught and advocated the violent overthrow of the government. He had with him books by Communist theoreticians, but Goodman's objections to any covering the period before 1938, when Stanley was naturalized, were sustained. Shortly after, court adjourned for the day.

Baxter testified most of the next day, which grew oppressively warm. In the somnolent atmosphere of the court during this long recital going back to 1932, Goodman sat with his hand over his eyes, appearing almost to drowse. That he was keenly following the testimony was indicated by his repeated objections, which were usually overruled. The long, wordy testimony continued until the government had what it desired. Goodman cross-examined briefly, and Baxter was excused.

Thaddeus Zygmunt was called to the stand, a tall, slender man, flashily dressed. His eyes gleamed and he had a fixed, smiling expression. His answers to questions were somewhat muffled; but once started, he became voluble. Zygmunt's role here was to show that Stanley had advocated forcible overthrow of the government many years before his naturalization, and that he was not "attached to the principles of the Constitution." He recalled in detail Stanley's alleged speeches of thirty years before. As the day wound down to a close, Goodman's cross-examination gently punched holes in Zygmunt's testimony, revealing contradictions and inconsistencies. The court soon adjourned, with cross-examination to continue in the morning.

On 23 July Goodman questioned Zygmunt about the previous day's testimony. In his examination by Hamborsky, Zygmunt had said he left the Communist party in 1937. Three times, Goodman asked whether he hadn't done so because he considered the party not militant or revolutionary enough; Zygmunt denied this.

"Wasn't it your position that American capitalism was reactionary and imperialistic and that you felt that the Communist party desired to maintain it instead of wanting to overthrow it? Wasn't that your position?"

"No, my belief was that the American government was much *better* than Russian government."

"And you felt the Communist party wanted to overthrow it?"

"Yes."

Goodman then produced a pamphlet published in Polish in 1938, which Zygmunt readily acknowledged he had written under the pseudonym of Konarski, in which he bitterly condemned the Communist party for not being revolutionary enough. This was the only evidence presented in relation to Zygmunt, and it completely contradicted much of his testimony in this hearing. Goodman read translated excerpts from the pamphlet, appealing to Polish members of the Communist party to break with it and join a "really revolutionary" organization, a group of Trotzky followers. Zygmunt tried to squirm out of his difficulty by saying he had not meant what he wrote. "That's not exactly lies, that's only maneuvering of the words. What I mean and what I wrote is two different things." Goodman had made his point and had no further questions. Zygmunt was temporarily excused, to be recalled for redirect examination, as Hamborsky wished to call another witness that afternoon.

After our return from the lunch break, an atmosphere of excitement was immediately evident. Many Catholic priests and sisters had come to sit in the visitor's section. Hamborsky was talking to some of them. The judge opened the session, and the court clerk called for Louis Francis Budenz, a former Communist party functionary who had resigned, recanted, and reembraced the Catholic church. In testifying for the government in immigration and Smith Act cases throughout the country, he had contradicted himself many times. Stanley had seen Budenz on only one occasion, in 1939 or 1940, when in Chicago to speak before the packinghouse workers. After the meeting, a stranger had introduced himself as Louis Budenz, editor of the *Midwest Record*, and asked for an interview concerning issues being debated in the Michigan Senate. On the basis of that interview, Budenz wrote a series of articles. They had not met since.

To dramatize his appearance and impress his audience of prominent Catholic officials and lay persons, Budenz entered the courtroom through a door behind the judge's stand, and went out of his way to pass the defendant's table and confront Stanley. His gaze wavered but he brazened it out, and as their eyes met and held, Stanley realized he was looking into the face of a sick man. Budenz then proceeded to the witness chair. It was soon evident that his purpose here was to place Stanley at closed party meetings. His testimony was similar to that given in other denaturalization or Smith Act cases. Goodman's cross-examination revealed inconsistencies and contradictions, and Budenz was soon released. Hamborsky requested an early adjournment so he could have Zygmunt's pamphlet translated into English and question him on it at the next session. Court adjourned until the following Tuesday (27 July), and Stanley and I accompanied Goodman to his office for a critical and significant session with Goodman and his legal staff.

The government would probably finish its presentation on Tuesday, and the defense would then have to present its case. Two decisions had to be made: Should any defense witnesses be called, and should Stanley take the stand in his own behalf? There were friends courageous enough to testify, but they would be thoroughly grilled as to political beliefs, associations, morals, and so on, to try and discredit them. Stanley felt he could not subject anyone to this. Both he and the attorneys agreed to call no witnesses.

Then came the question as to whether Stanley himself should take the stand. It had been expected that the government might call him as an unfriendly witness; but this had not happened, and it appeared unlikely. As the trial had proceeded, Stanley had become impatient to take the stand. If the government called him, he would have the constitutional protection of the Fifth Amendment and could possibly get some facts into the record. At the same time, he could refuse to name associates (to save them from labeling and harassment) or to answer misleading or loaded questions. If he took the stand voluntarily, he would forego any constitutional protection. While he could not be forced to testify against himself, he could be asked to name associates. Refusal would mean a charge of contempt of court and possible imprisonment. It was that simple, and it was happening throughout the country. Stanley and the attorneys debated back and forth, they insisting he should not subject himself to the risk.

In the Unity Caucus of the UAW, Stanley, Reuther, and many others had worked with all forces in the UAW of whatever political beliefs, often conferring with officials of various political parties to discuss issues and seek help and support in organizing various shops. This did not mean that such Unity Caucus members embraced the views of the political parties in working with them. Nevertheless, the sheer weight of the so called "evidence," the parade of government witnesses testifying to having seen Stanley at so-called "Communist" meetings, was enough to warrant presupposing membership in the Communist party. This was the government's contention. The government had only to ask Stanley if he were a member of the Communist party, and if he replied no, he could be charged with perjury because his testimony contradicted that of government witnesses. As his attorneys reviewed with Stanley the testimony thus far, all realized the trap was set and waiting for him.

From his seat by the window in Goodman's office, George Crockett, wise and seasoned counselor, smiled at Stanley's impatience: "What good would you accomplish in prison, Stanley? Would that help your case?"

"But maybe that wouldn't happen. Maybe I could get in some testimony to offset the lies and twisted facts."

"Stanley," said Crockett, "look at what has happened to others now in prison, charged with perjury in just such cases. The statements of government witnesses, however inaccurate, are accepted as truth because they were made by government witnesses. If your testimony contradicts them, it is your word against theirs. With the alleged role of Picard in your 1942 indictment and the eagerness of Hamborsky to entrap you, do you think you would fare any better than others now in prison for perjury? This isn't like your appearance before the House Un-American Activities Committee. There you had constitutional protection. Here you have none." With great reluctance, Stanley finally deferred to the opinions of his counselors. He came home very downcast, his whole being resisting the decision, yet realizing its wisdom.

At the hospital that night, we explained to Elissa and Dr. Bob our dilemma. He agreed with the attorneys, but she was thoroughly incensed over the lies and misrepresentations in the testimony and eager for her daddy to get on the witness stand and straighten everyone out. We explained the problem and the danger, and she finally realized there was no choice in spite of the unfavorable publicity that would inevitably follow. Stanley could not hide his heaviness of heart, and even Dr. Bob's cheerful efforts did not help much. Again we had a weekend of meetings and discussions with Stanley's defense committee and nationality groups. All urged him to follow our attorneys' advice.

On 27 July Stanley was still full of misgivings as we headed for the courtroom for what could be the last day of the trial. To add to our discomfort, we had suffered through an intolerably warm night; and the day was stiflingly hot.

In the courtroom the overhead fans were going, and the windows wide open again. An atmosphere of weariness and dejection seemed to pervade the whole room. Was it the wilting heat, we wondered, or just our downcast mood? The trial had been long and wearing, and everyone seemed to feel its effects.

Thaddeus Zygmunt took the stand, and Hamborsky questioned him about his pamphlet. The result was the same crazy-quilt kind of testimony as before — admissions and denials, a continuation of "maneuvering of the words," until he was excused.

It will be remembered that William Nowell had been excused earlier to refresh his memory as to testimony he had given before HUAC and the grand jury in 1942. He was now recalled for redirect examination by Hamborsky. Nothing new or startling came of it and he was excused.

And now came the dreaded moment. As Nowell left the witness stand, Judge Picard turned to Hamborsky: "All right, is that the government's case?"

"Yes, that is the government's case."

Picard then turned expectantly to Goodman. "The defendant," said Goodman, "will rest upon the case as it now stands. For the information of the court I want to indicate the particular position that we take in this case."

"All right," nodded Picard.

First, Goodman explained, the statute of 1928 prevented naturalization of aliens opposed to organized government, covering generally the category of political thinking known as *anarchists* and *polygamists,* and the statute did not at that time, and was not intended, to cover persons who belonged to organizations such as the Communist party. Second, he explained, the claim of fraud was based upon the testimony of two individuals without any corroborative testimony or evidence of any kind. The evidence introduced, Goodman maintained, was insufficient to meet the minimum standard provided by the Schneiderman case. Schneiderman had been an official of the Communist party and a naturalized citizen. An unsuccessful attempt had been made to strip him of citizenship on the basis of advocacy of violent overthrow of the government. The court declared in his favor, ruling that evidence in such a case had to be "clear, unequivocal, and convincing."

Third, continued Goodman, though the court probably had sufficient evidence to find for membership, the evidence as to what the aims and objectives of the organization were — even assuming the statute did apply to an organization of that kind — did not meet the minimum requirements. Zygmunt's 1938 pamphlet, in particular, raised a doubt concerning these aims.

"There isn't any doubt, is there," asked Picard, "that the aims and objectives up to and beyond the period we have in mind here, was the overthrow of this government by force and violence?"

"I disagree with that completely," said Goodman, "because the standard to be adopted in this case, according to the Schneiderman decision, is whether that aim and objective has been proved by clear, unequivocal, and convincing evidence. In the Schneiderman case, Your Honor may remember, Justice Murphy went on to point out that on the basis of the evidence there, the court *could* say that the aims and objectives of the Communist party was to overthrow the government by force and violence; but it could *also* be a tenable conclusion that the Communist party intended to change the form of government not by force and violence alone but by other methods and that force and violence would come into the struggle only because the existing order would refuse to submit to peaceful change." Zygmunt's testimony, Goodman argued, raised a similar doubt about the aims of the Party.

"I don't think the court is going to waste very much time with him," interposed Picard.

"The government would like the court to disregard his testimony entirely," commented Goodman drily.

"I don't know why they ever brought him in, in the first place," declared Picard.

"I don't want to disregard his testimony," Goodman stated.

Picard regarded him thoughtfully for a moment, then said, "Now I will be very frank with you. Right now, if I had to depend entirely upon the testimony of the two examiners, and this man had taken the stand and denied it, I would hesitate a long time before giving any merit to [their] testimony. But I don't feel the same way now. He doesn't deny that question at all."

"The question is," said Goodman, "whether there is testimony which measures up to the standard required—"

Picard interrupted: "I am going to give you a chance. I would even, within the next—" and then he looked at Goodman questioningly, as if not quite believing, "You are not going to put in any testimony at all?"

"No."

Picard shrugged. "All right. Now is there any testimony here as to the *knowledge* of this defendant as to the intents and purposes of the Communist party?" Hamborsky mentioned statements of various witnesses as to what they had alleged Stanley had said about his aims and objectives.

"This is a simple case," declared Picard, "in which the government has presented certain testimony, which, under the rule, must be viewed in the light most favorable to the government but must comply with the Schneiderman case in that it must be clear and convincing. And I don't take only one corner of it. I take all of it. You are going to have an opportunity. It isn't going to rest on any one thing. I will tell you that. You may adjourn court." And so the trial ended, on 27 July 1954.

The trial left both Stanley and me exhausted and drained. Elissa was recuperating at a nearby lake with friends. My mother was now with my sister so that she could have the attention she needed. She had become increasingly blind, and suffered several small strokes. This had weighed heavily upon us during the trial, for her bright spirit and loving presence had always been a comfort and inspiration to all of us. It was heartbreaking to see her slipping away, gradually but surely. We saw her frequently and talked to her daily by phone.

The Nowak Defense Committee continued its activities to raise funds for the enormous court costs and expenses. We fully expected an adverse decision from Judge Picard, but in the meantime we and the defense committee used every avenue to try and change the political climate. The committee decided that if Picard rendered an unfavorable decision we would appeal all the way to the Supreme Court if necessary.

Stanley began to work as a journalist and editor for *Glos ludowy* and continued organizing for various unions. I carried on my insurance work at home and worked with the Nowak Defense Committee. When fully recovered, Elissa entered Cass Technical High School's new performing arts curriculum.

As anticipated, Judge Picard's decision of 15 July 1955, was unfavorable. Attorney Goodman filed an appeal with the U.S. Court of Appeals, Sixth Circuit, in Cincinnati, and argued the case before that body. On 26 November 1956 that court upheld Picard's decision. Goodman then filed an appeal to the U.S. Supreme Court, which had refused to review such cases since its famous Schneiderman decision ten years earlier. We hoped that the kind of charges leveled against Stanley, after he had served ten years in the Michigan State Senate, might intrigue the members of the Supreme Court sufficiently to cause them to review the testimony in his case.

The *Detroit Free Press* of 2 April 1957 announced that the U.S. Supreme Court had agreed to review the case. Attorney Ernest Goodman's office immediately issued a press statement, which included the following comments:

> Many cases are appealed to the Supreme Court, but . . . the court selects only those in which it feels that constitutional or important legal aspects are involved. At times the high court wishes to review only certain aspects of a case. . . .
>
> The Supreme Court has decided to review the Stanley Nowak case in its entirety.
>
> For some time there has been a continuing attack upon the democratic rights of American citizens, both native and foreign-born.
>
> In 1941, the denaturalization case of William Schneiderman came before the U.S. Supreme Court for review. . . . The U.S. Supreme Court decided in favor of Schneiderman. . . . This set a historic pattern for courts throughout the nation. Since that time however, the movement

> against the foreign-born gained momentum and the lower courts throughout the land began to reflect this trend. Step by step the lower courts have deviated from the Schneiderman decision.
>
> Once again the high court has consented to consider the problem of denaturalization and citizenship. Obviously the Nowak decision will set a pattern for other courts to follow.

Subsequent statements and analyses of the Nowak case issued by Goodman's office contained the following comments:

> The government offered 10 witnesses, some of them government-paid professional informers . . . and it was on the basis of what these witnesses claim they remembered . . . that . . . his citizenship was ordered revoked. If a person's citizenship is dependent upon the professional informer or even upon the stale 30-year-old recollections of biased witnesses, how sure is a naturalized citizen that a change in political climate may not bring about the loss of citizenship?
>
> If citizenship, once granted, can be taken away on the basis of laws enacted long after the citizenship was granted, how permanent is the citizenship of any naturalized citizen?
>
> The government hopes in this case to get the Supreme Court to change its Schneiderman ruling. . . . The decision . . . in Senator Nowak's case will either reinforce that historic decision or will weaken or destroy its protection. . . . The fact that the Supreme Court has decided to accept the appeal indicates that the Court believes that the events of the 14 years since it decided the Schneiderman case makes it necessary to re-examine the legal basis upon which so many hundred have already lost their citizenship. Its decision in this case is likely to affect the rights of naturalized citizens for years to come.

Arguments before the Supreme Court would not be presented until the court's fall term of 1957, so we carried on with our lives as normally as possible until that time. It wasn't until 27 May 1958, Ernie Goodman phoned me about mid-morning: "Margaret, have you seen the morning *Free Press*?"

"No, I've been too busy. What's up?"

"The Supreme Court has reversed the lower courts on Stanley's case."

Afraid to believe, I asked, "Are you sure?"

"It's true. Read it for yourself in the paper. We'll know more about it as soon as we get a copy of the decision, and we should have that in a day or two."

Our phone rang all day. "How do you feel about it?" "Isn't it just great?" "Aren't you happy?" These were questions people kept asking as they phoned to congratulate us. I must admit I couldn't feel a thing. I was so exhausted and spent from the long ordeal that it just didn't seem real that it was over and we had won. It would be some time before I could release the crushing load that had hung over us for so long. Six years of our lives had gone into the struggle to raise funds and rally people and public opinion in our behalf. The trial had cost, in all so far, twenty thousand dollars, and there were still legal fees, court costs, and other bills facing us. Moreover, I was still coping with the death of my mother, followed in less than a year by the death of my eldest brother. Two cherished relationships gone within one year! This, added to Elissa's illness and the trial had been almost more than I could bear.

Within a few days, Goodman received and analyzed the decision. The Supreme Court substantiated our attorneys' contention that the government had failed to prove its case, as indicated by a few brief quotes from the decision:

> Evidence disclosing at best that the defendant prior to application for citizenship had been an active member and functionary of the Communist Party, was insufficient to prove charge of fraud. . . .
>
> Where citizenship is at stake the Government carries the heavy burden of proving its case by "clear, unequivocal and convincing" evidence which does not leave the issue in doubt. . . ." Especially is this so when the attack is made long after the time when the certificate of citizenship was granted and the citizen has meanwhile met his obligations and has committed no act of lawlessness.
>
> Applying the strict standard required of the Government by Schneiderman, we rule that the charge of fraud was not proved.
>
> . . . Virtually the only testimony at the trial bearing directly on Nowak's state of mind related to three statements attributed to him by former members of the Communist Party. . . . We cannot regard these fragmentary episodes as providing reliable support for the Government's case. Read in context, they can be taken merely as expression of opinions or predictions about future events, rather than as advocacy. . . . At no point does the record show that Nowak himself ever advocated action for violent overthrow. In addition, the record leaves us with the distinct impression that the testimony as to these episodes was quite uncertain, given . . . 17 to 19 years after the event. Indeed, some of the testimony was elicited only after persistent prodding by counsel for the Government.

In short, the court ruled that both the testimony of the two examiners and the testimony as to the aims of the Communist party failed to constitute "clear, unequivocal and convincing" evidence. In spite of what our ordeal had cost us in physical and emotional terms, there was one very real consolation. The decision threw out of the lower courts thousands of similar cases pending against naturalized citizens, most of whom did not have the human and financial resources that had been open to us because of the wide scope of Stanley's work and activities through the years. This kind of victory made our struggle meaningful and satisfying.

The fact that Stanley had not taken the witness stand during the trial had cost us some friends who assumed he was guilty because he failed to testify in his own behalf. We were sorry they could not understand the legal and political ramifications involved. Many faithful friends had remained, as witnessed by the continued fund-raising and work in our behalf while we had waited for the court decision.

On 20 June 1958, Parkside Hall on Fenkell near Wildemere was packed with friends and well-wishers to celebrate our victory. Carl Haessler, Ben Okshea, and other members of the Nowak Defense Committee were with us. And among the special guests were our old friend Leo Krzycki, former president of the American Slav Congress and vice president of the Amalgamated Clothing Workers; and Charles Lockwood, an attorney prominent in consumer affairs, who had defended many security cases. Of course, our own attorneys, Ernest Goodman and George Crockett, and their staff, were with us.

During the long fight for his citizenship, Stanley had always been my strength and inspiration when I grew weary and disheartened. His courage, insights, and strong faith in the future and in the U.S. people were sustaining to all who worked with him and were publicly acknowledged by our attorneys at the victory rally. Crockett summed it up when he said, "Stanley never knows when he's licked." Goodman and Crockett had handled the legal end of the defense but sometimes had doubts about the outcome. Not so with Stanley! He had great confidence in their ability but recognized that their approach was a legalistic one. In his travels around the country in an effort to change the social and political climate, he had sensed a real change growing against the oppressive atmosphere and had encountered a courageous determination on the part of the people to fight back. He had hoped this might be reflected in the court decision.

At the victory rally, Stanley pointed out the political significance of our triumph and almost broke down in tears when thanking everyone for their moral, political, and financial support. When I was called to speak, I took Stanley's hand and pulled him with me to the front of the speaker's platform. As we stood holding hands and looking out upon the dear faces of so many friends, I said, "Now, do you see what *you* have done?" The deafening applause answered me.

Stanley has always been full of surprises. Shortly after the rally, he startled me by saying, "Margaret, now that we don't *have* to go to Poland, would you like to go with me to see that country and the village where I was born?" It was a wonderful, exciting idea, just what I needed to jolt me out of my exhausted and numbed state and stimulate me into activity.

Elissa was at home that summer, recovering from mononucleosis and was not allowed to work. She could, however, look after my insurance work from our home office so that I could get away. We visited Stanley's Village of Ujkowica and the neighboring town of Przemysl, over a thousand years old. We saw other great, historic towns; saw the Tatra Mountains in their fall and winter glory; visited ancient castles now turned into museums and educational institutions; and tasted the rich and varied cultural life that abounds in Poland. In Warsaw, we visited Henry and Dolores Podolski and Jimmy Papandreau, all former Detroiters, victims of the McCarthy era and deportees under the Walter-McCarran Law. They had been provided with attractive apartments and were well adjusted to life in Poland. They were happy to see us and rejoiced in our victory. It was an unforgettable experience for us.

Stanley had assumed the editorship of *Glos ludowy* in 1955 or 1956, and the paper sent him to Poland several times. Podolski, in charge of Polish radio, wrote articles for the paper and often sent press releases. I had taken my portable typewriter to Poland in the summer of 1958, and I wrote a series of articles about my impressions of various aspects of Polish life for the English pages of *Glos ludowy.* We sent them by air mail to Detroit, where they were used immediately. In Warsaw in July, we watched the tremendous parade down Marshalkowska Street in celebration of the New Poland's twentieth birthday. It was a magnificent sight with thousands of Polish workers and young people, all in regional costumes, marching in many different formations to portray aspects of Polish history and performing athletic stunts on floats. The miners of Silesia were something to see in their beautiful black dress costumes and plumed hats. One special memory stands out—a contingent of twenty-year-olds bearing a streetwide, shoulder-high banner saying, "We Have Grown Up with the New Poland." During the three-hour parade there was much enthusiasm, joking, and interaction between the marchers and the spectators.

In 1960 Stanley visited Poland to make a silent film about the factories, mines, and steel mills being built and the continued reconstruction and growth of industry. On Stanley's return, he narrated the film at meetings in Detroit and around the country, arranging the meetings in between his duties as editor. That summer I was hired as bookkeeper for Ernie Goodman's office, then known as Goodman, Crockett, Eden, Robb, and Philo. I took the job while Stanley was in Poland, and he was much surprised to see attorney George Crockett at a conference in Warsaw and to learn that I was now working for that law firm.

Elissa graduated from Adelphi University in Long Island, New York the summer of 1964, with a B.A. degree in dance education. *Glos ludowy* sent Stanley to Poland again that summer to gather more material, and we borrowed enough money to finance Elissa's and my passage and hotel so we could accompany him. Elissa fell in love with the Polish folk dances and was invited to a summer dance camp. Stanley and I visited her there and met the director, a colonel in the Polish Army, in charge of cultural and educational matters. When the Nazis attacked Poland in 1939, he had escaped to the Soviet Union, where he joined one of the Polish brigades made up of Polish escapees like himself and marched with them and the Red Army to liberate Poland in 1944. He was much impressed by Elissa and wanted her to arrange a dance concert for the army. This she was able to do later with her students in Poland, for she managed to arrange with the Ministry of Culture to remain in Poland for two years on a stipend and study classical ballet and the Polish folk dances in return for teaching modern ballet.

Back in Detroit in 1964 I returned to work at the law office and Stanley resumed the editorship of the paper. He wrote a series of articles on Poland and lectured around the country on the progress made by Poland since his visit of 1960.

On her return to Detroit in 1966, Elissa was invited by the Detroit Community Music School to establish a dance department and teach the students. From her most promising dancers she organized a company, "Harbinger", which eventually outgrew the facilities of the music school and went on its own to become the first professional dance company in Detroit, dedicated to bringing dance to the people by performances in shopping malls, the streets, and the schools. She and her attorney husband, Dennis James, have presented us with two delightful grandchildren, who are a continuing joy to us.

In 1970, UN Year of the Woman, Stanley asked me to write a series of biographical sketches of some of the great women in U.S. history for the English pages of *Glos ludowy.* For two years I read and researched, and wrote perhaps a dozen such sketches of the great suffragists and abolitionists, Black and white, who had waged such a courageous battle for the rights of women in the United States. I was also asked to speak on this at women's gatherings. The Flint, Michigan Church of the Brethren, used this topic as their worship theme one Sunday morning.

Early in 1976 Stanley suffered a series of mild heart attacks and spent several weeks in the hospital. He was no sooner out and on his feet again than we were in an automobile accident, on 30 April, in which my neck was broken in two places, shoulder bone broken, and ribs cracked; and a severe concussion kept me unconscious for almost two weeks. I emerged from this to realize I had a metal circle cast attached to my skull with four screws, and a body cast to my hips. The long time in the hospital and recovering at home gave me time to think about what to do with the rest of my life, for I knew then I would probably never work again. Researching and writing this book became my goal.

As soon as I shed the body cast and the circle cast and was on my way to recovery, an invitation came for both Stanley and me from the Polish society in Warsaw in charge of relations with Poles abroad. The invitation was issued because of Stanley's contribution over the years to the rebuilding of Poland, as a Polish journalist and friend of Poland. We were invited to spend the summer at a beautiful retreat in the Tatra Mountains. The doctor forbade my traveling but said Stanley could go. He did not want to leave me; but I insisted, as he had been through a long ordeal with his heart attacks and then my accident and the long period of anxiety over my condition, which had been quite "iffy" at one point. I had a nurse's aid coming in half days and a nurse once a week. Neighbors and friends were available to get me to the bank, the doctor, or to do my shopping, and my sister and Elissa's family lived only a short distance away. So I persuaded Stanley to go.

He came home a month later feeling fit and ready for his work on the paper, which was now becoming quite a strain, as the generation of supporters and founders was dying one by one, and it was becoming more and more difficult to raise money to keep the paper going. Stanley kept it alive until about 1980, when the group of supporters was down to a mere handful and the need for language papers greatly diminished. The paper sold the building that housed its headquarters and all its equipment and furniture and merged its publication with a Polish paper in Toronto, Canada, *Kronika tygodniowa* (Weekly Chronicle). At first I missed the paper, as Stanley did; for during the last two years of its existence I had learned to operate the computer typewriter to set up the columns for the English pages.

By that time Solidarność (Solidarity) was making world headlines and friends came to us with questions we could not answer. The remnants of the small group that had supported *Glos ludowy* through the years decided that Stanley should go to Poland and see what was happening, and they raised the money for his transportation and expenses. We borrowed money for my share, and I went with him for our last trip to Poland in August of 1981. In Warsaw we stayed at the home of Mrs. Sofia Szyszko, with whom Stanley's delegation had traveled to Poland on the Queen Elizabeth in 1945. Stanley interviewed over fifty people from all walks of life, and sat for seven days as a press observer in the founding convention of Solidarity in the city of Gdansk, where I joined him part of the time. See the Appendix for a copy of Stanley's letter to the *Detroit Free Press* of 13 February 1984, giving his summation of Solidarity.

On our return to Detroit we both spoke at numerous organizations on what we had observed in Poland and the nature of Solidarity. Today, we feel that Poland is on its way to a better future.

Nineteen hundred eighty-five was a memorable year for us. We celebrated our fiftieth wedding anniversary at the same time that the UAW began celebrating its fifty years of existence. When we were married on 31 May 1935, the AFL was experiencing some severe birth pains, which resulted in the charter of the UAW at the AFL convention in Detroit in August at the Fort Shelby Hotel.

As we look back over the 50-plus years of the UAW, with which we were so closely allied in its infancy, we can see the enormous achievements it made in the auto industry, as other industrial unions have done in steel, rubber, farm equipment, and so on. Millions of workers were organized within a short period of time into an industrial and militant union. Such great corporations as GM, Ford, and Chrysler were compelled to recognize the UAW and sign contracts establishing grievance procedures and granting many benefits, among them pay raises, seniority rights, medical and hospital insurance, vacations with pay, and sick-leave and severance pay. The activities and influence of the UAW indirectly made possible a number of political achievements: unemployment compensation, social security and medicare, and improved workmen's compensation laws, to mention a few.

These accomplishments were made chiefly because of the *unity* prevailing in the UAW leadership, in spite of differences in political, religious, and ethnic backgrounds. The leaders were united on the basic principle of militant, industrial unionism. When World War II broke out in Europe, factions began to appear in the union, and rivalry for leadership developed. Nevertheless, the general principle of militant, industrial unionism held firm. Once the war ended, antilabor hysteria swept the country, antilabor legislation was enacted by Congress, and McCarthyism appeared, causing much damage in the political, academic, and cultural fields. Certain elements in the union took advantage of this atmosphere of reaction to seize the leadership. Free discussion was curbed, and many local unions amended their constitutions to exclude certain people from holding office. McCarthy hysteria swept the unions, resulting in some violence. Many devoted and dedicated people, who had worked hard and selflessly and sacrificed much to establish the union, were driven from its ranks.

In the meantime, great changes were taking place in our economy. Today we face monumental problems: growing unemployment due to plant closings and runaway factories and the increasing introduction of robots and other new technology, eliminating vast numbers of jobs permanently; the multinational character of big business, which builds factories in other countries wherever it can find the cheapest labor and make the greatest profit; and mass bankruptcy among small businesses and mergers of large corporations—all leading to the extreme concentration of wealth in the hands of fewer people. We face the growth of hunger; lack of medical attention; the cutting of funds for the poor and the elderly; and, worst, the *spending of vast sums on the military.* The problems today are infinitely more complex than were those of our generation, but we believe that today's workers are as capable of tackling their problems as we were in our day. The fifty years of the UAW's existence show that to confront these problems, two things are absolutely necessary: there must be free and thorough discussion of issues in the search for solutions; and complete *unity* within the ranks of labor.

The same unity is vital in the struggle for civil rights, an end to discrimination on the basis of race, religion, or sex, and in the efforts for disarmament, banning of nuclear weapons, and the establishment of peace. This has been an overriding concern of ours through the years and even today as we lend our support in any way we possibly can.

All his life, Stanley was able to work with socialists of many shades, communists, and conservatives on issues. The communists were the most numerous, knowledgeable, and courageous in whatever battles we faced, yet Stanley has never known one to advocate armed revolution and he certainly never did.

Stanley has been called many names and has denied none of them, for people of many ideologies have worked together for a better future wherever he found himself. It is a futile and shallow game to pin labels on people or try to fit them into certain categories. What does it matter? All people everywhere, regardless of political, religious, or social outlook, are going to have to work together on today's problems or be overwhelmed by them. Only by such a united effort can we bring into being a world in which peace and justice prevail.

Appendix

From the *Detroit Free Press,* 13 February 1984

From recent articles by Mariusź Ziomecki and others in the Detroit Free Press regarding Poland, I realize that the real facts as to the origin and demise of the Solidarity movement have not been told.

As a former editor of a Polish paper, I have followed closely the events in Poland since the new government emerged at the end of World War II. I was chairman of the first Polish-American delegation to Poland in 1945. Since then I have returned seven times, traveling throughout the country and talking to people from all walks of life. My last visit was in 1981 when I attended the founding convention of Solidarity in Gdansk and talked at length with many of the delegates about the convention, its aims and events leading up to it.

In the summer of 1980 a wave of strikes swept Poland, sporadic and without national leadership or organization. The demands were legitimate and deeply rooted in events following World War II.

National efforts had been concentrated on the building of heavy industry at the expense of consumer goods, particularly housing. Democratic centralism in managing industry had become bureaucratic centralism. The government and the Polish United Workers Party had lost touch

---

with the people. Foreign propagandists, mainly Radio Free Europe, hammered constantly on the low standard of living of the Poles and claimed the Soviets were robbing Poland of its production.

Individuals who had not been part of the strikes of 1980 and were not factory workers—professional intellectuals and political individuals who had opposed the people's government and its socialist economy for many years—offered their services to the strikers as advisers and were later promoted by them to the leadership of the union.

In August 1980, two large strikes occurred in the shipyards at Gdansk and Szczecin. After weeks of negotiations, the two strike committees independently arrived at agreements with the government and gained recognition for their union's independence, as well as the right to strike if negotiations failed. A substantial pay raise was also agreed to, and the committees, in turn, agreed to end the strikes, accept and respect the Constitution of Poland, and to recognize the government, the socialist economy and the leading role of the Polish United Workers Party. The strike committees also agreed to call a national convention to organize a new union under the name "Solidarity."

Solidarity was organized not as a labor union is, based on industry or work establishment, but rather as a political party is, on the basis of region. Anyone living in a particular city, county or region, regardless of what he did for a living, could join. According to the Credentials Committee of the founding convention, 56 percent of the delegates had a university education. Obviously, they were not industrial workers.

As I observed proceedings at Solidarity's founding convention, I could see how the extremist element imposed its leadership and orientation on the delegates. It became increasingly clear to me and to other journalists there that this dissident and extremist element wanted confrontation with the government and planned to use every possible means of creating economic confusion and anarchy.

The convention adopted an open letter to the people of all Eastern European countries, including the Soviet Union, calling for workers to support the Solidarity movement in Poland and rebel against their governments.

The majority of Polish workers, and the people generally, who had at first supported the ideas of Solidarity and a number of the economic reforms it had obtained, took careful note of events at the founding convention and became aware that the movement was heading toward civil war in Poland and possibly a confrontation with the Soviet Union. After that convention, workers began to withdraw their support of Solidarity and its collision course.

Every real or imaginary pretext was now used by Solidarity to call strikes—a shortage of matches, vodka or cigarets, or the removal of a plant manager. The government was forced to raise wages while production went down because of the frequent work stoppages. Drastic action became necessary to stop this destructive course, and voices from all sections of the population demanded government action.

The Polish Parliament assigned Gen. Wojciech Jaruzelski as prime minister, with instructions to form a new cabinet. His appeal to the workers to end the strikes and establish peace for 90 days was ignored by Solidarity's leaders, who not only continued the strikes but promoted them.

As a result, the Polish Parliament declared martial law and empowered Jaruzelski to enforce it. All strikes were banned, leaders and instigators of strikes were arrested, and Solidarity was declared illegal. Meetings, demonstrations and agitation were prohibited.

Those Solidarity leaders who escaped and went underground still issued appeals to the Polish workers to continue their strikes. However, they discovered that millions who had originally supported Solidarity now refused to follow its leadership and policies. Workers returned to the factories and work establishments, and only the young people, students, etc. would participate in the street demonstrations.

There are solid reasons behind the withdrawal of support from Solidarity. Two world wars have been fought on Polish soil, and many people there remember them. World War II took six million Polish lives and left Poland's cities reduced to rubble. The thought of another war, particularly nuclear war, strikes terror in the hearts of those who have paid such a high price in the rebuilding of Poland's cities and the industrializing of the nation to the point where it ranks 11th in the world.

The Polish Parliament has enacted new labor laws, giving workers the right to organize unions based on the industry or establishment where they are employed, and with complete independence from both the government and the Polish United Workers Party. Strikes are permitted only when negotiations fail. The new labor unions are now organized and number approximately 3.5 million in membership.

Many martial law restrictions have been lifted and amnesty has been declared for all former Solidarity activists. Something like 1,800 of them have abandoned Solidarity and agreed to accept and live by the new labor laws. It is generally recognized that martial law prevented civil war in Poland, which might well have brought about World War III.

Poland has emerged from three years of serious economic, political and ideological crises a healthier and more united nation. Poland today is probably more democratic than at any time in its history. Organized labor, in full partnership with the government and the Polish United Workers Party, is leading the nation into a better future.

STANLEY NOWAK
Detroit

Index